American University Studies

Series XXIV
American Literature

Vol. 62

PETER LANG
ew York • Washington, D.C./Baltimore • San Francisco
Bern • Frankfurt am Main • Berlin • Vienna • Paris

Cambridge Studies

Lurking Femin

Jenni Dyman

Lurking Feminism

The Ghost Stories
of Edith Wharton

PETER LANG
New York • Washington, D.C./Baltimore • San Francisco
Bern • Frankfurt am Main • Berlin • Vienna • Paris

Library of Congress Cataloging-in-Publication Data

Dyman, Jenni.
Lurking feminism: the ghost stories of Edith Wharton/ Jenni Dyman.
p.   cm. — (American university studies. Series XXIV, American Literature;
vol. 62)
Includes bibliographical references (p.).
1. Wharton, Edith, 1862–1937—Criticism and interpretation.
2. Ghost stories, American—History and criticism. 3. Feminism and
literature—United States—History. 4. Women and literature—United States—
History. I. Title. II. Series.
PS3545.H16Z644   813'.52—dc20   94-36238
ISBN 0-8204-2697-0
ISSN 0895-0512

Die Deutsche Bibliothek-CIP-Einheitsaufnahme

Dyman, Jenni:
Lurking feminism: the ghost stories of Edith Wharton/ Jenni Dyman.
- New York; Washington, D.C./Baltimore; San Francisco; Bern; Frankfurt am
Main; Berlin; Vienna; Paris: Lang.
(American university studies: Ser. 24, American literaure; Vol. 62)
ISBN 0-8204-2697-0
NE: American university studies/ 24

The paper in this book meets the guidelines for permanence and durability
of the Committee on Production Guidelines for Book Longevity
of the Council of Library Resources.

Printed in the United States of America.

For Ted and Ken

Acknowledgements

I wish to thank Simon and Schuster Inc. and the Watkins/Loomis Agency and estate of Edith Wharton for permission to quote from Wharton's work. I also would like to thank my mentor and friend Herb Eldridge who, many years ago, introduced me to Edith Wharton, and Dottie Eldridge, for their love and support; Cordelia Candelaria for her insightful perceptions, encouragement, and sharing of experience; Connie Willis for years of stimulating conversation, literary and otherwise; and my colleagues Claire Rogers and Polly Rogers for their daily confidence and *confidences*. Also to James Weber, President of Arapahoe Community College, Dean Herm Jantzen, librarians Jan Dawson and Marilyn Munsterman, and my student assistant Stephen Booth—I appreciate your professionalism and support. Thanks to Sally Dyson for her computer skills and efficiency. Finally, I thank my husband, Ted, and my son, Ken. This project would have never been started or completed without you.

Contents

Preface

It is in the warm darkness of the prenatal fluid far below conscious reason that the faculty dwells with which we apprehend the ghosts we may not be endowed with the gift of seeing.

Preface to *Ghosts*, 1937

From Edith Wharton's death in 1937 until well through the 1960s, limited and mostly uniform conclusions emerged from discussion of her work: Wharton was a distinguished novelist of manners until her work dwindled into women's magazine fiction after 1920; a realist, but not as good as Henry James, her mentor; a master of irony, but not as good as Sinclair Lewis whom she accidentally defeated for the Pulitzer Prize; a stiff patrician "lady" from Old New York who attacked the conventions of her heritage, but who lived according to their dictates. She was considered a talented writer, but with a limited range, confined almost by duty to one subject, the resurrection of New York of the 1870s and 1880s, referred to by Wharton herself as "a vanished city as Atlantis or the lowest layer of Schliemann's Troy" (*Backward Glance* 55). The *Literary History of the United States* (1959) sums up Wharton's career: "Historically, [she] is likely to survive as a memorialist of dying aristocracy" (Spiller 1211). This view of Wharton was perpetuated by anthology selections emphasizing her short fiction and reflecting a narrow range of her subjects and themes. The one exception was *Ethan Frome*, considered uncharacteristic because it was not about Old New York.

Today, the view of Wharton has changed. The multiplicity of contemporary critical approaches and the loosening of the American literary canon have encouraged this. Major changes occurred after Yale opened the Wharton archives to researchers in 1968 and the Morton Fullerton letters surfaced in the early 1970s. Both events produced new data, rendering earlier biographical work on Wharton biased or incomplete (Lubbock, Kellogg) and leading critics to move beyond Blake Nevius's measured view of Wharton's talent, even beyond the intelligent, but limited, analyses of Wharton's work collected by Irving Howe in 1962, which he considered at the time the small body of "first-rate criticism" available (1).

Critics and students are drawing new conclusions about Wharton. Beginning in the 1970s, especially with R.W.B. Lewis's Pulitzer-prize-winning biography (1975), the fresh perspectives disclose that Wharton was not only prolific, but also wide-ranging in subject matter, theme, and technique. In life, Wharton's affair with Morton Fullerton, and in art, the erotic "Beatrice Palmato" fragment have modified the portrait of the puritanical "lady." Lewis describes the woman rather than the legend when he writes, "There was, after all, a fund of passion and of laughter in her, and almost unbelievable energy" (*Biography* xii). Contradicting Irving Howe's dictum that she was "a writer of limited scope" looms three or four feet of work on a wide variety of subjects and themes, increasingly viewed as rich in complexity and subtlety (3).

Although Wharton did not publish her first book until 1897 when she was 35 years old (*The Decoration of Houses*, an interior design treatise written with architect Ogden Codman, Jr.), or her first collection of short stories until 1899 (*The Greater Inclination*), or her first novel until 1900 (*The Touchstone*), she went on to publish 47 volumes of fiction and non-fiction before her death in August 1937 at age 75. The literary criticism on what were previously considered her major works (*Ethan Frome, The Age of Innocence, The House of Mirth*) is now supplemented by investigations of long neglected novels such as *The Reef, The Custom of the Country, Summer, The Mother's Recompense, Hudson River Bracketed, The Buccaneers,* and many neglected short stories. The increasing body of contemporary criticism on Wharton from the 1970s and 1980s and continuing to develop in the 1990s shows Wharton's legacy extends beyond realism and social satire. As adept a psychologist as Henry James, she was also an early clarifier of gender issues and feminist concerns. She could "unpack from her treasures" romantic imagery and symbolism as well as she could present incisive realistic detail.[1]

Until the 1990s, little criticism dealt directly with Wharton's ghost stories, works which confirm her versatility and skill. In October of 1937, Appleton-Century published posthumously a volume titled *Ghosts* including ten of Wharton's previously published tales (1902-1931) and a new, unpublished one, "All Souls." Wharton completed the preface for this volume before her death. This final collection of short fiction, supplemented by other stories which are or might be construed as ghost stories, establish Wharton as a key figure in the supernatural tradition.[2] Her ghost stories also present a strong case for what Blake Nevius refers to as her "lurking feminism" (85).[3] Indeed she uses the ghost story to explore the status of women and men in society: their gender roles, relationships, marriages, communication patterns, creativity, and sexuality. Functioning within the male literary tradition to produce her texts, relying on the extensive symbolism and figuration of the supernatural tradition which offered her a rich idiom for subtextual expression of her feminist concerns, working from her observations as a woman and a writer in a patrician class, she sought to reveal society's restrictions, both external and internalized, on the individual.[4]

Wharton provides no discussion of the themes of any of her ghost stories. Her silence here parallels her silence regarding her other work. She only occasionally commented about her work, usually when she was displeased with a specific response to it and then mostly in brief remarks in letters. She wrote prefaces for only three of her volumes, *The House of Mirth, Ethan Frome,* and *Ghosts;* they do not directly address her themes. Her comments about her work can even be misleading. In the preface to *Ghosts,* she emphasizes that the success of a ghost story depends on its "thermometrical quality; if it sends a cold shiver down one's spine, it has done its job and done it well."[5] She also states that the "moral question" has little to do with the ghost story (*Ghost Stories* 4). However, in *The Writing of Fiction,* she writes that a good subject for any story "must contain in itself something that sheds a light on our moral experience," and the body of her work provides evidence for this conviction (28). In commenting on *The Turn of the Screw,* she does not overlook the "moral question," although she stresses the "thermometrical quality": "It is true that the tale is strongly held together by its appalling moral significance; but most readers will admit that, long before they are conscious of this, fear, simple shivering animal fear has them by the throat; which, after all, is what writers of ghost stories are after" (40-41). In practice, she demonstrates that the ghost story requires both "the subtlest artifice" and "moral significance" (37, 40). The ghost story, as any of her short stories, is "not a loose web spread over the surface of life," but "at its best, as a shaft driven into the heart of human experience" (31, 36).

Although there are occasional designated villains in Wharton's ghost stories, her understanding of life is too complex for formulaic Gothic characterizations, but Gothic symbolism and techniques provide her with a framework. She depicts a male-dominated culture that restricts women to small worlds represented by Gothic enclosures. Women are relegated to safe, but isolated, home spheres whereas men roam the world conducting business and seeking pleasure. Presented sympathetically as victims of

male domination, the codes of the marriage institution, and internal conflicts between prescribed gender roles and their own needs, the women,
lacking outlets for personal expression, live as estranged, silent, and often
sexually repressed individuals. They are generally passive, but in one tale,
a woman may have murdered her abusive husband; in another, a woman
becomes a frightening witch-like dominator as she aggressively attempts
to retaliate against isolation and confinement and compete with a rival
woman. Ironically, women in competition with one another play into patriarchal codes to control other women and also themselves. In these tales,
women look to men for authority, safety, and self-esteem. There is little
evidence of nurturing maternal support or independent female role models
for women. The internalized role of the traditional or conventional woman
creates conflict for the New Woman who must contend with the growth-
hindering pull of the past. New Women must rely on their own resources
which are limited and frequently exhausted.

Wharton's ghost stories also show men as disadvantaged as women by
the cultural codes that govern gender roles and relationships. Men are
frequently shown as selfish and insensitive, evoking at times the Gothic
villain, yet they are also portrayed as confused and unhappy individuals.
Their possessiveness leads to cruelty, or their passivity, detachment, or
lack of commitment to a full life causes them to be psychologically blind.
Often the male characters are egotistical bachelors, possibly with homosexual tendencies, who are themselves trying to escape the defined gender
roles of the society. These men live restricted lives that are as confined
and repressed as the women's.

Finally, the larger picture of the culture is not attractive, strongly suggesting the need for change. Wharton portrays the institution of marriage
and narrowly defined gender identities as repressive structures. Her victimized characters, both males and females, blindly follow internalized
cultural codes with disastrous consequences. Outbursts of cruelty, violence, and madness suggest problems of communication, power, sexuality. Compatible, intimate relationships between men and women simply
do not exist or survive here.

The purpose of this book is to provide an introduction to Wharton's
ghost stories, to chart a progression of ideas constituting her "lurking feminism," and to show how the conventions of the supernatural tradition and
the transmuted material of her own life provide Wharton with a powerful
means of expression. I enter the dialogue of Wharton criticism using primarily feminist, psychological, and contextual approaches. My intent is

to "open up" Wharton's work rather than to enclose it in reductive ideology. To this end, I have integrated various critical perspectives into my explorations to illustrate the rich criticism available and to emphasize the complexity of Wharton's work, which operates on many levels and uses an array of techniques. I see texts and critical interpretations as interactive, text informing interpretation, interpretation informing text, in cycles of awareness, understanding, and appreciation. I focus on the eleven stories in *Ghosts* with some discussion of other stories that might also be designated as ghost stories. Because I discuss Wharton's stories in the context of her personal and cultural concerns, I present them chronologically and connect them to biographical and intertextual material. As Barbara White has noted in her study of Wharton's eighty-five short stories, the "stories of any particular time period resemble each other more than the . . . stories of another era" (xiii).

Some of the themes of Wharton's ghost stories undoubtedly spring from personal experience transmuted into fantastic events. Critics have generally agreed that Wharton's work is infused with her personal background. The limitations Wharton felt in her own life, such as her childhood fears and isolation, her growth-stunting relationship with her parents, the restrictive societal codes in the world of Old New York, the disappointment and sexual repression in her marriage to Teddy Wharton, shaped her identity and contributed to the text and subtext of her work. Her affair with Morton Fullerton, her relationship with Walter Berry, and her friendships with many males, who were mostly bachelors, gave her subject matter and affected her themes. The interaction with a society which saw her stereotypically as a woman and therefore as a "lady," with little need or right to become a writer, colored her experience and her literary creations. Lewis goes as far as to say that "personal experience was never entirely real for her until it had been converted into literature" (*Biography* 244).[6]

It is still with caution that I move to draw parallels between Wharton's life and work, especially in looking at the emotions and ideas that charge the ghost stories with their dynamic quality and their ultimate horror. Wharton describes in her autobiography "what seems to have gone to the making of my books . . . . I can only say that the process, though it takes place in some secret region on the sheer edge of consciousness, is always illuminated by the full light of my critical attention" (*Backward Glance* 197, 205). She was annoyed with the reductive *roman-à-clef* approach to her work. She considered the *roman à clef* a fiction of a "low order . . . never written by a born novelist." And she writes that "nothing can be more trying to the creative writer than to have a clumsy finger point at one of the beings born in that mysterious other-world of invention, with the playful accusation: 'Of course we all recognize your Aunt Eliza!'" In spite of Wharton's irritation over the *roman-à-clef* approach, a number of critics have made convincing arguments for partial correspondences between characters and people in Wharton's life.[7] Wharton does confirm that "No 'character' can be made out of nothing . . . . Experience, observation, the looks and ways and words of 'real people,' all melted and fused in the white heat of the creative fires—such is the mingled stuff which the novelist pours into the firm mold of the narrative" (*Backward Glance* 210-11). Accordingly, I explore in the ghost stories how, consciously or unconsciously, Wharton's conflicts as well as her observations of "real people" appear to have driven her work.[8]

Interestingly, Wharton's ghost stories are not thematically a radical departure from her other work: her lifelong themes create the framework for her focus in the ghostly tales. Blake Nevius was the first to point out that Wharton's great subject was the "trapped sensibility." Wharton, he writes, "focused on the waste of spiritual and human resources" (8, 73). Further, Wharton's "psychic horrors," strikingly modern and feminist, lie within the boundaries of the traditional, or I might say traditionally subversive, themes of supernatural literature: oppression of the past (the sins of the fathers—and the mothers), the oppression of sexism (male domination), the obsessive quest of knowledge or pleasure (resulting in a lack of humanness and human compassion), and the limitations of human perceptions. Influences from a number of earlier supernatural works haunt Wharton's tales.

In the Introduction, I place Wharton in the supernatural tradition and discuss theoretically how she found a voice through its possibilities. In chapter 1, I discuss in some detail her earliest ghost story which appears in *Ghosts*, "The Lady's Maid's Bell" (1902), along with brief analyses of several other early stories. Subsequently, each chapter will group and discuss two stories: chapter 2, "Afterward" and "The Eyes," both written 1909-1910; chapter 3, "The Triumph of Night," also written in 1910, and "Kerfol," written between 1910 and 1914, both pre-war stories; chapter 4, "Bewitched" and "Miss Mary Pask," both post-war stories first published in 1925; chapter 5, "A Bottle of Perrier" and "Mr. Jones," from the period of 1926-1930; and finally in chapter 6, two stories from the 1930s, "Pomegranate Seed" and "All Souls."

Wharton's ghost stories provide an illuminating look at her personal conflicts and concerns projected on a cultural screen. Her work is still relevant and revealing today. Predicting patterns of late-twentieth-century thought, her work shows a progression from protest against male domination and patriarchal codes to the complexities of exploring sexuality, power struggles in relationships, and the individual's internal conflict between debilitating, but safe, codes of traditional thought and behavior, and the desire for growth.

Notes

1   I have used an expression of Wharton's out of context. In a letter to W. Morton Fullerton, early March 1908, Wharton writes, "And I'm so afraid that the treasures I long to unpack for you, that have come to me in magic ships from enchanted islands, are only to you the old familiar red calico & beads of the clever trader . . . ." (*Letters* 135).

2   Throughout my book, I have referenced Scribner's 1973 reprint of Wharton's ghost stories, a volume which is easily obtainable. This reprint was reissued in 1985. In the reprint, "The Looking Glass" replaces "A Bottle of Perrier." For the text of "A Bottle of Perrier," I have referenced R.W.B. Lewis's *The Collected Short Stories of Edith Wharton*, vol. 2.

In addition to "The Looking Glass," critics have considered the following stories as either ghost stories or closely related to the ghost story genre: "The Fullness of Life" (1893), "The Duchess at Prayer" (1900), "The Angel at the Grave" (1901), "The Moving Finger" (1901), "The House of the Dead Hand" (1904), and "After Holbein" (1930)." These dates are publication dates. For publication dates of Wharton's stories, I have relied on Barbara A. White, *Edith Wharton: A Study of the Short Fiction*, 173-175.

In the original Appleton-Century volume of *Ghosts*, 1937, the stories come after the preface in the following order: "All Souls," "The Eyes," "Afterward," "The Lady's Maid's Bell," "Kerfol," "The Triumph of Night," "Miss Mary Pask," "Bewitched," "Mr. Jones," "Pomegranate Seed," "A Bottle of Perrier."

3   In his 1953 study of Wharton's fiction (*Edith Wharton: A Study of Her Fiction*), Nevius uses the phrase "lurking feminism," which I have borrowed for my title, to refer to Wharton's feminist consciousness. In chapter V, "The Republic of the Spirit," Nevius writes: "In a sense Edith Wharton's fiction represents a continuous effort to define the good society." He then proceeds to summarize Wharton's ideas contained in a series of articles collected in *French Ways and Their Meaning*, which he says are important because they offer "the most concise formulation of her social ideal." In commenting on Wharton's concept of the superiority of the Frenchwoman over the American woman, he says:

> There is of course a lurking feminism in Mrs. Wharton's brief, which can be detected elsewhere in her implied criticism of the double standard of morality and in the appearance in so many of her stories of the emotionally low-charged, overscrupulous male protagonist (granted that this kind of logic makes Henry James, too, a feminist); but it is not the feminism, either

in kind or degree, of Willa Cather or Ellen Glasgow, for she regards men in abstract neither as junior partners nor as enemies. (85)

For a discussion of Wharton's concept of the Frenchwoman, see chapter 3 on "Afterward" in this book.

4   The term "feminism" has become a difficult term in that it implies a focus only on women's concerns rather than on societal and personal gender dynamics affecting both men and women. I strongly use the term to apply to a concern with societal and interpersonal constructs which limit individuals, male and female, within the society.

5   Wharton writes that it is not easy for a writer to achieve the "thermometrical quality." "All these tales, in which the effect sought is completely achieved, are models of the subtlest artifice. It is not enough to believe in ghosts, or even to have seen one, to be able to write a good ghost story." What is required first is that the writer must gain the reader's confidence.

> One of the chief obligations in a short story is to give the reader an immediate sense of security . . . . The greater the improbability to be overcome the more studied must be the approach, the more perfectly maintained the air of naturalness, the easy assumption that things are always likely to happen in that way.

Once the reader's confidence has been gained, "he may be lured on to the most incredible adventures." Wharton writes:

> The next rule of the game is to avoid distracting and splintering up [the reader's] attention. Many a would-be tale of horror becomes innocuous through the very multiplication and variety of its horrors. Above all, if they are multiplied they should be cumulative and not dispersed. But the fewer the better: once preliminary horror is posited, it is the harping on the same string—the same nerve—that does the trick.

She also cautions that "The least touch of irrelevance, the least chill of inattention, will instantly undo the spell . . . ." (*Writing of Fiction* 37-39).

6   Critics generally agree with Blake Nevius "that the stresses in her private life were reproduced in her fiction" (249). In his introduction to Wharton's collected stories, R.W.B. Lewis briefly considers the material that fueled her ghost stories:

> To what extent . . . was Edith Wharton's imagination working with her own private passions, impulses, and fears? To what extent was she 'distancing' elements in her personal life by converting them into the eerie or setting them in a foregone age or both . . . . To a very considerable extent, I should suppose. (*Collected Stories* xvii-xviii)

Leon Edel writes that Wharton survived in her life "by converting the stuff of experience—including her emotional helplessness—into the stuff of art . . . . Her art became the expression of her inward life" ("Stone in the Mirror" 830). Cynthia Griffin Wolff's extensive biocriticism of Wharton (*A Feast of Words: The Triumph of Edith Wharton*) illuminates many parallel relationships between Wharton's life and work.

> Once she began to create the visionary worlds of her fictions, her deepest feelings began to find expression in them . . . . Wharton was angry at the ways in which society had hedged the opportunities for even its most promising women. (Wolff, "Visionary Imagination" 26)

More recently, Lev Raphael's analysis of the psychology of shame in Wharton's life and fiction (*Edith Wharton's Prisoners of Shame*), Gloria Erlich's *The Sexual Education of Edith Wharton*, and Shari Benstock's biography, *No Gifts from Chance*, corroborate this widely demonstrated view. I agree that Wharton's personal conflicts and emotions heavily affect her views invested in her work.

7   For example, see R.B. Dooley's "A Footnote to Edith Wharton" (1954) on *The Age of Innocence and Old New York* and recently (1994), Shari Benstock's look at "A Line of Least Resistance" (*Gifts* 11).

8   To what extent was Wharton aware of this? A debated question. Dr. Henry Friedman ("The Masochistic Character in the Work of Edith Wharton") suggests that

> Since she is not basically an autobiographical novelist, there is always much work done in disguising the source of her basic themes. It does not appear to me that the disguise is a conscious one. In other words, as a psychiatrist reading these novels and comparing them to the available events of Mrs. Wharton's life, it does not appear that she was aware of the emergence of certain themes from her own life in her works. (317)

I agree that Wharton (as perhaps is any author's case) was not always fully aware of the ramifications of her work. Even so, I hesitate to underestimate her intuitive flashes of understanding of herself and her work. I also see her writing as a form of personal therapy. Wharton appears to have had a strong desire to communicate what she was learning to others.

Introduction

The Supernatural Tradition
and Wharton's Feminist Vision

It is, in fact, not easy to write a ghost story.

Preface to *Ghosts,* 1937

The ghost story with its oppressive Gothic atmosphere, its "vague shapes," and "filmy textures" provided Wharton with a perfect vehicle to create her feminist vision (Howells v). Having read a great deal of classical poetry, Elizabethan drama, and German and English Romantic poetry in which the supernatural often plays its part, she was familiar with and appreciated the supernatural tradition in literature. In a letter to Morton Fullerton in 1908, Wharton exhorts him to tell her all the details about the "mysterious Stenheil murder" saying "You know I adore horror & mysteries, and your friend Aidé never had a more impassioned reader of his 'creepy stories' than I was in my youth" (*Letters* 147).[1] In *The Writing of Fiction* (1925), she defends the "eerie" tale citing "Almost all the best tales of Scott, Hawthorne, and Poe" as belonging "to that peculiar category of the eerie that lies outside of the classic tradition" (34). As influences on her work, she refers to Scott, Poe's "awful hallucinations," Le Fanu, Stevenson, and Henry James, the "last great master of the eerie in English" (36-37). In the preface to *Ghosts,* she puts "her attempts . . . under the protection of those who first stimulated [her] to make the experiment."

> The earliest, I believe, was Stevenson, with 'Thrawn Janet' and 'Markheim'; two remarkable ghost stories, though far from the high level of such wizards as Sheridan Le Fanu and Fitz James O'Brien. I doubt if these have ever been surpassed, though Marion Crawfurd's isolated effort, "The Upper Berth," comes very near to the crawling horror of O'Brien's "What Is It?"

She adds that "For imaginative handling of the supernatural no one, to my mind, has touched Henry James in 'The Turn of the Screw.'" Wharton has dedicated *Ghosts* to Walter de la Mare, whose protection she had special reason to call upon, for she saw him in 1937 as "The only modern ghost evoker whom I place in the first rank" (*Ghost Stories* 3-4).[2]

Many critics and authors in the early twentieth century claimed that the ghost story, particularly popular in the Victorian era, was a worn-out genre. Dorothy Scarborough in her 1917 study of supernatural fiction disagrees, noting that the genre had benefited from modern developments in the writing of fiction and psychology. "Like every other phase of Man's [sic] thought, ghostly fiction shows the increasing complexity of form and matter, the wealth of added material and abounding richness of style, the fine subtleties that only modernity can give."[3] Like Scarborough, Wharton did not doubt that writers existed who could invest meaning into an old form. She questioned, however, the twentieth-century reader's ability to enjoy and understand the subtle ghost story. In the preface to *Ghosts*, she writes: "I have made the depressing discovery that the faculty required for . . . enjoyment [of the ghost story] has become almost atrophied in modern man. The creative faculty (for reading should be a creative act as well as writing) is rapidly withering, together with the power of sustained attention." Wharton laments the generation gap between her generation "for whom everything which used to nourish the imagination . . . had to be won by an effort, and then slowly assimilated" to the new generation who "is now served up" everything "cooked, seasoned and chopped into little bits." Citing the instance of "a host of inquirers" writing to know the meaning of the title of "Pomegranate Seed" (one of the stories in *Ghosts*, published originally in 1931), she writes that she deplores the current lack of cultural literacy and notes parenthetically, "In the dark ages of my childhood an acquaintance with classical fairy lore was as much a part of our stock of knowledge as Grimm and Andersen." She also regrets her readers' lack of imagination because they insist on asking "how a ghost could write a letter, or put it into a letter box."[4] What she requires for the reading of one of her ghost stories is "a common medium between myself and my readers, of their meeting me halfway among the primeval shadows, and filling in the gaps in my narrative with sensations and divinations akin to my own" (*Ghost Stories* 1-2).

Wharton's interest in ghosts lay in her sensitivity to attitudes and behaviors that control our lives. She had no actual interest or belief in spiritualism or the occult. She discussed occult phenomena with her friend, Philomène de Lévis-Mirepoix (Countess de la Forest-Divonne), but Wharton wrote to Bernard Berenson that Philomène dwelled on "third-rate flashy rubbish, of the kind that most enervates the mental muscle—'occultism,' the Sar Peladan, mediums ('after all, there *is* something in it'), vital fluids, & all the lyre—or the lie." In another letter to Berenson, she notes that "Philomène is now absorbed in Coue-ism & spiritualism, and I find our talks rather boring . . . ." (*Letters* 450-51, 454). In the preface to *Ghosts* , Wharton, however, quite seriously refers to the "ghost-feeler" as opposed to the "ghost-seer" as a "person sensible of invisible currents . . . ." She says that "The celebrated reply . . . 'No, I don't believe in ghosts, but I'm afraid of them,' is much more than the cheap paradox it seems to many" (2).

In her ghost stories, Wharton relied upon possibilities inherent in the supernatural genre to create her feminist themes. Researchers in the supernatural field generally agree that elements of fantasy literature connect directly to the sociological and the psychological, to cultural taboos and unconscious desires.[5] In his famous essay on "The Uncanny," Freud attributes the feeling of the uncanny (such as one would have upon seeing a ghost) to two possible causes: repressed infantile complexes revived by some impression, or discarded primitive beliefs once more confirmed. He associates the uncanny with that which is hidden, concealed, repressed. "It may be true that the uncanny is nothing else than a hidden, familiar thing that has undergone repression and then emerged from it" (153). Freud connects the uncanny with cultural taboos. In his view, repressed knowledge which erupts into consciousness must be buried again for the maintenance of individual psychological stability and cultural order.

Rosemary Jackson, in her study of the fantastic, challenges Freud's conservative view. She agrees that "the fantastic traces the unsaid and the unseen of culture: that which has been silenced, made invisible, covered over and made 'absent' . . . . Themes of the fantastic in literature revolve around this problem of making visible the un-seen, of articulating the unsaid" (48, 4).[6] However, Jackson claims that fantastic literature is subversive, attempting to bring the unconscious to the conscious level, to unleash the repressed, to reveal that which is taboo, in order to bring about new awarenesses and psychological and social change.

According to Jackson, conservative "safe" texts of fantasy echo Freud in their attempts to preserve the existing culture. For example, *Dracula* (1897) explores cultural sexual taboos. Dracula's dark sexuality threatens, but Mina Harker and company, representing bourgeois British values, triumph. Van Helsing, representing reason and scientific thought, in effect the backbone of the British patriarchy, brings back order and stability. The conservative themes preserve the existing social order. On the other hand, Jackson argues that the subject matter of the narrative is radical and taboo, the subtext ultimately subversive, representing rebellion against repressive

Victorian sexual mores. "Fantasy is preoccupied with limits, with limiting categories . . . . Subversive texts activate a dialogue . . . directing their energy towards a dissolution of repressive structure" (48).

Post-Freudian psychologists tend to side with Jackson, viewing this subversive tendency as healthier than the repressive mode which is seen as debilitating to the individual and to the society. Ironically, given Freud's theories, Jackson sees re-repression as a "death drive . . . a desire to cease 'to be,' a longing to transcend or escape the human" (156). Her view suggests an integrative Jungian model of self rather than a repressive Freudian model. The Jungian "shadow" is not repressed, but integrated into a new self and a new society.

Thus Jackson describes the fantasy writer as a creator of a subtext, both personal and cultural, whether working from conscious thought or subconscious impulse. She emphasizes that the fantasy writer may also create from the perspective of a subculture or counterculture apart from prevailing orthodoxy. Her theories explain, in part, the reticence of some to accept supernatural literature wholeheartedly. Instead, they relegate it to a subgenre in the realm of outcast popular literature. In effect, the writer of fantasy, whether consciously intending to or not, writes from a "wild zone" that presents a threat to cultural order, requiring new knowledge of self or society to be repressed again or acknowledged and integrated.

Jackson's subversive theory of fantasy presents a striking parallel to the concept of the "wild zone" developed by Oxford anthropologists Shirley and Edwin Ardener as a model of women's culture, a theory which has had an impact on the marginalized female literary tradition. The Ardeners' model of women's culture shows women as a "muted group," the boundaries of whose culture overlap with the dominant male culture. The two cultures can be represented by intersecting circles. Most of the muted female circle falls within the boundaries of the dominant male circle, but there is a crescent of the female circle which lies outside the dominant boundary and is therefore labelled "wild." As Elaine Showalter points out, the "muted" aspect of the "wild zone" suggests problems both of power and language:

> Both muted and dominant groups generate beliefs on ordering ideas of social reality at the unconscious level, but dominant groups control the forms or structures in which consciousness can be articulated. Thus muted groups must mediate their beliefs through the allowable forms of dominant structures. Another way of putting this would be to say that all language is the language of the dominant order, and women, if they speak at all, must speak through it. Through

ritual and art, the muted group can speak, although the messages are screened by the forms of the dominant structure and must be deciphered and interpreted. ("Feminist Criticism" 261-262)

This cultural model suggests that women writers live a duality, "as members of the general culture and as partakers of women's culture" (Lerner, qtd. in Showalter 261). They pass back and forth between male-centered literary tradition and themes, and female-centered concerns, yet women writers have been forced by the desire for publication and recognition to appear to be male-centered.

A woman writer, such as Wharton, emerging from a male-centered tradition, but nonetheless working from the "wild zone," often produces a dual text, a text in the dominant language observing traditional forms, and a subtext which, breaking the bonds of the dominant language through a sub-language, conveys her perspective. Showalter calls this dual text a "double-voiced discourse" containing a "dominant" and a "muted" story. "Two oscillating texts" are

> simultaneously in view . . . . The orthodox plot recedes, and another plot, hitherto submerged in the anonymity of the background, stands out in bold relief like a thumbprint . . . . Through the voluntary entry into the wild zone . . . a woman can write her way out of the 'cramped confines of patriarchal space.' ("Feminist Criticism" 266, 263)

One of the most difficult problems with writing from the "wild zone" of women's culture is living with a "divided consciousness." For women, "existing in the dominant system of meanings and values that structure culture and society may be a painful, or amusing, double dance, clicking in, clicking out . . . ." (Duplessis 285). Another difficult problem is finding the forms and language to present a dual text. As Alicia Ostriker puts it, "women have always tried to steal the language" (315). Annette Kolodny writes that "women writers, coming into a tradition of literary language and conventional forms already appropriated for centuries, to the purposes of male expression, will be forced to 'wrestle' with that language in an effort to 'remake' it a language adequate to [their] conceptual processes" ("Minefield" 148).[7]

Women writers, like many other artists struggling with new visions that are not acceptable to or understood by the dominant culture, turn to the available, subtle literary techniques of imagery, symbolism, euphemism, circumlocution, implication, innuendo, dramatic irony, and the importance of what is "not said" to convey their plots and themes, even innovatively expanding the limits of these techniques. Showalter notes that "women's literature is still haunted by ghosts of repressed language . . . . The feminist content of feminine art is typically oblique, displaced, ironic, and subversive; one has to read it between the lines, in the missed possibilities of the text" (256). This "female aesthetic" challenges the reader to creative interpretation and evaluation.[8] At first, themes may appear to be submerged and murky, narrative techniques ineffective. Standards of judgment and taste drawn from a male tradition of criticism designed for the work of mainstream male writers may no longer apply as originally conceived.

Reading the text of Wharton's feminism in her ghost stories depends on exploring a "buried" feminist text and a female aesthetic made possible by the subversive nature and odd conventions of supernatural fiction. Supernatural fiction, as a literary stepchild, emerging from a need to probe muted concerns, offered Wharton a ready-made form with few drawbacks. Mainstream male writers were writing supernatural fiction, and it was a popular, lucrative genre. The world of the supernatural with its accepted conventions offered a language that could readily be turned to her purposes.

Employing the ghost story, Wharton masters the evocation of terror and horror. "Terror" and "horror," terms often used loosely and synonymously, have been defined, debated, even confused by many.[9] Devendra Varma clarifies the terms: "The difference between Terror and Horror is the difference between awful apprehension and sickening realization: between the smell of death and stumbling against the corpse" (130). Wharton strives for both apprehension, or dread, and realization in her tales. Using suspense to increase terror, Wharton often delays revelations, emphasizing their ultimate horror. The horror, always psychological in her work, not physical, lies often more fully with the reader than with the characters who may not consciously understand what they have experienced, who may only be beginning to understand what they have experienced, or who may quickly re-repress threatening knowledge of themselves or their circumstances.

Using symbolic imagery, Wharton sets up a dialectic on personal and cultural concerns. As Margaret McDowell has pointed out, the ghost "always conveys some inescapable symbolic truth" ("Ghost Stories" 135). Wharton's ghosts inevitably, disturbingly, represent suppressed and repressed knowledge. Creating strange turns of plot and abrupt endings which defy conventional aesthetics, Wharton raises questions about "acceptable" codes of character and conduct. Ingeniously incorporating implication, innuendo, and strategic gaps of information, Wharton subtly presents her subversive themes. She also marshalls for her own purposes other techniques developed by masters of supernatural fiction: the confused or unaware single consciousness as narrator or register, a technique pioneered and advanced by Radcliffe, Poe, and James, and James' process of adumbration, a technique of non-specification which makes the reader "think the evil . . . think it for himself" (*Art of Criticism* 343).

In the stories collected in *Ghosts*, Edith Wharton took up the challenge to invest the ghost story with fresh impact. Her ghosts are not just weak reflections of a worn-out Gothic tradition, but highly charged images with subversive intent. Drawing energy from the "wild zone" of the supernatural and the "wild zone" of women's culture, she produced eleven tales of horror, seemingly writing towards the dissolution of repressive structures leading to the evolution of what we term today "a masculinist-feminist culture, a culture whose styles and structures will no longer be patriarchal in the old way" (Gilbert, "Volcano" 43). Her ghost stories reflect the complexity of her conflicts and grievances suggesting an "improved reordering of the present and the future," which, sadly, is never realized for her characters or for herself (Kolodny, "Minefield" 162). Her work plunges the reader into the depths of the repressed unconscious, psychologically and culturally. What Wharton achieves is a vision of the brutal domination of patriarchal and capitalistic codes in western culture, the debilitating limitations of cultural gender identity, and the blindness and suffering of men and women, both victims of restrictive social conventions.

Notes

1   The supernatural tradition, as I use the term, refers to fantasy literature or literature of the fantastic containing supernatural elements, either confirmed or implied. As Wharton notes, she was interested in mystery and horror with or without the supernatural elements. Her interests and her work embrace the Gothic tradition (the heart of which is the Gothic atmosphere of oppression and repression), mystery, tales of terror and horror. Her ghost stories, specifically part of the supernatural tradition, reflect these elements. A further discussion of "terror" and "horror" follows in this introduction. See the Works Cited list for books that offer discussions of these various genres.

Helen Killoran's "Edith Wharton's Reading in European Languages and Its Influence on Her Work" and Richard Lawson's *Edith Wharton and German Literature* are particularly helpful in finding out what books Wharton owned and likely read. Her letters frequently discuss what she is reading. Hamilton Aidé (1826-1907) was a friend of Henry James and Morton Fullerton. Wharton had read his book *Morals and Mysteries* (1872) when she was younger.

2   For a discussion of relationships between Wharton's ghost stories and those of de la Mare, see Margaret McDowell's "Edith Wharton's Ghost Tales Reconsidered," 298-312.

3   Referring to primitive Gothic forms, Scarborough (*The Supernatural in Modern English Fiction*, 1917) writes:

> The modern supernaturalism is more complex, more psychological than the terroristic . . . . Humanity still wants ghosts, as ever, but they must be more cleverly presented to be convincing. The ghostly thrill is as ardently desired by the reading public, as eagerly striven for by the writers as ever, though it is more difficult of achievement now than formerly. Yet when it is attained, it is more poignant and lasting in its effects because more subtle in its art. The apparition that eludes analysis haunts the memory more than do the comparatively simple forms of the past. Compare, for instance, the spirits evoked by Henry James and Katherine Fullerton Gerould with the crude claptrap of cloistered spooks and armored knights of Gothic times. How cheap and melodramatic the earlier attempts seem. (71-72)

Writer Katherine Fullerton Gerould was a cousin of Morton Fullerton who was raised in his family. She was at one time engaged to Fullerton.

4   Interestingly, she attributes this literalness to the "two world-wide enemies of the imagination, the wireless and the cinema" (Preface, *Ghost Stories* 1-2).

5   In a study of the Gothic tradition (*The Literature of Terror: A History of Gothic Fictions from 1765 to the Present Day*), David Punter writes: "Gothic fiction becomes a process of cultural self-analysis, and the images it throws up become the dream-figures of a troubled social group" (425). In a study of the tale of terror (*The Delights of Terror: An Aesthetics of the Tale of Terror*), Terry Heller writes:

> Fantasy gains it particular power to terrify by presenting images of the culturally forbidden, which is the content of our unconscious . . . . Horrors become charged with vague and disturbing meanings . . . . Though [the] monsters have actions to perform in their plots, they also act directly upon the reader, threatening to bring repressed fears into consciousness. (40, 33, 47)

Julia Briggs, in a study of the ghost story (*Night Visitors: The Rise and Fall of the English Ghost Story*), suggests that the supernatural represents repressed, inadmissible truths concerning the inner life or the outer world (22-23).

6   Critics generally agree with this concept. See also Todorov, Lovecraft, Messent, Penzoldt, Rabkin, Sullivan, Thompson.

7   For discussions of these feminist concepts, see Elaine Showalter's *The New Feminist Criticism: Essays on Women, Literature, and Theory*, and the work of Sandra M. Gilbert and Susan Gubar. In particular, see the essay on Wharton "Angel of Devastation: Edith Wharton on the Arts of the Enslaved" in *Sexchanges*, vol. 2 of *No Man's Land: The Place of the Woman Writer in the Twentieth Century*.

8   In "For the Etruscans," Rachel Blau Duplessis writes:

> The female aesthetic turns out to be a specialized name for all social practices which wish to criticize, to differentiate from, to overturn the dominant forms of knowing and understanding with which they are saturated . . . . Female aesthetic begins when women take, investigate, the structures of feeling that are [theirs] . . . . Following the female aesthetic will produce artworks that incorporate contradiction and nonlinear movement into the heart of the text." (278)

9   Radcliffe ("On the Supernatural in Poetry") writes that terror and horror are opposites. Terror is fear "which expands the soul, and awakens the faculties to a high degree of life. Horror contracts, freezes, and annihilates them" (149). H.P. Lovecraft (*Supernatural Horror in Literature*) blurs the two terms by tying terror and horror to atmosphere; he sacrifices precision of definition to a captivating metaphor: "The one test of the really weird is simply this—whether or not there be excited in the reader a profound sense of dread, and of contact with unknown spheres and powers; a subtle attitude of awed listening, as if for the beating of black wings on the scratching of outside shapes and entities on the known universe's utmost rim" (16). Barton Levi St. Armand (*The Roots of Horror in the Fiction of H.P. Lovecraft*), following Radcliffe's lead, distinctly separates terror and horror: "Terror expands the soul outward . . . . Horror overtakes the soul from inside" (2). Others connect horrors only to physical dangers and gruesome physical realities, not necessarily psychological dangers, which are Wharton's focus.

One

"The Lady's Maid's Bell"

Success had convinced her of her vocation. She was sure now that it was her
duty to lay bare the secret plague spots of society.

"Expiation," 1904

"The Lady's Maid's Bell" is the oldest story appearing in *Ghosts*. It was
first published in *Scribner's Magazine*, November, 1902, and reprinted in
1904 in the story collection *The Descent of Man*. Wharton wrote the tale
during an incredibly intense period of literary activity just after she finished her novel *The Valley of Decision* (Lewis, "Powers of Darkness" 644),
and sent it to Burlingame, editor of *Scribner's Magazine*, in January, 1902.
R.W.B. Lewis writes that it was "the first in a series of ghost stories which
were to establish her as a major practitioner in this possibly minor genre,
and a sign that her own ghost-haunted days could now be drawn upon to
expert literary and psychological use" (*Biography* 107).[1] Wharton's "ghost-
haunted days" indeed seemed to be behind her or in perspective as she, at
forty years of age, moved from a dalliance with literary pursuits to a professional commitment to writing, and began to create for herself a personal identity and life style compatible with her talents and interests. Behind
her lay a stifled childhood, failed romances, entry into an unhappy marriage, and years of debilitating illness. "The Lady's Maid's Bell" reso-
nates with echoes from these circumstances.[2]

Born Edith Newbold Jones into a family with two older brothers soon
to leave the household, Wharton, in effect, grew up an "only" child. She
travelled extensively, learned languages, and developed a love for the beauty
of Europe over the drabness of New York. She lived in well-to-do circumstances in Europe, New York City, and Newport, and had privileged social
opportunities. Despite the advantages of her wealth and social situation,
we know from her autobiography that her main childhood remembrances
are of a lonely little girl reading in her father's library and compulsively
"making up" stories. Although these experiences demonstrate her imagination and early love of language, they also isolated her. She felt even

more isolated because of her mother who seemed to dominate her life. She experienced her mother's influence in contradictory extremes, alternately "hot and cold," leaving her feeling insecure and rejected. Both R.W.B. Lewis and Cynthia Griffin Wolff have well outlined the repressive effect of Lucretia Jones on her daughter. More recent studies have also explored the negative attachment of Wharton to her lonely father "haunted by something always unexpressed and unattained" (*Backward Glance* 39).[3] The social restrictions of Old New York also created a repressive environment for Wharton in her youth. Her world was made up of strict social codes and proper behavior that could be abandoned only at risk of being "cut" and ostracized. Wharton's mother was a fine product and embodiment of the social codes which she pressed on her daughter to insure her survival within the folds of their privileged society.

However, Wharton's lonely childhood and her escape through books and imagination led her to a different path: she was drawn to literature and art. By adolescence, she had written enough verse to fill a small volume that was privately printed by her family and had written a first novel (*Fast and Loose*) that remained unpublished. She notes in her autobiography that these pursuits were considered trivial in her world: "In the eyes of our provincial society authorship was still regarded as something between a black art and a form of manual labor" (*Backward Glance* 68-69). Wolff points out that the unresolved crises of Wharton's childhood—loneliness, rejection, repression, painful shyness, and the conflict between her interests and talents and the right thing for a young woman in her set to pursue—"left a residue—a language that instinctively turns to evocations of heat and cold or starvation and suffocation, and a view of the world that focuses excessively upon the dangers of emotion and the threat of isolation" (*Feast* 24).

The proper path for Wharton and other young women in her society normally led to marriage. However, her efforts to walk this path met with disappointment and failure. Her alliance with Harry Stevens ended in a broken engagement. Her next serious encounter with romance was with Walter Berry, a promising young lawyer whom she met at Newport in 1883, who could have provided the marriage she needed socially as well as have been, according to her, her soulmate for life, but Berry did not propose. According to his account, he considered marriage, but delayed action to pursue his career. Berry would enter Wharton's life again fourteen years later and become her dearest friend. She acknowledges this in her autobiography: "His character, his deepest personality, were interwoven with mine" (*Backward Glance* 116).

In 1885, Wharton did marry at the age of twenty-four, narrowly escaping society's idea of spinsterhood, and took up a life of social obligations and travel. She married Edward (Teddy) Wharton, an affable, socially well-connected, handsome Harvard graduate with a poor intellectual record. They shared an interest in the country and horses, but Teddy preferred hunting and fishing over literature and the arts. They were incompatible for the long twenty-eight years of their marriage. Wharton's good friend, Henry James, said that, in marrying Teddy Wharton, she had done "an almost—or rather an utterly—inconceivable thing" (qtd. in Lewis, *Biography* 52). Apparently the incompatibility of talents and interests was compounded by sexual incompatibility as well. According to Lewis, "The marriage was not consummated for three weeks . . . . There is no question that the sexual side of the marriage was a disaster" (*Biography* 53). Marrying to escape from earlier conflicts and social stigma did not lead to fulfillment, but to further conflict that threatened Wharton's physical health and emotional stability.

In a letter to Sara Norton, April 12, 1908, Wharton refers to years of "neurasthenia" that plagued her life. She writes:

> For twelve years I seldom knew what it was to be, for more than an hour or two of the twenty-four, without an intense feeling of nausea, and such unutterable fatigue that when I got up I was always more tired than when I lay down. This form of neurasthenia consumed the best years of my youth, and left, in some sort, an irreparable shade on my life. *Mais quoi!* I worked through it, and came out on the other side. (*Letters* 139-140)

The twelve years of illness started after her marriage and did not end until 1900 after Wharton stepped up her literary activity and literally began to write her way to the "other side."[4] In her autobiography, she writes:

> I had yet no real personality of my own, and was not to acquire one till my first volume of short stories was published—and that was not until 1899 . . . . At last I had groped my way through to my vocation, and thereafter I never doubted that story-telling was my job. (*Backward Glance* 112)

Of the ensuing active writing years until 1903, she writes:

> These years were perhaps the happiest I was to know as regards literary hopes and achievements. My long experimenting had resulted in two or three books which brought me more encouragement than I had ever dreamed of obtaining, and were the means of making some of the happiest friendships of my life. The reception of my books gave me the self-confidence I had so long lacked, and in the company of people who shared my tastes, and treated me as their equal, I

ceased to suffer from the agonizing shyness which used to rob such encounters of all pleasure." (*Backward Glance* 133)

In 1902, when Wharton turned to the ghost story, the circumstances of her life were changing. Emerging from years of conflict and ill health, Wharton began to build her career and a new life. Her mother, with whom relations had cooled over the years, died in Paris in June, 1901. Wharton probably last saw her mother the summer of 1900 during her annual trip to Europe, but in June of 1901, occupied by literary pursuits, Wharton was not at her mother's death bed nor did she attend the funeral. Lewis connects the death of Wharton's mother with her writing of ghost stories: "With the source of her childhood terrors removed, the mature writer could now deploy her memory of them to expert literary purpose" ("Powers of Darkness" 644).[5] In 1897, Walter Berry had re-entered her life as friend, mentor, critic, and one with whom she could share her greatest artistic pleasures. Berry, Wharton, and her husband formed a trio, suspiciously like a love triangle. But according to Lewis, Berry and Teddy Wharton had a cheerful relationship (*Biography* 209). Yet Teddy Wharton, too, slowly began to change. As a leisured gentleman, he managed The Mount, the new estate he shared with his wife, which was primarily built and supported by her monies, pursued his sporting interests, tolerated his wife's literary friends who were the most frequent household guests, and as his wife blossomed, he began to decline, his difficulties ultimately leading to financial irregularities and emotional instability that would precipitate their divorce.

Not surprisingly, Wharton incorporated many of the conflicts of her life into her first ghost story.[6] "The Lady's Maid's Bell" is a tale of a stifling, repressive environment, debilitating illness, an unhappy marriage, and a triangular relationship. The setting of the tale is Wharton's milieu: an upper-class household of New York. When Alice Hartley, a young Englishwoman, arrives at Brympton Place on the Hudson as the new lady's maid, she finds Mrs. Brympton, an unhappy, invalid mistress; Mr. Brympton, an unhappy, unpleasant master; and a third party, Mr. Ranford, a kindly young neighbor who, in the absence of the husband, takes long walks with the wife and reads her books. Hartley also finds a ghost: Emma Saxon, the former lady's maid of twenty years whom Mrs. Brympton "loved like a sister" (*Ghost Stories* 10).[7] As narrator of the tale, Hartley appears to tell her story honestly, but her interpretation of the events at Brympton Place is an unreliable one. Beyond Hartley's superficial, biased interpretation of events, the story offers the reader a subtext created by implication, dramatic irony, symbolism, and the use of calculated absences.

The reader's challenge is to probe the subtext to discover the secret that the "gloomy house" and the ghostly presence represent.

Wharton set the scene through Gothic architectural imagery. The reading of the "text" of the house and its inhabitants is a classic motif from early Gothic fiction that has been subsequently borrowed by many other writers of supernatural fiction, including Poe in "The Fall of the House of Usher" (1839), Hawthorne in *The House of the Seven Gables* (1851), and James in *The Turn of the Screw* (1898). The foreboding castle or manor house of Gothic fiction represents an isolated, repressive environment. Similarly, Brympton Place, which depresses Hartley at first sight, evinces a stifling atmosphere where horrors lurk. Hartley reports: "The moment I caught sight of the house again my heart dropped down like a stone in a well. It was not a gloomy house exactly, yet I never entered it but a feeling of gloom came over me." When Hartley leaves the house to go to town to shop, she feels "high glee," leaving behind the repressive emotional atmosphere as though she were released from prison (13). Wharton was readily drawn to this conventional imagery because of her lifelong interest in architecture and also because of the symbolic potential and her conviction that the knowledge of characters' lives could be conveyed through setting. She writes: "The impression produced by a landscape, a street or a house should always . . . be an event in the history of a soul" (*Writing of Fiction* 85).[8]

Drawing further on literary tradition, Wharton selected a naive and unreliable narrator whose confusion fragments the tale and builds suspense. Wharton thought that the writer should select as reflector the "mind that can take the widest possible view . . . . It is the story-teller's first care to choose this reflecting mind deliberately" (*Writing of Fiction* 46). In the supernatural tale, the selection of the narrator requires "view" in terms of what the narrator can observe, but not necessarily "view" in terms of what the narrator can comprehend. Hartley, in her position as the servant permitted in Mrs. Brympton's quarters, can report what goes on in private chambers, but her interpretation of events is limited and biased. Yet her views are persuasive because she speaks earnestly from her frame of reference. Because she plays into classic Gothic stereotypes familiar to the reader, she easily captures the reader's imagination.

Arriving at Brympton Place, Hartley has little information about her new post, but she does not ask questions. Nevertheless, she quickly begins to draw conclusions about her master, her mistress, and the frequent visitor, Ranford. To her, Mrs. Brympton is a wonderful woman, a "delicate-looking lady" whose smile made her feel "there was nothing [she] wouldn't do for her" (8-9). Hartley sees her mistress as the victim of an "unhappy match" (12). Brympton is, in Hartley's eyes, a brute. She describes him as a man with "bad-tempered blue eyes" and a "red and savage" face, "an angry red spot coming out on his forehead." From her first meeting with him, Hartley infers that Brympton is a philanderer. He looks her over "in a trice." She says: "I knew what that look meant, from having experienced it once or twice in my former places." When Brympton turns his back on her, Hartley concludes: "I knew what that meant, too. I was not the kind of morsel he was after" (11). She also finds Brympton generally unpleasant, "cursing the dullness and solitude, grumbling at everything . . . ." She observes him sitting "half the night over the old Brympton port and madeira . . . drinking a good deal more than was good for him." One night she observes him coming upstairs "in such a state that [she] turned sick to think of what some ladies have to endure and hold their tongues about" (12). This questionable interpretation of the Brymptons' sex life is accepted by R.W.B. Lewis who writes: "The action turns on the brutish physical demands made by one Brympton upon his fastidious wife . . . ." (*Collected Stories* xvii). Hartley sums up her opinion of Brympton as "coarse, loud and pleasure-loving." She corroborates her views by saying: "Nobody loved him below stairs" (10).

In contrast to Brympton, Mr. Ranford, the third member of the triangle, is something of a saint to Hartley; he is "a slight, tall gentleman . . . rather melancholy looking till I saw his smile, which had a kind of surprise in it, like the first warm day in spring" (11-12). The "servants all like him" and "we were glad to think that Mrs. Brympton had a pleasurable companionable gentleman like that to keep her company when the master was away." Hartley remarks that Brympton and Ranford were on "excellent terms" (12). "The gentlemen seemed fast friends," although she "couldn't but wonder that two gentlemen so unlike each other should be so friendly" (17, 12). According to Hartley, there is no romance or love affair between Mrs. Brympton and Ranford. The morning when her mistress sends her with a note to Ranford, urging her to be back before Brympton gets up, Hartley suspects that something is going on, but she squelches her suspicions, saying, "I would have staked my head on my mistress' goodness" (17).

Hartley holds decided opinions of her employers and Ranford; however, she has no opinion of the household ghost, Emma Saxon. To her, the ghost of Mrs. Brympton's former lady's maid (identified from a picture) represents a great mystery which she cannot fathom. Each appearance of the ghost is a reproach, making her feel compelled to try to solve some mystery for her mistress which seems to be connected to Ranford. "I had never thought harm of my mistress and Mr. Ranford, but I was sure now that, from one cause or another, some dreadful thing hung over them. She [the ghost] knew what it was . . . ." But Emma Saxon never speaks, and Hartley never understands Emma's mission. "I had not been able to guess what she wanted. Her last look had pierced me to the marrow; and yet it had not told me . . . . It seemed as if she had left me all alone to carry the weight of the secret I couldn't guess" (24).

Hartley is unable to interpret Emma's presence, but even if she were to come to a view, her lack of perception as a register of events would undermine her interpretation. Wharton loads the story with hints to show that Hartley is not a reliable narrator. Coming to Brympton Place after a bout with typhoid fever, "weak and tottery" (6), Hartley describes herself as one not prone to ask questions, not impulsive, and not likely to lie. As the story progresses, her actions belie her words. So many mysteries confront her that she begins to ask questions, but ironically, no one in the repressive atmosphere of the Brympton household talks. Mrs. Blinder the cook (as blind as Mrs. Gross in *The Turn of the Screw*) avoids answering questions by changing the subject or leaving the room. Finally, Hartley wants to ask Mr. Blinder and the butler, Mr. Wace, about the ghost, because she thinks they are "the only two in the house who appeared to have an inkling of what was going on," but she does not ask, for she had the feeling that "they would deny everything" (18). Not able to get information, Hartley begins to speculate wildly. When Mrs. Brympton sends her to have a prescription filled, she hysterically asks the pharmacist if it is safe, worried that Mrs. Brympton might be depressed enough to commit suicide. The prescription is safe. When Brympton asks her if she has been out the morning she takes Mrs. Brympton's note to Ranford, she lies and tells him she was not out. Growing very nervous after she has been at Brympton Place a short time, Hartley begins to doubt her own perceptions. "I grew so nervous that the least sound made me jump . . . . I fancied I heard noises" (13). Repeatedly she says, "I think I must be dreaming." When she appears at Mrs. Brympton's door the first time the lady's maid's bell rings, she thinks Brympton has been drinking, yet when he walks down the hall, she confesses "To my surprise, I saw that he walked as straight as a sober man" (16). The next day a comment by Brympton further puts her view in question: "I suppose you thought I was drunk last night? A pretty notion my servants have of me" (18). The second time she answers the ring of the bell and appears at Mrs. Brympton's door, she is rebuked by her: "I didn't ring. You must have been dreaming" (25). Increasingly, Hartley, who cannot sleep well anymore, becomes distraught as the demands of a situation she cannot understand overwhelm her. Basically an honest, earnest narrator, Hartley is nonetheless not a reliable one. In addition to her lack of information and shaky conclusions, she imposes the gender biases of her own class and a conventional value system on the Brymptons; she does not understand how debilitating the restrictions of social structures and conventions can be. The reader must look beyond Hartley's interpretations to the subtext to understand what might actually be going on in the Brympton household.

Hartley's conclusions do not take into account many details which she almost inadvertently conveys to the reader. She virtually ignores Brympton's jealousy of Ranford. She overhears Brympton say to his wife: "One would suppose he was the only person fit for you to talk to." On another occasion, he asks her, "Where's Ranford? He hasn't been near the house for a week? Does he keep away because I'm here?" Mrs. Brympton's answer is inaudible. Brympton says: "Well, two's company and three's trumpery; I'm sorry to be in Ranford's way, and I suppose I shall have to take myself off again in a day or two and give him a show" (14). When Brympton arrives home unexpectedly the eve of his wife's death, as he pushes past Hartley and Mrs. Brympton to go to the dressing room, he tells Hartley he is "going to meet a friend." When Hartley admonishes him to look at his wife, he says, "It seems that's done for me" (26). At Mrs. Brympton's funeral, Hartley reports that Brympton stares at Ranford "instead of following the prayers as a mourner should" (26). Although not interpreted by Hartley, it is suggested to the reader through dramatic irony that Brympton suspects an affair and that his surprise visit home is an attempt to confront the situation.

Brympton's jealousy is not likely ill-founded. Other details reported by Hartley, but not interpreted, imply clandestine meetings between Mrs. Brympton and Ranford. On the night Brympton arrives home unexpectedly, but before his arrival, Hartley hears a suspicious noise. "Once I thought I heard a door open and close again below: it might have been the glass door that led to the gardens" (24). Also when Hartley's bell rings and she arrives at her mistress's door, she sees that Mrs. Brympton "had not undressed for the night" and gives her a "startled look" (25). This information hints at a midnight rendezvous between Mrs. Brympton and

Ranford which Brympton intends to interrupt. The reader might even con-jecture, from the footsteps that Hartley hears in the hall, that Ranford some-times hides out in Emma Saxon's old room, making noises at night, and after hours, sneaking into Mrs. Brympton's rooms.

The dreadful secret that Hartley seems on the verge of discovering, but resists acknowledging, is the possibility of a romance or affair be-tween Ranford and Mrs. Brympton, that their "goodness" is a sham. Yet Wharton's story is not completely told after she implies the possibility of a Brympton-Ranford liaison. Emma Saxon's symbolic significance provides the key to levels of understanding beyond this literal level and beyond Hartley's limited comprehension. For Emma does not ring the bell on Mrs. Brympton to announce a scandal. Not a conventionally moralistic ghost, Emma appears to be Mrs. Brympton's guardian angel, protecting her in her efforts to escape the constraints of an unhappy marriage which must be maintained for social reasons. Or Emma may be read as Mrs. Brympton's double, her shadow self, embodying the emotional desires and conflicts which she normally represses to maintain the conventional front of a stable marriage.[9] Carol Sapora has shown how Wharton uses literary doubling, a widely used Gothic convention to show "division and con-flict" within a character or the public self versus the private self. Sapora notes that "Deceit and hypocrisy are essential ingredients of a woman's socially acceptable self, necessary to the appearance—if not the fact—of the purity and innocence of ideal womanhood."[10] Emma represents Mrs. Brympton's other self and her inner needs and desires for expression, es-cape, and finally selfhood.

Susan Goodman's conclusion in studying Wharton's canon is that al-though societal code fosters competition among women, Wharton valued female relationships and saw cooperation between women essential in women's gaining independence in a patriarchy. According to Goodman,

> Wharton is adamant: mothers need to nurture and spiritually mentor their daugh-ters, and women need to direct their energies inward. If one behaves with hon-esty and openness, other women can be a source of help, a reef in 'the flux of tides.' Only then can there be a 'new' woman and a new world. (*Edith Wharton's Women* 66)

When Emma (the ghost woman) rings the lady's maid's bell, she calls for a live woman's support for Mrs. Brympton's emerging self who is desper-ately trying to find expression and survive. The ringing of the bell, the bell of the title of the story, seems significant. It is the means of communication

that Emma/Mrs. Brympton use to seek help and to reveal the truth to another; it is an extension of themselves. In effect, Wharton's story is her
own "Lady's Maid's Bell," sounding the alarm for women, and finally
also men, in a society not sensitive to their needs or their true selves.[11]

The ghost for Wharton in this tale and in her subsequent ghost stories
becomes a figure that "shatters complacency" and forces new awareness,
very much like the female intruder described by Carol Wershoven as a
pervasive pattern in Wharton's work. Emma Saxon, as a female intruder,
offers "a kind of reproach to the false values of society."[12] For in the
Brympton world, as was the case in Wharton's society, images and marriages must be maintained, however miserable the situation might be. To
uphold the marriage code, couples must put up a good front, creating repressive, unhealthy environments. What Wharton shows is that social codes
and conventions not only dictate, but also destroy lives.

Wharton presents Mrs. Brympton and her need to escape and survive
sympathetically. At the time she wrote the tale however, most readers
would likely have condemned her character. Consider, for example, some
of the audience responses at the turn of the century to fiction that dared to
deal with illicit relations or any material that would affront social conventions. In a letter in response to *Crucial Instances* (1901), which included
"Souls Belated" and other tales sympathetic to women who are trapped by
social conventions, a reader exhorts Wharton: "Dear Madam, have you
never known a respectable woman? If you have, in the name of decency
write about her" (*Backward Glance* 126). A fastidious critic responding to
"The Lady's Maid's Bell" overlooks the possible affair, but charges that
"It was hard to believe that a ghost created by so refined a writer as Mrs.
Wharton would do anything so gross as to ring a bell!" (*Backward Glance*
126). Wharton reminds us of the remarkable prudery of her age:

> My career began in the days when Thomas Hardy, in order to bring out "Jude
> the Obscure" in a leading New York periodical, was compelled to turn the chil-
> dren of Jude and Sue into adopted orphans; when the most popular young people's
> magazine in America excluded all stories containing any reference to "religion,
> love, politics, alcohol or fairies" . . . the days when a well-known New York
> editor, offering me a large sum for the serial rights of a projected novel, stipu-
> lated only that no reference to an 'unlawful attachment' should figure in it;
> when Theodore Roosevelt [Wharton's cousin by marriage] gently rebuked me
> for not having caused the reigning Duke of Pianura (in "The Valley of Deci-
> sion") to make an honest woman of the humble bookseller's daughter who loved
> him; and when the translator of Dante, my beloved friend, Professor Charles
> Eliot Norton, hearing (after the appearance of "The House of Mirth" [1905])

that I was preparing another "society" novel, wrote in alarm imploring me to remember that "no great work of imagination has ever been based on illicit passion"! (*Backward Glance* 126-127).

Given the tenor of the times, Wharton writes "The Lady's Maid's Bell" as a conservative text which flirts with sexual taboos (adultery and "brutish physical demands")[13] and a woman's desire for growth and independence.

A further technique Wharton uses to create her subtext, the use of elisions or absences, offers an even more textured interpretation of events. Rosemary Jackson notes:

> By attempting to make visible that which is culturally invisible . . . the fantastic introduces absences. The cultural, or countercultural, implications of [the] assertion of non-signification are far-reaching, for it represents a dissolution of a culture's signifying practice, the very means by which it establishes meaning . . . . Un-doing those unifying structures and significations upon which social order depends, fantasy functions to subvert and undermine cultural stability. (69)

Through the absence of information, a tendency towards "non-signification," Wharton subtly suggests her themes. The ghostly Emma Saxon, symbolically significant as the keeper of the secrets in the Brympton household, functions as an uncanny evocation of absent knowledge, information suppressed or repressed. If we read her as Mrs. Brympton's double who knows the full sense of her secret self, Emma's physical absence and absence of voice lend even more poignancy to the tale. Emma is dead and mute. What she cannot say and do makes her appearances seem urgent. She is pleading for someone to understand and assist with what she, in her absence, cannot address. She solemnly leads Hartley first, to Brympton, second, to Ranford, and third, to Mrs. Brympton as though they are equally involved in some suffering that Hartley must alleviate. As Mrs. Brympton's double, she tries to speak for her, for Mrs. Brympton is also mute; she is hemmed in by social restrictions and cannot speak for herself. Carol Sapora suggests that the doubling of a female character indicates problems of language and independence. "Wharton . . . made the convention work not only to criticize society but also to characterize what she saw as the most significant restriction on women, their lack of access to language and, more importantly, their consequent inability to use language as independent adults" (381).

Other absences haunt the tale. The Brymptons have had and lost two children (6). How or when they are lost is never explained; they are never spoken of in the household. Their absence, however, points to past suffering and a difficult adjustment to a childless household. Also, Hartley sees that the Brymptons are incompatible, and she sizes up Brympton as a man who savagely insists on his marital rights. Real information, however, on the Brymptons' sexual relationship is absent in the story; it is possible that relations are absent altogether. Another problematical detail is Mrs. Brympton's illness. Hartley conjectures that her waxy look might indicate heart disease, but the medicine that Hartley picks up at the pharmacy turns out to be harmless limewater which the pharmacist says could be fed "to a baby by the bottle full" (17). Mrs. Brympton may have no actual physical ailment, but rather psychosomatic illness brought on by her unhappy marriage.[14]

The only character shown trying to communicate openly in a household where open emotion and communication are notably absent is Brympton, yet his communication is daunting because he always sounds angry. Everyone else in the household is mute, quiet, or inaudible. The only time the servants speak freely is when Brympton is supposedly in the West Indies. They have a "merry dinner" and register their dislike of him. Even then the religious Mr. Wace cautions that to speak too freely might be disastrous. Hartley says, "Mr. Wace said the bears would eat us" (20). Open expression and honesty of emotion are not characteristic of the "gloomy house" and are, in fact, considered dangerous. What Wharton portrays, undoubtedly drawn from the social world she grew up in, is a socially proper, repressive atmosphere in a household where everyone keeps up a good, but for the most part, decidedly false, front. Ironically, Hartley notes admiringly: "I knew how the real quality can keep their feelings to themselves" (12). In order to maintain a childless (child-lost), possibly sexless, possibly loveless, and definitely non-communicating relationship, and a socially proper household, the Brymptons and their servants who are trained to follow suit "keep their feelings to themselves," even if this creates repression, illness, and misery.

This reading of "The Lady's Maid's Bell" moves beyond the facile stereotypes of the villain husband, delicate Victorian lady, and kind friend, or the brute husband and the fallen, adulterous pair, to portraits of three sympathetic characters, all frustrated and suffering because of rigid social conventions and training. In her autobiography, Wharton clarifies her approach to creating characters in her fiction:

> The poor novelists who were my contemporaries (in English-speaking countries) had to fight hard for the right to turn the wooden dolls about which they

were expected to make believe into struggling suffering human beings . . . . It is
as hard to get dramatic interest out of a mob of irresponsible criminals as out of
the Puritan marionettes who formed our stock-in-trade. Authentic human
nature lies somewhere between the two . . . . (*Backward Glance* 127)

Wharton's subtext pushes the reader to look at her characters as "authentic" human beings whose situations are more complex than appearances would suggest. Brympton's outbursts appear ungentlemanly and even savage to Hartley. However, to be socially correct, when he suspects adultery, he must move to defend his honor. The greatest suffering actually shown in the story is Brympton's. The red spot on his forehead appears to Hartley to be an evil brand, yet the angry flush also suggests high emotion. The man's drinking habits indicate a weak and cruel character to Hartley, yet they also suggest loneliness and frustration. Brympton is angry, he drinks, and although Hartley thinks he is a philanderer, as far as we know he lacks the sometime pleasure of a pleasant, compatible companion as Mrs. Brympton has. His social schedule is notably absent, as is any evidence of joy and happiness in his life. Although he exemplifies patriarchal power, he, like the other members of the triangle, is trapped in an intolerably unhappy situation. Slavish adherence to the marriage contract, the necessity to defend honor, the habit of repression punctuated with sporadic outbursts of anger and frustration make Brympton also miserable. Julie Olin-Ammentorp concludes that in Wharton's work "the system of marriage wastes male potential as it does female . . . . Despite the weakness of Wharton's males—a weakness that has become almost proverbial among Wharton critics—Wharton presents her male characters as meriting as much (or perhaps almost as much) sympathy as her female characters" ("Edith Wharton's Challenge" 239, 238).

It is interesting why readers tend to believe Hartley's profile of Brympton when she is unreliable about interpreting practically everything else. Intuitively, she does sense the unhappiness and repression in the Brympton household, represented by her seeing Emma Saxon. But on a conscious, rational level, she seems to have no clue about the complicated cultural systems and complex personality interactions that surround her. Undoubtedly, Brympton wishes to have a sexual relationship with his wife, and he may periodically try to force himself on her. Certainly, Hartley implies this interpretation in her view of Brympton as "the consummate Gothic villain" (Fedorko 94).[15] But Mrs. Brympton's illness as a defense may deflect these demands. I can imagine a core scene that replays occasionally throughout the marriage when Brympton presses his demands.

However, whether he is sexually successful is debatable. His and his wife's behavior suggest individuals who exhaust their energy through unsuccessful means to express and resolve their conflicts. It seems that this is the pattern Edith and Teddy Wharton sustained in their own marriage.

Another aspect of Brympton is that he is a ghost-seer along with Hartley. When Hartley appears at Mrs. Brympton's door after the first time the bell rings, Mr. Brympton comes to the door and says, "How many of there are you?" suggesting that he has already seen one lady's maid. That he may see Emma Saxon may indicate an effective defense by the ghost to deflect his demands on Mrs. Brympton. However, it may also indicate his sensitivity to denial and repression which are stunting his growth as well as his wife's. When Brympton arrives unexpectedly in the last scene, Hartley reports that he saw Emma. "He threw up his hands as if to hide his face from her" (26). Do we believe Hartley's report in this case? If so, Emma's appearance is open communication of all that threatens Brympton: his wife having an affair, his wife's desire for independence, their lack of intimacy. Emma's presence blinds him in its intensity. This final expression of the house's secrets is even more than Mrs. Brympton can survive. Neither spouse has the resources to deal with the secrets of Brympton Place out in the open.

Although the friends or lovers may have each other, they are as trapped as Brympton, and Wharton again shows this through absence. Ranford and Mrs. Brympton meet publicly less and less as the story proceeds. Finally they either cease to see each other, or they seek each other's company through clandestine meetings. Mrs. Brympton responds to the situation with illness (absence of health) and, less convincingly in the framework of the story, with death (absence of life). A modern reading of the story suggests the "fallen" couple are pitiable and their conduct understandable. Social conventions, governing feelings and behavior in the tale, imprison them. Stolen companionship or infidelity seems the only way out. Divorce, although increasingly more common at the turn of the century, was still socially unacceptable at the time Wharton was writing, but she subversively questions the institution of marriage and the repressive social codes that keep a bad marriage intact.

This reading echoes Wharton's own unhappy situation. In a 1908 diary entry, Wharton wrote what any unhappy wife or husband trapped in an incompatible, unworkable situation might privately write: "I heard the key turn in my prison-lock. That is the answer to everything worthwhile! Oh, Gods of derision! And you've given me over twenty years of it" (qtd.

in Wolff, *Feast* 51). Whether unconsciously or consciously based, the circumstances in the story seem remarkably similar to her own. The portrait of Brympton can hardly be said to be Teddy Wharton's portrait, but Brympton as a fellow sufferer in a *ménage à trois* suggests the sympathy that Wharton, when her own anger and frustration did not have the upper hand, must have at times felt for her husband whose circumstances she could consider as unfortunate as hers. Brympton uncannily foreshadows Teddy Wharton's unhappiness when he later revolted against Wharton's growing independence.[16] But to what extent was Wharton in control of her material and deliberately undermining cultural conventions and values as this reading suggests?

Evidence exists intertextually to address this question. In "Expiation," another tale in the *The Descent of Man*, Wharton introduces a character who resembles herself, a well-to-do author with a husband who is her intellectual inferior. Paula Fetherel is quite distraught because her new book has been misunderstood by the reviewers. The reviews have been favorable, referring to her novel as "sweetly inoffensive" and a "distinctly pretty story" (*Collected Stories* 1: 447).[17] However, Paula Fetherel finds the reviews "odious." The reviewers have missed her point altogether. She confides to her cousin that she is afraid of her work being a "*succès de scandale*," but nonetheless she says that she has "handled the subject without kid gloves," and she is prepared to face the consequences (439, 440). She says: "A writer who dares to show up the hollowness of social conventions must have the courage of her convictions and be willing to accept the consequences of defying society." She admits to being nervous because "so much is at stake; I've put so much of myself into this book and I'm so afraid of being misunderstood . . . of being, as it were in advance of my time . . ." (440). But out of conviction she perseveres.

> It has always seemed to me that the message I had to deliver was not for myself alone, but for all the other women in the world who have felt the hollowness of our social shams but have lacked either the courage or the power to proclaim their independence.

She hopes that her confidante, her cousin who has divorced, will provide her support. "I have fancied . . . that, however severely society might punish me for revealing its weaknesses, I could count on the sympathy of those who like you . . . have passed through the deep waters" (441). As the plot unfolds, Paula Fetherel, in order to help her uncle, the Bishop of Ossining, has him denounce her book, thus explaining its actual intent to the public. For in the end, she is more annoyed at being misunderstood than she is fearful of the scandalous revelation of her intent.

Paula Fetherel provides a mouthpiece for Wharton's conflicting views on her task as a writer in her particular society. Wharton, like Fetherel, seems determined to express her observations honestly regardless of possible censure. Also—ultimately— censure is not the worst fate: not being understood is. Again, the reader's creative ability comes into question. In a review of *Ghosts* in the *Times Literary Supplement* in 1937, the reviewer cites several of Wharton's tales including "The Lady's Maid's Bell" as "so fogged that, although the reader may be thrilled, he is likely to be very uncertain what happened" (Anon. 823). Up to the last year of her life, Wharton found, as Paula Fetherel did, that the limitations of many of her readers left little for her to worry about in the way of producing a *"succès de scandale."*

Wharton's concern with the "marriage question" is evident in many of her early stories. Starting with "The Fullness of Life" in 1893 until 1902, almost half of thirty short stories Wharton wrote deal with the lack of fulfillment in marriage, the disillusionment of women with men they loved, and the pain of triangular relationships.[18] "The Lamp of Psyche," "The Valley of Childish Things and Other Emblems," "Souls Belated," and "The Twilight of the God" come to mind. Two tales, "The Fullness of Life" and "The Duchess at Prayer," seem particularly related to the themes and techniques of "The Lady's Maid's Bell" because both contain supernatural elements.

"The Fullness of Life," published in *Scribner's Magazine*, December, 1893, was Wharton's second published story. It is a fantasy tale about the life after death of a woman whose marriage was not fulfilling. When she arrives on the other side of life and finds "death is not the end after all," she hopes that "she shall now know what it is to live," lamenting that she has never "known that fullness of life which we all feel ourselves capable of knowing." The Spirit of Life asks her, "You were married, yet you did not find the fullness of life in your marriage?" She replies, "Oh, dear, no, my marriage was a very incomplete affair" (*Collected Stories* 1: 13-14).[19] Yet given the opportunity to spend eternity with "a kindred soul" to whom she can reveal her "inmost being," the wife chooses to wait for her husband to join her (16). Her husband's door slamming, creaking boots and affinity for reading railway novels and sporting advertisements annoy her, but she admits fondness for him and expresses concern over his helplessness if she should desert him. Bound in the duty and dependency of her marriage, she tells her soulmate that she cannot possibly go with him and resolutely seats herself to wait for her husband.

As Lewis points out, this early story is a "fairly direct literary translation" of Wharton's discontented married life and her early resolution of the conflicts in a socially acceptable manner as the faithful, devoted wife, an image which her conventional readers would no doubt applaud. In the story, she uses "one of her most elaborate images, drawn . . . from the interior of a house, to provide an almost nakedly revealing summary of her psychological and sexual relationship with her husband" (Lewis, *Biography* 65). The image, a fine instance of Wharton's use of architectural symbolic imagery to "reveal the soul," is a comparison between a "woman's nature" and a "great house full of rooms."

> There is the hall, through which everyone passes going in and out; the drawing room, where one receives formal visits; the sitting room, where members of the family come and go as they list; but beyond that, far beyond are other rooms, the handles of whose doors perhaps are never turned; no one knows the way to them, no one knows whither they lead; and in the innermost room, the holy of holies, the soul sits alone and waits for a footstep that never comes. (14)

The wife reveals that her husband never got beyond the sitting room, and even worse, "he was quite content to remain there . . . admiring its commonplace furniture." He was incapable of locating and entering the rooms "full of treasures and wonders . . . rooms that no step has crossed" (14).

The image of the house of the woman's soul reveals Wharton's feelings of isolation, deprivation, and sorrow. Lewis says it is "too direct an expression of her personal situation" and "almost a lament about it" (*Biography* 86).[20] Wharton seemed aware of what she might have revealed in the story after she sent it to Burlingame. He thought the story a "capital conception" (Lewis, *Biography 65),* perhaps because of the laudable faithfulness of the wife, and asked only for minor revisions which Wharton was never able to supply. The story was finally published without revision, but never reprinted in Wharton's lifetime. In 1898, when Burlingame wrote to Wharton about inclusion of some of her earliest work in *The Greater Inclination*, she wrote to him:

> As to the old stories of which you speak so kindly, I regard them as excesses of my youth. They were all written 'at the top of my voice,' & The Fulness of Life [sic] is one long shriek. I may not write any better, but at least I hope that I write in a lower key, & I fear that the voice of those early tales will drown all others: it is for that reason that I prefer not to publish them." (*Letters* 36)

In time Wharton did learn to lower her voice. Her subsequent work distances her personal history, allowing her to attack personal and cultural grievances more angrily and in more unconventional ways.

Another tale of unhappy marriage, distanced and muted, written before "The Lady's Maid's Bell," is "The Duchess at Prayer," first published in *Scribner's*, August, 1900. A more controlled story than "The Lady's Maid's Bell," "The Duchess at Prayer" is set far away in time and space from Wharton's environment.[21] The tale starts with the image of another "great house" like Brympton Place that must be entered to understand the terrible sorrow within. "Have you ever questioned the long shuttered front of an old Italian house, that motionless mask, smooth, mute, equivocal as the face of a priest behind which buzz the secrets of the confessional?" (*Collected Stories* 1: 229).[22] The villa of Duke Ercole II and his Duchess contains memories of violent agonies beyond the levels of frustration in "The Lady's Maid's Bell," although the stories are quite similar. The young Duchess, isolated and alone in the villa while her scholar husband buries himself in the library in Vicenza, spends a great deal of time with a companion, Cavaliere Ascanio, the Duke's cousin. After a visit by the Duke who finds Ascanio present, Ascanio ceases to visit often, but the Duchess increases her religious activities, spending an inordinate amount of time in solitude in the crypt below her chapel. The suspicious Duke arrives unexpectedly one evening bringing "a kneeling figure wrapped in deathclothes," a marble statue of the Duchess at prayer done by Bernini, and he orders it placed on the floor covering the door to the crypt (239). The Duchess, in vain, pleads for modification or delay of the order. The deed done, the Duke and Duchess retire to her chambers for a feast where the Duke drinks a toast to Ascanio: "I drink to his very long life—and you, Madam?" In a "wild voice," the Duchess toasts "to his happy death," drinks her full goblet of wine, and falls down on the floor (243). She dies before morning.

As in "The Lady's Maid's Bell," the impact of the tale lies in implications, dramatic irony, and absences that point to romance and illicit passion and, in this case, accomplished revenge. The narrator of the Duchess's story is an old man showing the villa to a gentleman visitor who is the primary narrator. The old man, an unreliable narrator, incredibly claims that the tale, which he tells with detailed dialogue, was told to him by his grandmother, although the Duchess has been dead two hundred years. He tells the story without drawing unpleasant conclusions about the Duchess' personal life or Ascanio's and the Duchess's deaths. The telling of the tale is provoked by the primary narrator's shock upon looking at the face of the statue of the Duchess: "It was a frozen horror. Never have hate, revolt and agony so possessed a human countenance . . . " (231). According to the old man, the statue originally had the beautiful face which the visitor sees in a portrait of the Duchess, but the morning after the Duchess' death, the face of the statue changed. The old man's grandmother reported entering the chapel, hearing a "low moaning," and seeing the "sweet and smiling" face of the statue contorted, the moaning seeming "to come from its lips" (244).

"The Duchess at Prayer" and "The Lady's Maid's Bell" share similar characters: the isolated, lonely wife (although the Duchess is a happy and gay young woman while Mrs. Brympton is older, ill, and melancholy), a frequently absent, jealous husband (although the Duke's character is more coldly drawn than Brympton), and the companion (lover) desired by the wife; a similar plot ending with the unexpected appearance of the husband and the deaths of the wives (in this respect, Brympton seems less diabolical than the Duke); and a narrative technique using an unreliable narrator and dramatic irony to create an erotic subtext. The ghostly "frozen horror" of the Duchess symbolizes the suppressed knowledge of a marital situation which poisons lives as Emma Saxon's mute appearances speak of the dreadful waste of lives at Brympton Place.

In "The Duchess at Prayer," Wharton again questions cultural conventions. She underscores the cruel code in the patriarchal marriage tradition which has moved men to violent means to preserve their marriages and their honor. The Duke, reminiscent of Browning's Duke of Ferrara, seems irredeemably cruel in his entombment of the lover in the crypt and the poisoning of his wife. In "The Lady's Maid's Bell," Brympton seems to abuse himself as much as he abuses others, although Wharton gives no indication of what he might have done had Ranford been cornered in Mrs. Brympton's dressing room. A modern husband, Brympton makes life miserable for everyone, including himself. Unlike the Italian Duke, he does not have the license to practice swift and violent retribution. "The Duchess at Prayer" makes a strong statement on the confinement of marriage, the isolation and lack of expression of women, the unfair freedom of men, and the cruelty emerging from the required defense of honor. The characters are, however, more flat and allegorical than the characters in "The Lady's Maid's Bell." The Duke symbolizes the cruel patriarchy and its restrictive conventions of marriage that uphold the rights of the man and preserve his honor. Brympton is a more "authentic" character, a genuine sufferer trapped himself by the patriarchal code. The Duke is portrayed as an unequivocal brute, Brympton as a troubled man.

"The Lady's Maid's Bell" is not considered the best crafted of Wharton's ghost stories, yet as a reflection of Wharton's early concerns, themes, and techniques, it is an interesting and illuminating piece of work. Margaret McDowell cites this tale and three other Wharton ghost stories "wherein the supernatural is evoked to little purpose, wherein technique obtrudes at the expense of mental conflict, moral complexity, and psychological penetration" ("Ghost Stories" 143).[23] On the contrary, Emma Saxon is not evoked "to little purpose" for she has major symbolic significance, but she is evoked too often, becoming too substantial a presence to be terrifying. The walk from Hartley's door to Ranford's house is a long time for a ghostly presence to be sustained.[24] Wharton soon learned that the literalness of a ghost was not a necessity. In fact, a too literal ghost destroys atmosphere and symbolic impact. In future ghost stories, Wharton uses James' process of adumbration and curbs the appearances and substantiality of her ghosts (except for Mary Pask who requires presence and substantiality).

One bothersome aspect of the tale is Mrs. Brympton's death. What does she die of so abruptly and rather unconvincingly? Her death emphasizes the tragedy of the circumstances, but it seems precipitous and out of context. The only literal explanation is the one Hartley suspects, that Mrs. Brympton has a heart condition. The death of the Duchess in "The Duchess at Prayer" also seems precipitous and particularly cruel and violent, although the implication of poisoning and the desire of the Duke to be rid of an unfaithful wife does logically explain her demise. Wolff notes that Wharton's early stories have intrusions which indicate lack of control on her part, "violent imagery that is inappropriate to the story and plots that may be adequately explained only by a reversion to the author's personal history" (*Feast* 86). The deaths of Mrs. Brympton and the Duchess, which seem excessive, appear to be Wharton's means of expressing the emotional devastation she felt in her own marriage, a death-in-life situation, which she felt was the situation for many women who had little independence in a society controlled by patriarchal codes of behavior.

Although "The Lady Maid's Tale" lacks Wharton's highest level of artistry, and "reversion to the author's personal history" may be necessary in unravelling the tale, this early ghost story exhibits many of Wharton's strengths of storytelling and her ability to create a subversive subtext. She effectively uses a believable, but unreliable, narrator; suspense; dramatic irony; and symbolic imagery. She invokes the Gothic to create an eerie, stifling environment, suggesting oppressive social conventions and unhealthy repression. She experiments with the use of implications and absences in the text. And importantly, her "lurking feminism" questions cultural codes. What she achieves is only one step in her career-long effort to voice her anger over the constraints of marriage and gender roles. Although an apprenticeship work, "The Lady's Maid's Bell" is a fascinating preview to the supernatural and natural realms Wharton would continue to explore in her later stories. By 1910, Wharton had produced two more ghost stories, one of which has been referred to as her masterpiece in the genre.

Notes

1 Lewis's reference to a "possibly minor" genre seems to indicate a concern about whether supernatural fiction, or specifically the ghost story, is legitimate fiction.

2 At the time of my initial work for this book, the "definitive" biography of Wharton was R.W.B Lewis's 1975 volume, *Edith Wharton: A Biography.* I wish to thank Haper Collins Publishers, Inc. for permission to quote from Lewis' work. I also relied on Cyntha Griffin Wolff's 1977 biocriticism of Wharton, *A Feast of Words: The Triumph of Edith Wharton.* And I wish to thank Oxford University Press for permission to quote from Wolff's work. Shari Benstock's 1994 biography of Wharton, *No Gifts From Chance*, expands the information available on Wharton's life and re-assesses some major assumptions about her. Also now available is another 1994 biography by Eleanor Dwight, *Edith Wharton: An Extraordinary Life*, which focuses on Wharton's world and her passions for houses and gardens. This work offers an extensive collection of photographs.

3 Criticism during the 1970s focused on the negative influence of Wharton's mother on her life. In the 1980s and especially in the 1990s, critics have explored more fully Wharton's relationship with her father. The "Beatrice Palmato" fragment and the prevalence of incest imagery in Wharton's work have led some to believe that Wharton suffered not only from an unresolved emotional attachment to her father, but that as a child, she was a victim of incest. For various readings on Wharton's relationship with her father (and her mother), see Cynthia Griffin Wolff, *A Feast of Words;* Adeline R. Tintner, "Mothers, Daughter, and Incest in the Late Novels of Edith Wharton"; Gloria C. Erlich, *The Sexual Education of Edith Wharton*; David Holbrook, *Edith Wharton and the Unsatisfactory Man;* and Barbara White, *Edith Wharton: A Study of the Short Fiction.* See also note 4 for this chapter.

4 Scholarship of the 1970s and 1980s concludes that Wharton had, at points, "nervous" or emotional breakdowns. Some critics have reported that in 1898, Wharton underwent a breakdown and sought help from Philadelphia neurologist, S. Weir Mitchell, now well known through Charlotte Perkins Gilman's *exposé* of the ineffectiveness of his infantilizing rest cure in her story "The Yellow Wallpaper" (1892). Shari Benstock finds that Wharton was not a patient of Mitchell's and did not undergo the infamous rest cure. Wharton did, however, go to Philadelphia in 1898 to consult with a Dr. George McClellan in regard to severe allergy- and sinus-related bronchial problems that may have eventually weakened her heart. She stayed at the Stenton Hotel for three months. According to Benstock, "Although Edith Wharton faced difficult challenges in her development as a woman and a writer, there is no evidence that she experienced nervous breakdowns" (Introduction, *House of Mirth* 9). Also see Benstock, *No Gifts From Chance*, 93-97. Wharton's ill health, especially

during the twelve years of "neurasthenia" she refers to (at other times, she denied she was neurasthenic), probably resulted from a combination of problems: allergy, sinus, bronchial conditions; stress from the conflicts in her marriage; stress from the challenges she faced in developing as a person and as a writer; overwork; depression; perhaps the tendency to use illness to secure time and space for creative efforts. In addition, some critics of the 1980s and 1990s now suggest that Wharton may have been a victim of incest in her childhood. Barbara White, in her study of Wharton's short fiction, says she was. As evidence, she notes that the symptoms and patterns reported by Wharton during her illnesses tally with those reported by incest victims, and she cites the incest imagery in Wharton's work (42-56). Her argument is persuasive, although the conclusion is highly debatable and, as White notes, impossible to prove. Her symptoms may be attributable to the physiological and psychological causes already discussed. The incest imagery in her work may figuratively convey the conflicts she felt trying to gain independence in a restrictive patriarchal environment. The father or father figure becomes the symbol of patriarchal restriction of women and their dependency. Whatever the sources were of Wharton's ill health, what finally stands out is her energy, willingness, and ability to work through her problems to create a life for herself. Her writing became a form of therapy, allowing her to work through conflicts and deal with anger.

5   Here again the specter of who haunted Wharton the most arises. Who was the "source of her childhood terrors"? Her mother? Her father? Her father died in 1882 (Wharton was 20); this was twenty years prior to her mother's death. On the mother as the focus of her "terrors," see Lewis's speculation in his "Powers of Darkness," 644-645, sparked by an anecdote reported by Wharton in an autobiographical fragment titled "Life and I." On the father, see Barbara White's re-evaluation of Lewis' assessment in *Edith Wharton: A Study of the Short Fiction*, 48-49. Also see the conclusion of this book for further discussion of the fragment from "Life and I."

6   I have designated this tale as her first ghost story although this is not her first story using supernatural elements. See discussions in this chapter of "The Fullness of Life" (1893) and "The Duchess at Prayer" (1900). Other early tales that atmospherically and thematically function like ghost stories are "The Angel at the Grave" and "The Moving Finger" (both 1901). These stories are discussed in Chapter 6.

7   All page references from the text of "The Lady's Maid's Bell" are from *The Ghost Stories of Edith Wharton*, Scribner's, 1973.

8   See Sarah M. McGinty "Houses and Interiors as Characters in Edith Wharton's Novels" and Jan Cohn's "The House of Fiction: Domestic Architecture in Howells and Edith Wharton" on Wharton's perception of architecture and interior design as forces shaping and defining character.

9   Kathy Fedorko ("Edith Wharton's Haunted Fiction: 'The Lady's Maid's Bell' and *The House of Mirth*") sees Emma Saxon as Hartley's "dark double" rather than as Mrs. Brympton's double (89). Indeed Hartley has taken Emma's former job and Mrs. Brympton sometimes mistakes Hartley for Emma. Ellen Powers Stengel ("Edith

Wharton Rings 'The Lady's Maid's Bell'") sees the text as a tale of Hartley's repressed homoeroticism. Both Hartley and Emma Saxon protect Mrs. Brympton from heterosexuality (6-7).

10   Carol Sapora's work focuses on Lily Bart in *The House of Mirth* (1905). Historically, Sapora reports "From ancient myth, primitive folklore, early philosophy, and religion, the doubled or divided character has appeared as a metaphor for people's feeling of division, from themselves, from their society, or from their culture." She also clarifies how Wharton uses the double for female characters: "Wharton shows that for a woman in a patriarchal society the real struggle is not between a good and evil self but between a dependent and independent self." For comments on doubling in the male tradition of good and evil selves, see the discussion of the *doppelgänger* in relation to "The Eyes" in chapter 2.

11   Several critics have connected the supportive Emma with Wharton's nursemaid, Doyley, whom Wharton claimed provided her with maternal nurturing as a child. Barbara White writes in relation to "The Lady's Maid's Bell," "It can hardly be accidental that the main protector in Wharton's childhood was her nursemaid, whose presence established 'the warm cocoon in which my infancy lived safe and sheltered; the atmosphere without which I could not have breathed' [qtd. from *A Backward Glance* 26] (69). Barbara White also points out that "Wharton's title, as is often the case with her titles, reflects the controlling metaphor of the story . . . ."

12   For characteristics of the female intruder, see Carol Wershoven, *The Female Intruder in the Novels of Edith Wharton*, 15. Although Wharton's ghosts function basically as censuring intruders, not all of her ghosts are female, or even human.

13   A number of critics have discussed how sexual themes are conveyed indirectly in Wharton's work. As early as 1961, Kenneth Bernard wrote in "Imagery and Symbolism in *Ethan Frome*" that sexual problems lay at the heart of the Frome's failed marriage and showed how Wharton rendered all the sexual themes indirectly through images. The veiling of sexual themes is particularly relevant to the ghost stories which have erotic intensity and reflect problems with selfhood and sexuality.

14   An interesting side note, as Carol Wershoven points out, is that "One of the most pervasive reservations about Wharton's work is the accusation that it lacks moral positives" (12). Susan Goodman has added that "Wharton [herself] was largely defined by a series of absences: lack of love, lack of children, lack of compassion, lack of social sensitivity, lack of 'femaleness'" (2). Ironically, Wharton's adroit, but perplexing, use of absences has helped to produce these perceptions.

15   Kathy Fedorko's reading of Brympton follows R.W.B. Lewis's lead. She concludes that "Emma's ghost serves to tell us that a wrong has been committed, and her appearance is an appeal for justice or a preventive against its recurrence. The clues tell us that the wrong has to do with the tyrant's sexual assault on the weakened woman" (7).

16   Barbara White points out that Wharton's father may have influenced the develop-
     ment of Brympton as a character. She notes that Brympton has the "'ruddy complex-
     ion' of Wharton's description of her father. He even drinks 'the ole Brympton port
     and Madeira,' reminding us of the celebrated Jones Madeira Wharton's father drank"
     [qtd. from Wharton, *A Backward Glance*, 2, 58] (68). If Wharton's father lies behind
     the Brympton portrait, another interpretation emerges. Following White's idea that
     Wharton was a child incest victim, Wharton indeed may be implying "brutish sexual
     demands" on Brympton's part. In this reading, Emma Saxon mirrors Wharton's nurse-
     maid, Doyley, whose presence, at times, may have protected her as a child. How-
     ever, the resemblances to Teddy Wharton and George Frederic Jones may illustrate
     how Wharton draws composite characters from her life experience. The ambiva-
     lence shown towards Brympton suggests, on the one hand, Wharton's anger towards
     the men in her life and, on the other hand, her sympathy for their own restricted,
     unfulfilling existences. She sees individuals as not only culpable, but themselves
     caught in cultural webs.

17   "Expiation" first appeared in *Heart's International-Cosmopolitan* in December, 1903.
     All page references for "Expiation" are from *The Collected Stories of Edith Wharton*,
     vol. 1, 438-456.

18   Wolff writes that "the theme of the unhappy marriage in her early fiction is too obvi-
     ous to need mentioning" (*Feast* 103). Lewis notes that the early stories deal with the
     theme "in an atmosphere which is a curious and artful blend of the passionate and
     violent with the muted and remote" (Introduction, *Collected Stories* xv).

19   All page references for "The Fullness of Life" are from *The Collected Stories of
     Edith Wharton*, vol. 1, 12-20.

20   Wolff writes of Wharton's early stories that "Her choices of subject very often reflected
     her sense of herself and her own problems . . . however, she had so little control over the
     passions that were attached to these problems that the first fictions did not even stand
     clearly separated from them." They were "expressions, in however muted and indirect a
     way of . . . hitherto-repressed emotions and conflicts" (*Feast* 86).

21   As early as 1929, Jane E. Downy in *Creative Imagination: Studies in the Psychol-
     ogy of Literature*, compares Wharton's "The Duchess at Prayer" with Poe's "Cask of
     Amontillado" and Balzac's "La Grande Bretêche." She notes that the three stories
     create "aesthetic detachment," regarding Wharton's tale the most distanced or "given
     of objectivity in every possible way." She concludes that these stories illustrate how
     life generally may be transformed into art; she does not, however, explore Wharton's
     personal motivation for her effective distancing in the tale. Wharton admired "La
     Grande Bretêche"; she acknowledged the influence of Balzac's tale on "Kerfol,"
     which is also a story like "Bretêche" that, as Downey says, is "many times filtered in
     the telling" (207, 203). In *The Writing of Fiction*, Wharton writes that in "La Grande
     Bretêche," Balzac showed "what depth, mystery, and verisimilitude may be given to
     a tale by causing it to be reflected, in fractions, in the minds of a series of accidental
     participants or mere lookers-on" (92).

22 All page references for "The Duchess at Prayer" are from *The Collected Stories of Edith Wharton*, vol. 1, 229-244.

23 McDowell writes: "In 'The Lady's Maid's Bell,'" Mrs. Wharton was not yet fully in command of her craft nor deeply enough involved in the situation she developed, that of a sickly, sensitive wife persecuted by her husband and protected by the ghost of her former maid. As a result she only partially elicits the complex relationships she needs to chart" ("Ghost Stories" 144). Although I do not see "The Lady's Maid's Bell" as Wharton's best ghost story, I disagree with McDowell's assessment. Sensitivity to Wharton's subtext yields a different view. Wharton plies her craft in ways which will be her stock-in-trade throughout her ghost stories; she is personally engaged in the conflicts she portrays, and her relationships are more complex than at first meet the eye. The other tales that McDowell cites are "Mr. Jones," "Afterward," and "A Bottle of Perrier."

24 In addition to the ghost's too substantial presence, Hartley's identification of the ghost is contrived. As Hartley works at the sewing machine in her room, a machine "that had never been used since Emma Saxon's death," a drawer which she "had never been able to open slid forward and a photograph fell out" (18). The photograph of Emma Saxon is conveniently identified for Hartley by Mrs. Blinder.

Two

"Afterward" and "The Eyes"

[She] had begun to perceive that the fair surface of life was honeycombed by a vast system of moral sewage.

Sanctuary, 1903

There are moments when a man's imagination, so easily subdued to what it lives in, suddenly rises above its daily level and surveys the long windings of destiny.

The Age of Innocence, 1920

By mid-1909, Wharton was at work on the stories which would appear in *Tales of Men and Ghosts* published by Scribner's in October, 1910 (Wolff, *Feast* 153). Response to Wharton's fifth collection of short fiction was ambivalent. Lewis writes that *"Tales of Men and Ghosts* had come out . . . to a mixed and even confused reception . . . . Some reviewers dismissed [all the stories] as no better than run-of-the-mill magazine fiction; others, on the contrary, accused Mrs. Wharton of an excess of subtlety beyond anything the average magazine reader could enjoy."[1] Lewis calls "The Eyes," one of the two ghost stories in this volume, " a small masterpiece"; however, he says that the other, "Afterward," begins "promisingly but wilts into melodrama . . ." (*Biography* 296). Wharton also produced a third ghost story in this period of her life, "The Triumph of Night," written in 1910, which did not appear in print until 1914.[2] Of her literary activity in 1910, Lewis notes that she was "writing a little; considering the nightmare she was going through, she was writing ghost stories . . . ." (*Biography* 280).

The "nightmare" of Wharton's life in 1910 arose from the culmination of her affair with Morton Fullerton and the impending dissolution of her marriage to Teddy Wharton. More positively, the literary successes of the turn of the century continued for Wharton through the century's first decade, moving her firmly from a "drifting amateur into a professional" (*Backward Glance* 209). From extensive tours of Europe, she produced three "travel" books. Life on the continent was mobile, frantic, and enchanting with the coming of the "motor" which Wharton felt "restored the romance of travel" (Lewis, *Biography* 129). Life in general became a "moveable feast" with summers at The Mount (from 1902-1911, the Wharton home in Lenox, Massachusetts), winters in New York (after 1907, in Paris), and spring back in Europe again. As she made her seasonal rotations of scene, Wharton's literary entourage increased; her renown led to meetings with writers in New York and abroad. Most dear to her would become what her circle called the "inner group" (*Backward Glance* 192), including Henry James, Walter Berry, Bay Lodge, Gaillard Lapsley, Robert Norton, John Hugh Smith, and Howard Sturgis, all of whom partook of the gentle summer life at The Mount and memorable conversations on the terrace overlooking Wharton's carefully planned gardens. From 1904-1910, in addition to travel books and three short story collections, Wharton published three novels and a book of poetry. With *The House of Mirth* (1905), Wharton enjoyed her greatest success and avowed that she had become a writer, working with "systematic daily effort" (*Backward Glance* 209). She had established habits that would take hold for the rest of her life.

As new habits, new opportunities, and new zest entered Wharton's professional life, her "nightmare" began. Teddy Wharton responded to his wife's success, shifts in life style, and acquiring of new friends with his own "neurasthenia." The environment she built for herself seemed to suffocate her husband, just as his environment had constrained her for years. His discomfort first manifested itself with aches and pains attributed to gout, but progressed to severe manic depression. His behaviors included embezzlement of Wharton's funds, sexual promiscuity, and finally pathetic pleading for forgiveness. His condition was exacerbated by Wharton's increasing desire to remain in Paris, where she was comfortable amid her friends, most of whom lived in Europe, and was stimulated by the intellectual excitement of Europe during *la belle époque*. He may have also become aware of Wharton's affair with Morton Fullerton which lasted from the fall of 1907 to the summer of 1910. On October 29, 1907, she began a private journal called "The Life Apart," subtitled "L'Ame Close" (The Shut-In Soul), to Fullerton, a journalist for the *London Times* in Paris. Her soul at last "open," she responded sexually, emotionally, and intellectually to Fullerton, whose charming speech and attentions captivated her. As Lewis points out, although Teddy Wharton may have accommodated Walter Berry's presence, he could not have avoided seeing that Morton Fullerton came only to see his wife and that his presence sparked more response than the dry Berry, who as close as he was to Wharton in friendship and spirit, was probably never her lover. In the end, resigned to the irreconcilable situation, Wharton finally acquiesced to the inevitable, but still socially and personally offensive, solution of divorce in 1913.

In the 1908 story collection, *The Hermit and the Wild Woman*, the familiar themes of domination and entrapment seen in earlier work, especially in the early supernatural tales, were laced with the intense longing for escape and failed attempts at it (Lewis, *Biography* 233). In her own life, Wharton managed to escape at last, immersing herself in romantic oblivion before surfacing to find a tangled reality: an ailing, rebelling husband and a fading romance with a lover who was bisexually promiscuous, and whose relationships with women, she discovered, were usually not sustained for more than two or three years. Her temporary escape proved to be a dream. She awakened to a nightmare reality, but also to new self-understanding and emotional maturity. Accordingly, the theme of awakening to horrors which bring new insight recurs in the ghost tales of 1910 that emerged from the "lower depths of her psyche" (Lewis, *Biography* 280).[3]

In both "Afterward," first printed in *Century Magazine* in January, 1910, and "The Eyes," first printed in *Scribner's Magazine* in June, 1910, the main characters become aware of horrors earlier repressed. Initially blind to reality, through contact with supernatural apparitions, they eventually gain new knowledge. As in many of Henry James's ghost stories, the apparitions are instruments of insight.[4] This pattern of the development of insight or epiphany is not confined to Wharton's ghost stories; in her other fiction, Wharton's characters often cannot face things as they are because they cannot "see." The characters eventually, usually through some unexpected stimulus (the intruder), develop new ways of seeing, leading to psychological and moral dilemma. Another constant of Wharton's fiction is that the social order contributes to the prolonging of the immaturity and blindness of the characters (Lindberg 55). They are trapped in habits of consciousness conditioned by social codes and lifestyles. In particular, in the two ghost stories in *Tales of Men and Ghosts*, Wharton illuminates class and gender dilemmas of the leisured class. The subtexts of the two tales focus on gender roles which are accepted without question by individuals because they are safe roles. The acceptance of these roles leads to selfishness, dependency, and immorality.

"Afterward" tells Mary Boyne's story of awakening from a dream world of privileged security, where she resides with the husband she loves and trusts, to the sheer "horror . . . sweeping over [her] in great deafening waves" (*Ghost Stories* 73).[5] Mary Boyne depends on the protection of her husband to provide a secure world. She is a well-to-do American wife, detached from her husband's world of business, who basks in the sunny warmth of an artificial environment that shields her from the complexities and unpleasantness of the human condition, but also assures her entrapment as a submissive, dependent, immature woman. In "Afterward," Wharton abandons the first-person narration of "The Lady's Maid's Bell" for limited omniscience which allows her to shape events into a sharply focused drama. As the register or reflector of events, Mary Boyne, like Hartley, is uninformed, limited in her knowledge and powers of analysis, and increasingly confused, yet she intuitively feels that there is a secret to discover, some key feature of her life that she cannot grasp. Eventually, Mary Boyne becomes aware of the dubious moral underpinnings of her life.

As in "The Lady's Maid's Bell," the setting suggests classic Gothic, and the task confronting the potential ghost-seer is the "reading" of the house. The Boynes, "two romantic Americans," purchase Lyng in Dorsetshire because it is "really Tudor" and remote, a place with "special charm" showing "marks of commerce with a protracted past" (48, 50). There they can indulge in the "harmonious activities" of a well-ordered life of retirement from the "irregular hours" of the business world (50, 66). Ned Boyne, a mining engineer who has made his fortune from the Blue Star Mine, works on a book, "The Economic Basis of Culture," while Mary Boyne indulges her fancy for gardening, spending whatever money is needed, "luxuriating in a lavish play of figures" (63). The "central, the pivotal 'feature'" of Lyng is the library which Mary, "like a novel heroine," thinks is "full of secrets. They seemed to be piling themselves up . . . like the layers and layers of velvet shadow dropping from the low ceiling, the rows of books, the smoke-blurred sculpture of the hearth" (48, 51). Throughout her ordeal, Mary, who vainly gropes for understanding, feels intuitively that what she cannot understand "the house knows, the library . . . knew" (71). The library, like the Willows' library in Wharton's *Hudson River Bracketed*, functions both literally and figuratively as a repository of knowledge.[6] Mary, however, cannot "read" its knowledge because along with her sheltered existence, she has accepted limited vision. She tries to read the text of the house, but "revelation never came" (71). Only after her husband's disappearance and the arrival of the lawyer Parvis, who brings her additional information, does she, in horror, begin to understand the "pattern of the long long story [the house] sat there weaving in the sun"

(62). Mary, as so many women have done before her, has accepted the status quo of long-standing tradition. Men have power, control, and knowledge; women live in dependency, subserviency, and ignorance. In effect, the books of the library contain the knowledge of the past bound up in patriarchal code and language. As Parvis, astonished with Mary, attempts to confront her ignorance, he futilely looks "up and down the long line of books, as if one of them might have supplied him with the definition he sought" (73). As Mary finally begins to understand the moral morass that surrounds her, she feels "The walls of books rush toward her, like inward falling ruins" (77).

Wharton creates her mysterious setting and "secret" motif by drawing on Gothic convention and symbolism, but in creating the ghost of "Afterward," she deftly departs from supernatural tradition. Not a defined presence, the identity of the ghost of Lyng depends on the story of the particular inhabitants of the house. Also the ghost is not identifiable as a ghost until after its appearance. In the Boynes' case, the ghost is a thoroughly modern presence, a slight "greyish" man with a "faintly American" accent and a "soft felt hat" who looks merely like a "person arriving on business" (62). Not ghostly at all, he appears in broad daylight, in full view, and proceeds to speak and act. The matter-of-fact daylight ghost of Lyng reflects Wharton's belief that modernity will not destroy the ghost story. However, symbolically, like the more haunting presence of Emma Saxon, he represents suppressed and repressed knowledge. The ghost, a man named Elway whom Boyne cheated out of a share of the Blue Star Mine, appears first after attempting suicide and then after succeeding at it. However, "Afterward" is not as much a postmortem account of Elway as it is of Mary Boyne who, unaware of her husband's business practices or the Elway incident, lives an unexamined, half-alive existence. Not until long after the appearance of the ghost does she know who he is or what he represents for her husband or for herself.

Several critics have read the ghost of Lyng as primarily a sign of marital estrangement. Janet Ruth Heller writes that "Afterward" is "a psychological study about the emotional alienation of a husband and his wife," resulting from "Ned's dishonesty and Mary's escapism." Heller's reading targets "avoidance of real intimacy" as a major theme (18, 19). Richard A. Kaye has taken such a reading a step further, alleging that Ned's desire to escape intimacy (his disappearance finally) suggests his homosexual predisposition. In effect, Ned's secret includes more than his questionable business dealings; he is being summoned by a "male paramour" to a "deadly underground" (12). The tale becomes "a woman's emerging realization that her husband has been 'homoerotically abducted.'" Kaye points out that in the tale "homosexuality . . . indicates an enviably sensual universe that has been denied women: patriarchy's forbidden fruit" (13).[7] These readings add to the complexity and ambivalence of the tale.

Although the overt text of this tightly crafted ghost story focuses on a controlled release of information about Ned Boyne's villainy and Robert Elway's ghostly revenge or return, the buried text probes much more. The primary focus in the tale is on the consciousness of Mary Boyne as the reflector, leading to the "portrait of a lady," the dependent American wife who blindly relies on her wealthy husband to order her world. Her moral failing is her inattention to her husband's moral failings. Mary Boyne lives life based on what is unknown, unseen, unarticulated. She lives with an absence of information, "negative information" (70), and lack of communication, because she has been conditioned and encouraged by her husband and by the social code defining the female's life to prefer dependent security over independence of thought and action. As a "lady" inhabiting her proper world, she has been socialized to repress any information that threatens her safety or that might emotionally overwhelm her. Her life at Lyng assumes a "Benedictine regularity" fostered by Boyne who "cultivated the last refinements of punctuality and monotony, discouraging his wife's fancy for the unexpected, and declaring that to a delicate taste there were infinite gradations of pleasure in the recurrences of habits" (66).

In keeping with the social code and her husband's desires, Mary Boyne has developed habits of submissiveness, repression, and absence of direct communication in her daily life. For instance, when Ned Boyne begins to look worried, she conjectures that he may be ill or may have seen the Lyng ghost, but rather than ask about his anxiety, she is "tongue-tied in his presence as though it were she who had a secret to keep from him" (51). The first time Elway appears and Ned Boyne panics, Mary acts as though she believes her husband's fabricated explanation for suddenly dashing off without a word, but she really feels "her husband's explanation . . . to have been invalidated by the look of anxiety on his face" and later his "look of relief" when the stranger vanishes. When Boyne receives the letter about Elway's suicide, she sees he is worried at first. When Boyne's "lines of tension had vanished" (57), she remains silent and does not ask about what has troubled him.

Mary's need for preservation of the status quo is so strong that she conveniently ignores or forgets any information that might alter her life. When she receives a letter with a newspaper clipping about Elway, she finds she knows nothing about "the squabble over interests in the Blue Star." Boyne says he told her earlier about it. "I must have forgotten," she says. "Vainly she strained back among memories." She does not press for details when Boyne reminds her, "It's all rather technical and complicated. I thought that kind of thing bored you." Although "it startled her a little to find how little she knew of the material foundation on which her happiness was built," she does not question at all the appearance of the business-like stranger whom she directs to Boyne (59). When Boyne does not appear for lunch, she questions the servants about him, at first not even remembering the visit of the stranger. When Parvis, the lawyer, arrives, Mary Boyne admits, "I know nothing." He is "surprised at her continued ignorance . . . . Was it possible that she really knew as little as she said?" (72). It is only when Parvis raises the curtain on the sordid affair: Boyne's cheating Elway out of a share of the mine, Elway's attempted suicide and eventual death, the impoverished condition of Elway's family, that her "confused perceptions, and imperfectly initiated vision" allow her to finally see "something dishonorable" about her husband's actions (72-73). Looking at a news photo of Elway, at last she realizes that Elway is the ghost of Lyng and the dis-embodiment of the "dreadful moral secret that haunted her." She hears "the faint boom of half-forgotten words," "You won't know till afterward . . . . You won't know till long, long afterward" (77).[8]

Mary's repressive tendency, however, is not airtight; nagging questions sometimes surface. She "could not say that any one of these questions had occurred to her [earlier], yet, from the promptness with which they now marshalled themselves at her summons, she had a sense that they must all along have been there, waiting their hour" (55-56). There is really nothing wrong with Mary's memory. When Boyne disappears, she has an "unwonted exactness of visual memory" that his papers "lay precisely as they had lain" (66). Under stress, she is capable of "leaping back to an image . . . lost under layers of subsequent impressions" (69). She has within her recesses and resources that she does not explore or tap, similar to Lily Bart in *The House of Mirth* . Lily was "always scrupulous about keeping up appearances to herself. Her personal fastidiousness had a moral equivalent, and when she made a tour of inspection in her own mind there were certain closed doors she did not open" (Benstock ed. 93-94). Society's role of "lady" requires women to deny the uncomfortable material realities around them.

One door that Mary Boyne, in her childish dependency, never opens on her own is the door to an understanding of American business and her husband's part in it. "Theoretically, she deprecated the American wife's detachment from her husband's professional interests, but in practice she had always found it difficult to fix her attention on Boyne's report of the transactions in which his varied interests involved him." She had always preferred during their leisure "escape from immediate preoccupations, a flight to the life they always dreamed of living" (59). Mary rationalizes her lack of interest and attention to business and the financial foundation of her life. "If she had indeed been careless of her husband's affairs, it was . . . because her faith in him instinctively justified such carelessness" (60-61). When Ned assures her that everything is "all right" with the Blue Star Mine, she thinks that "his right to her faith had now affirmed itself in the very face of menace and suspicion" (58, 61).

Wharton uses telling imagery to describe Mary's dependent, immature existence. Like a child, she is soothed and comforted by Boyne. She seats herself on the sofa beside him. He clasps her hand. As she experiences a "flood of . . . dissolving doubts," he tells her things were "never righter" and holds her close (60). Mary is soothed by the father authority figure who knows all, tells little, and promises her safety. Several times Wharton compares Mary to a child. Mary has the conviction that "[The house's] secrets were all beneficent, kept, as they said to children, 'for one's good' . . ." (62). Mary is also compared to "a savage on whom the meaningless processes of civilization make but the faintest impression" (71). And she is described as an object acted upon, "part of the routine, a spoke of the wheel, revolving with its motion; she felt almost like the furniture of the room in which she sat, an insensate object to be dusted and pushed about with the chairs and tables" (71). In her repressive and dependent state, she is ignorant of the actual world that sustains her. When Parvis finally breaks through her shell and tells her that her husband's business dealings were questionable ("I don't say it wasn't straight, and yet I don't say it was straight. It was business" [73]), her first impulse is to do what she has always done, deny disturbing reality. Parvis gives her a sensational news clipping about her husband, and "she felt it would be impossible to read what was said of him, and closed her eyes with the sharpness of pain" (75). Finally then, she can deny no longer. She understands the information that threatens not only her physical world and her husband's reputation, but also the entire internal construct by which she has lived her life: "She nodded at Parvis with the look of triumph of a child who has worked out a difficult puzzle" (77).

The life at Lyng condemns modern American business practices which alarmed Wharton. Parvis suggests that what Ned Boyne has done is both morally questionable and commonplace: "It's the kind of thing that happens every day in business. I guess it's what the scientists call the survival of the fittest . . . " (73). Wharton admired the vitality of the mercantile New Yorkers of the twentieth century and attacked the passivity and rigidity of Old New York, but she came to value and satirize aspects of both the old and new orders. In her autobiography written in her seventies, she, in retrospect, says she wants to "atone" for her "unappreciativeness" of Old New York (*Backward Glance* 5). In particular, she points out the value of "scrupulous probity in business and private affairs" of the old order (21). In *The Custom of the Country* (1913), she assaults the voraciously greedy new order of American business that subdues the old by whatever tactics work, regardless of moral principle.

Moreover, the life at Lyng condemns the American woman's status in relation to economic and political affairs. In *The Custom of the Country*, Wharton addresses "a general view of the whole problem of American marriages" (757). The theory presented in the novel is based on the "fact that the average American looks down upon his wife." For proof, Charles Bowen (Wharton's mouthpiece) asks, "How much does he let her share in the real business of life? How much does he rely on her judgment and help in the conduct of serious affairs?" (758). The male concentrates on "the big steal" in business; the female is placated by "the money and the motors and the clothes . . . the big bribe she's paid for keeping out of some man's way" (758-759). The trade off in the American marriage creates separate lives. Mutual effort and understanding and mature love are sacrificed. The wife, like Mary Boyne, becomes an ignorant dependent. Bowen points out the contrast between the American and the European woman. "Why does the European woman interest herself so much more in what the men are doing? Because she's so important to them that they make it worth her while! She's not a parenthesis, as she is here—she's in the very middle of the picture" (758).

Wharton returned to this theme in *French Ways and Their Meaning* (1919) written twelve years after her shift in residence to France. In this work, she praises the French "intellectual honesty" (58-59), and she describes the Frenchwoman as "in nearly all respects, as different as possible from the average American woman" (100). The Frenchwoman's advantage "is simply that, like the men of her race, [she] is grown up. Compared with the women of France the average American woman is still in the kindergarten" (100-101). The American woman is like a "Montessori infant" living in a controlled, artificial environment where she pretends to have individuality and where she and other women are "to a great extent each other's only companions . . . . They seem, compared to women who play an intellectual and social part in the lives of men, like children in a baby-school" (102). The Frenchwoman is "her husband's business partner" (103), yet she is more important to her husband than business. "For if Frenchmen care too much about other things to care as we do about making money, the chief reason is largely because their relations with women are more interesting" (111). Wharton writes that the "more civilised a society is, the wider is the range of the women's influence over men, and of each man's influence over women." In a grown-up world, the "power of each sex is balanced by that of the other" (112, 113). The stifling existence of a dependent relationship with male and female confined to "communing with their own households" gives way to a world of equality where there are different points of view, "the refreshment of new ideas . . . [and] new faces" (112).

Julie Olin-Ammentorp has questioned the reading of Wharton's argument in *French Ways and Their Meaning* as a "feminist statement" ("Wharton's Views"15). As Margaret McDowell says and Olin-Ammentorp acknowledges, "The exact nature of Edith Wharton's feminism resists easy definition"("Viewing" 253). I agree. Wharton was known as sometimes impatient with women or condescending to them, which her portrait of Mary Boyne may suggest. And Wharton, as an intellectual and a writer, not finding a place with most women, resorted to preferring the company of males.[9] As Olin-Ammentorp points out, this does not make her a misogynist. I also think that her sometime sense of superiority, condescension, and even contempt for women do not disqualify her from being a feminist. She is neither a feminist in the traditional sense of the activist suffragette nor do some of her comments and behaviors tally with the image of the thoroughly modern feminist, but one theme throughout her work is the exposure of problems with gender roles and relationships, a feminist endeavor. In her praise of the Frenchwoman and condemnation of the American woman, she is blind to some patriarchal conventions that she is continuing to support, and she overgeneralizes, but this does not mean, as Olin-Ammentorp states, that she believes in "the fundamental inferiority of women," the very charge Wharton herself levels at the American male.[10] If anything, her portrait of Mary Boyne and her entire canon suggest that women may become sensitized to their entrapment and grow. Wharton wrote "Alas, I should like to get up on the house-tops and cry to all who come after us: 'Take your own life, every one of you'" (qtd. in Lewis,

Biography 238). Yet Wharton's position as a feminist waivers and vacillates according to her situation. Her feelings when she was trapped in her marriage, or castigated by society for not being the lady she was supposed to be, seem to drive characters and plot and feminist themes in her work, although after her affair and divorce, during the War, with women waiting for their men to return from the battlefront, her feelings of exclusion from the "normal" woman's world seemed to have resulted in a longing to be included—and moments when she herself turned blind eyes to the restrictions of the patriarchy she had previously so ruthlessly exposed.

Wharton's *exposé* of Mary Boyne, as a representative American wife of the leisured class and as "an adult who has chosen dependency [and] must remain an incomplete and undeveloped human being" (Wolff, *Feast* 173), reflects struggles in Wharton's own life and themes in other fiction she wrote soon after "Afterward." Confined by a marriage of dependency and the conventions of the wife's role bequeathed to her by Old New York, Wharton tried escape through her romantic affair, finally faced her situation, and developed an independent life in France. In *Ethan Frome* (1911) and in *The Reef* (1912), she creates fictional worlds where her characters struggle unsuccessfully with repression and dependency. Ethan Frome, a man who lacks vision, is trapped in immaturity and unable to assert his independence. Instead of a full life, he chooses a half life like a scared child clinging to the familiar. In *The Reef*, Anna Leath, like Mary Boyne, awakens to deception and discovery. She is a "Sleeping Beauty" who has adopted the deluded fantasy that she will be rescued and protected by marriage to a "prince" (Ammons, "Fairy-Tale Love" 616). In Anna's case, however, we follow her as she develops a fuller understanding of her life. "She looked back with melancholy derision on her old conception of life, as a line of well-lit and well-policed suburbs to dark places one need never know about. Here they were, these dark places, in her own bosom . . . . " (*The Reef* 339).

Similarly, in "The Letters," which appears in *Tales of Men and Ghosts* following "Afterward," Lizzie West Deering, as Mary Boyne and so many women in Wharton's early fiction ("The Fullness of Life," "The Lamp of Psyche," and "The Valley of Childish Things," for example), faces disillusionment about the man she loves. This is a "theme that obsessed Wharton's imagination for years" (Lewis, *Biography* 77). Janet Heller writes that in Wharton's stories "wives fail to comprehend [men's] character flaws because Wharton's heroines tend to idealize husbands and lovers" (19). Ammons' view of the themes of Wharton's fiction is that "fairy-tale visions of love and marriage imprison rather than liberate men and women" (*Argument* 61).[11] In "The Letters," when Lizzie Deering discovers her husband's duplicity that indicates he married her for her money, she tries to fashion a new reality beyond illusion, but her first impulse is to try to preserve the life she had. "She wanted to keep his image intact . . . . Every nerve in her clamored for her lost happiness" (*Collected Stories 2:* 203, 204).[12] She faces the horror of the revelation and, disoriented, questions whether life can be built out of the ruins.

It was horrible to know too much. There was always blood in the foundation. Parents kept things from children, protected them from all the dark secrets of pain and evil and was life livable unless it was thus protected? Could one look in the Medusa's face and live?" (204)

Unlike the passive Ethan Frome who tries a futile, suicidal escape from reality and the fastidious Anna Leath who may not be able to accept her old or new imperfect existences, Lizzy Deering tries to make adjustments. Although perhaps still too romantic and idealistic in her approach, she at least faces her disillusionment squarely and has hope for the future. "The years had not been exactly what she had dreamed; but if they had taken away certain illusions they had left rich realities in their stead" (206).

In all of these fictions, the horrors of illusion and disillusionment are explored, but only in "Afterward" does Wharton show so clearly the conventional and dependent life-style of the American wife who lives in a state of ignorance and immaturity. Not surprisingly, some critics have missed the story's buried text. Lewis dismisses "Afterward" as mere melodrama. Superficially, the tale is the plight of a Gothic heroine trapped in a labyrinth; it has melodramatic twists and turns of plot. However, the overt tale is a cover for the buried tale, which is not a melodrama or Gothic romance, but a feminist parody of one with a carefully crafted, psychologically and morally significant subtext. Because Mary Boyne's repression and ignorance are fundamental to plot and theme, Wharton's challenge was to tell her story, as she did in "The Lady's Maid's Bell," through the use of absences: absence of information, communication, memory, clear thought, and independent judgment. Elway's absence (through death) and Ned Boyne's absence (disappearance) further create the mystery of Lyng and Mary Boyne's absence of understanding. Missing Wharton's technique, Margaret McDowell groups "Afterward" with "The Lady's Maid's Bell" as an inept early story. She writes: "Mrs. Wharton does not develop fully enough . . . the perceiving consciousness of the story . . . . The result is that the appearance of the ghost . . . and the husband's disappearance do not register decisively" ("Ghost Stories" 144). However, the ghost and the husband do not "register decisively" because in my mind, they are not the primary focus of the story, nor is marital discord or the husband's behavior, however construed, whether as dishonest business dealings or homosexual adultery. Wharton's focus is on the "perceiving consciousness," Mary Boyne, whose psychological and ethical blindness are subtly, but well developed through symbolism, imagery, and absences in the text. As Allan Gardner Smith points out, the ghost of Lyng dramatizes Ned Boyne's guilt, but also the difficulty Mary Boyne experiences in bringing "material to consciousness and recognition or becoming aware of the foundations of her domestic milieu" (154). Through "silence and stillness," Wharton moves her character from a conventionally "shortsighted" perception to "defamiliarized perception" (155), which changes her life.[13]

In "The Eyes," again Wharton's final stroke is to bring an immature character to new insight. The reviewer for the *Times Literary Supplement* who charged that "The Lady's Maid's Bell" was "fogged" brought the same charge against "The Eyes" (Anon. 823), but other critics demur. "The Eyes" has been the most widely commented on of Wharton's ghost stories, and many think that it is Wharton's best horror tale. A well crafted story of a selfish man who, like Oscar Wilde's Dorian Gray, finally faces the horror of his own moral decay, the tale portrays a familiar Wharton type: the effete American bachelor. Wharton often castigated these men in her fiction for their inability to live fulfilling, committed lives. This insensitive male is frequently a dilettante, sometimes an artist *manqué*, often homosexual, or if heterosexual, unable to establish a lasting (or a sexual) relationship with a woman. Like Mary Boyne in "Afterward," the well-to-do leisured bachelor is immature, lacks vision, and is confined to a restricted and "safe" life by the particular gender role that he has assumed.

Wharton uses a frame tale in "The Eyes." The narrator is a member of an all-male salon created by an effete bachelor, Andrew Culwin.[14] As the story opens, only the narrator and a naive young man, Phil Frenham, a neophyte to the group, remain late in the evening in Andrew Culwin's library after an "excellent dinner" and the telling of ghost stories by the guests (28). Prodded by Frenham, Culwin tells his ghostly tale. Wharton's use of the frame tale probably stems from her reading of the German Romanticists who frequently used this technique (Lawson 65). The frame tale, a popular device in supernatural fiction (Emily Brontë's *Wuthering Heights* [1847], James's *The Turn of the Screw* [1898], and more recently

Peter Straub's *Ghost Story* [1979], for example), provides distance and
perspective to a story. Wharton points out the value of the technique in
reference to the frame tale of *Ethan Frome*: "Only the narrator of the tale
has scope enough to see it all, to resolve it back into simplicity, and to put
it in its rightful place among his larger categories" (Modern Student's Library ed., intro ix). In "The Eyes," the perspective of the narrator height-
ens the effect of the story's final revelation as it is the narrator who reflects
for the reader Culwin's dreadful moment of recognition.

The Gothic setting of "The Eyes" is minimal and incidental, almost a
textual abbreviation for readers who have come to expect it. Wharton sets
the scene in one bold stroke: "Culwin's library, with its oak walls and dark
old bindings, made a good setting for such evocations" (28). Culwin's
first experience with the supernatural occurred in his aunt's "damp Gothic
villa" after he halfheartedly promised marriage to his young cousin in the
"Gothic library" of the house (31, 32). Beyond these explicit and quick
descriptions, the image of the "hateful" eyes that appears to Culwin on
two occasions creates the atmosphere of dread (36). Wharton does not
produce horror from Gothic trappings, but from psychological depth.

The narrator, more realistic than the idealistic Frenham who seems to
idolize Andrew Culwin, tells the reader quite a bit about Culwin before
Culwin, in relating his ghost story, unwittingly reveals his shadow self.
Culwin is a dilettante, a man of leisure who cultivates his capacities for
intellect and sensation. Not committed to job or family or career, he is a
traveller and a taster, "essentially a spectator, a humorous detached ob-
server of the immense muddled variety show of life . . . . None of the
disturbances common to human experience seemed to have crossed his
sky" (28, 29). Culwin's "ghost" appears twice to him in the form of "the
very worst eyes" he has ever seen which hover in the darkness above his
bed at night. The eyes represent repressed knowledge: Culwin's lack of
understanding of his own immoral behavior. He proposes to his cousin,
Alice Nowell, even though he finds her an insipid creature, and he deceives himself into thinking that this is "the first good action [he] had ever
consciously committed" (33). Then the eyes appear to him with an "expression of vicious security." He thinks they "seemed to belong to a man
who had done a lot of harm in his life, but had always kept just inside the
danger lines" (34). Harassed by the eyes, Culwin flees to Europe without
even notifying his *fiancée*. In Europe he courts the favor of a young poet,
Gilbert Noyes, whom he finds to have disappointingly severe intellectual
limitations. Loathe to give up what appears to be a homosexual relationship,

he lies to Noyes, telling him he has talent. Culwin deceives himself into thinking that his lies are morally acceptable "with a sense of self complacency that is supposed to attend the footsteps of the just." The eyes again haunt him. He says:

> I saw now what I hadn't seen before: that they were eyes which had grown hideous gradually, which had built up their baseness coralwise, bit by bit out of a series of small turpitudes slowly accumulated through the industrious years . . . . It came to me that what made them so bad was that they'd grown bad so slowly. (42)

In spite of this accurate perception of the nature of the eyes, Culwin is totally unable to make any connections between the appearances of the eyes and his life's circumstances.

Through Culwin's obtuseness, Wharton parodies the man who lacks imagination. Culwin "belonged to the stout Positivist tradition"; he is "not the kind of man likely to be favored with visions though he had imagination enough to enjoy, without envying, the superior privileges of his guests" (28). He tries desperately to explain the presence of the eyes "on scientific principles" as some sort of "optical or digestive delusion" (36, 31). When his hypotheses fail, he posits that he is hallucinating, but he cannot tally the "projection of [his] inner consciousness" with any "morbid pathological state" (36). Empirical data failing him, he turns to logic and tries to draw a cause/effect conclusion. He is stumped. For him the eyes have no cause. They are an irrational phenomenon: it was the "insane irrelevance of their coming that made it so horrible" (41). Culwin lacks the perceptive faculty to reach the interpretation that becomes apparent to his listeners.

Through dramatic irony, Wharton guides Culwin's listeners and the reader to understanding. Phil Frenham is sickened by Culwin's account, and he bows his head with "stricken awareness that he is next in line to be seduced and then destroyed by his 'benefactor'" (Lewis, "Powers of Darkness" 644). The narrator, who also understands the situation, shrewdly records Culwin's moment of recognition. Looking in a small mirror on a table behind Frenham, Culwin sees his reflection "as if scarcely recognizing the countenance in it as his own." However, his expression gradually changes and "he and the image in the glass" confront each other "with a glare of slowly gathering hate" (46). At last he understands that the reprehensible phantom eyes are his double.

In the telling of his tale, Culwin reveals his dubious moral character. He is an egoist and manipulator whose selfish desires reign supreme. He is also a man who lives under the shadow of repression and self-delusion.

Wharton initially conveys this figuratively. As Culwin prepares to tell his story, he cowers "gnomelike among his cushions, dissembling himself in a protective cloud of smoke" from a cigar (30). In telling the story of Alice Nowell, he reveals his selfishness and his condescending attitudes towards women. He describes Alice in deprecating terms: she is neither "beautiful [n]or intelligent," rather "a nice girl, but uninteresting" (32). He toys with her. He wants to find out how she can be content to be so uninteresting. In describing her eyes, he provides an ironic contrast to the horrible eyes he will later encounter. Hers are "not remarkable eyes . . . wholesome as fresh water, and if she had had more imagination—or longer lashes—their expression might have been interesting." (36). Women are no more to Culwin than servants or objects. He found "women necessary only because someone had to do the cooking" (29), or they are only valuable if they help to build his own self-esteem. He says: "I had an idea that a nice girl was what I needed to restore my faith in human nature, and principally myself." When Alice kisses Culwin, his egotism and selfishness are clear. As she is bravely and sincerely about to reveal her emotions, he focuses not on her, but on an object, a lamp on his desk, which he describes in detail to his listeners. His focus is always on himself and his own gain. He fantasizes: "I'll marry her, and when my aunt dies she'll leave us this house, and I'll sit here at the desk and go on with my book; and Alice will sit over there with her embroidery and look at me as she's looking now" (33). Culwin's fantasy is not enough to sustain his interest in Alice. After the frightening appearance of the eyes, he deserts her. The eyes may be a reproach, but he uses them as an excuse to bolt.

Culwin's relationship with Gilbert Noyes suggests that his flight from Alice also resulted from homosexual panic at the thought of an impending liaison with a woman. The relationship with Noyes provides further evidence for Culwin's selfishness and destructive manipulation of others. Noyes is a beautiful young man, "slender and smooth and hyacinthine" with "blissful eyes" (38, 41). The narrator reports that Culwin "liked 'em juicy" (29). Noyes, however, turns out to be as insipid to Culwin as Alice. He says acidly: "I used to wonder what had put into that radiant head the detestable delusion that it held a brain" (39). He manipulates Noyes to keep him in their relationship by lying to him about his writing, his "lamentable twaddle" (43). He justifies his behavior by thinking that "telling [Noyes] the truth would have been about as pleasant as slitting the throat of some small animal" (39).[15] Culwin's attitude towards Noyes is the same as his attitude towards women. Noyes is an object for his use and pleasure. He is no more than a pet or a "charming parasitic thing" (43). Culwin finally decides to break with Noyes because he begins to feel hedged in by his commitment. He realized "what I might be letting myself in for . . . . I shall have him for life . . . . I'd never seen anyone, man or woman, whom I was quite sure of wanting on those terms" (41). Honest only momentarily, in "an impulse of egotism," he decides to keep Noyes and lies again, rushing "straight into Gilbert's arms." Deceiving himself, Culwin thinks he has done the right thing, forgetting his wrong reason, and declares himself in a "state of grace." The eyes reappear representing the truth that he has repressed. He reports: "They reminded me of vampires with a taste for young flesh . . . . Since I'd made Gilbert happy they simply wouldn't loosen their fangs" (42). Culwin, sexually and psychologically a vampire, motivated by his selfish desires, feeds off Noyes' dependence on him.

An egotist and an escapist, Culwin attempts to flee not only from personal ethical behavior, but also from the responsibilities that a male is called on to assume in the patriarchal society. He criticizes Noyes' intellectual attempts as "simply protective mimicry—an instinctive ruse to get away from family life and an office desk" (39). This has also been Culwin's ploy. He says that with money, leisure, and pleasure Noyes would be an "inoffensive idler." Culwin, himself, apparently with all three, has not written his great works and has turned into an idler, however an offensive one. When the narrator asks Culwin what became of Noyes, he replies "nothing became of him—because he became nothing . . . . He vegetated in an office . . . and finally got a clerkship in a consulate, and married drearily in China" (45). Like Noyes, Culwin has become nothing, although he has avoided the dreary job and marriage. His primary motivation has been pleasure through the avoidance of responsibility and commitment. Ironically, although he appears free and independent in his choices and his travels, in reality, he moves in a very limited environment dependent upon the naive men who provide him solace and security. The worlds he creates easily collapse, and he finds it necessary to create new situations successively. His salon is constantly fed by newcomers, for the long-term members catch on to his game, even though for their own ends (a good dinner and conversation), they may choose to continue to participate. Culwin operates from several basic principles: he finds a homosexual relationship safer than a heterosexual one; he thinks no human being is worth commitment; he needs relationships which he can dominate and control; he rationalizes his behavior so he can live with himself as a just man. To achieve his goals, he creates a separate world, apart from the conventional patriarchy, his own "republic of the spirit" (*House of Mirth*). The eyes, however, an uncanny representation of the repressed knowledge of what he is doing haunt him in his worst, or as he determines, his best hours.

The eyes as "other" are another instance of Wharton's use of literary doubling; they are a *doppelgänger* image corresponding with modern theories of psychology that explore divided selves and stages of development. Culwin's eyes, like Jekyll's Mr. Hyde (Stevenson) and William Wilson's double (Poe), reflect concealed selves, repressed facets of identity. In the case of Jekyll, the other self is an abysmally evil self, while in the case of Wilson, it is the reverse, a good conscience attempting to deter the destruction of the individual's moral character. Culwin's double is not a person, only a phantom body part, but the dreadful eyes represent the faculty of true sight and offer a damning moral assessment of the behavior he exhibits, an assessment he represses.

Otto Rank, in his psychoanalytic study of the double based on Freudian theory, describes Wilde's Dorian Gray as a man who, like Culwin, splits his ego, repressing conscious knowledge of his undesirable self, in order to pursue a narcissistic, selfish life. The narcissism (self-love) leads to an inability to love others and homosexual tendencies (love of one's ideal self-image) (71-74). Dorian Gray and Andrew Culwin are similar instances of the arrested development of self. They are unable to proceed through normal stages of development: narcissism, attachment of loved objects (love for others), and realization of and surrender to necessity and reality. Jacques Lacan, extending Freudian theory, writes of a stage of human development which he calls the "stade du miroir" or the mirror stage. This stage falls between Freud's first and second stages of development.

> What is formed in this stage is a recognition of self as object, as if seen in a mirror, the mirror constituted by the looks of others. This self is the ego and becomes the means of self definition and identification. The mirror phase effects a shift from the 'body in fragments' and an 'asubjectivity of total presence' [Lacan] to the ideal of a whole body with a unified (constructed) subjectivity. (Jackson 88-89)

This theory provides a salient gloss on exactly what happens to Culwin when he is able to locate the phantom eyes in his own face as he literally looks in a mirror. Culwin prefers primary narcissism and avoids the mirror stage, because it may lead to frustration of his natural, selfish desires. But his unexpected glimpse of himself in the mirror and the attendant recognition break through his long practiced repression.

As Rosemary Jackson points out, in fantasy literature, "Frequently the mirror is employed as a motif or device to introduce a double, or *doppelgänger* effect: the reflection in the glass is the subject's other . . ." (45). Modern fantasy in its subversive mode is preoccupied with "problems of vision and visibility," with making the invisible visible, the unseen of self or culture seen; thus "spectral imagery" is frequently used. Jackson writes, "It is remarkable how many fantasies introduce mirrors, glasses, reflections, portraits, eyes . . ." (43). The function of the spectral imagery such as the mirror is to produce a distance. "It establishes a different space, where our notions of self undergo radical change" (87). In Culwin's case, the eyes themselves are spectral images which haunt him, threatening to reveal his true self. But Culwin is so grounded in narcissism and repression that it takes a second spectral image (the mirror) and a sudden encounter with the reflection of his eyes to break through his defenses and provide him with the unwanted knowledge of his character. Culwin's listeners and the reader recognize with horror Culwin's degradation in the first spectral image (the phantom eyes). The horror increases in the tale with the realization that he does not understand this himself and increases to its greatest intensity, the last turn of the screw, at the sickening moment when he, facing the second spectral image, finally grasps the truth like a blast of wind from hell.

That Wharton's story is a mirror of psychological theory accounts for the strength of the tale and some of its critical acclaim. Wharton read Freud, but was Wharton reflecting Freud or simply reflecting what she perceived personally and culturally? Blake Nevius claims that Wharton worked from manners rather than from psychological theory.

> To her way of thinking, reality was to be sought for in the present and visible, not in the realm of the ideal, in a romantic primitivism, or in the findings of modern psychology. Freud became available to her too late, and then only to be rejected, and the importance of the subconscious she acknowledged only indirectly in her ghost stories and such psychological horror stories as 'The Eyes'. In the quest for reality, manners were almost her only guide." (73)

Wharton, like other literary artists through the ages, was involved in pioneering psychological concepts. Psychiatrist Henry Friedman writes, "It is my impression that a writer like Mrs. Wharton, who was dealing in her writing unconsciously with personal conflicts managed to express artistically the concepts that later were put into theoretical and clinical understanding" (317). Freud himself acknowledged his debt to the creative imagination: "The poets and philosophers before me discovered the unconscious" (Trilling 45). He used narrative as a strategy for reporting his case histories that support his theories. Tzvetan Todorov's statement (1975) on one of the values of fantasy literature adds perspective to Wharton's accomplishment: "The themes of fantasy literature have become, literally, the very themes of psychological investigations of the last fifty years" (161).

Nevius notes that Culwin was a fictional double for a type Wharton was familiar with, for whom she had a "special and apparently irresistible, although disagreeable, fascination":

> "The Eyes" gives her least flattering analysis of a type necessarily prominent in the peculiar world she inhabited, a world suspended, as it were, by equal attraction between the worlds of society and letters, in which the prevalence of leisure, independent means and a taste for art and letters encouraged the various kinds of dilettantism reflected in her fiction. (98)

The cultured bachelor was indeed a part of Wharton's sphere. Lewis points out that

> Married men were not missing from Edith Wharton's early New York group, though they never appear as such in her recollections of them; but there was a notable proportion of bachelors and widowers. It is our first occasion for seeing Edith's tendency to surround herself with unmarried males . . . . (*Biography* 57)

Later, the "inner group" was made up of primarily unmarried males, and James, Berry, and Fullerton, the men who were her closest friends in 1910, were all bachelors with known or suspected homoerotic tendencies. Before her divorce, these flexible men were the male company available to a wife, and even after her divorce, as an older woman, she was often more comfortable with men and could spend more time with men whose relationships with their wives were not a factor in a relationship with her. Although Wharton had many close relationships with women, her friendships with men knowledgeable about art, literature, and the world in general were central in her life, allowing her to expand her own world through conversation and the sharing of ideas.

Before knowledge of the Fullerton affair came out in the 1970s, critics tended to see Andrew Culwin as a portrait of Walter Berry's characteristics which most irritated Wharton, taken to the extreme, and perhaps as revenge against Berry because of his unwillingness to commit himself more fully to her. Now it appears that a primary inspiration and target may have been Morton Fullerton, "a man who lived almost entirely in the moment" (Lewis, *Biography* 203), who, unlike Berry, is known to have had homosexual relationships.

> The traces of Fullerton are there to recognize in the portrait of Culwin: what might be called a sort of sexual indecisiveness, the sense of unrealized literary gifts, the cunning use of language in conversation; even more, the engagement to a first cousin [Katherine Fullerton Gerould], followed by flight to Europe and absolute silence. One of the phrases used about Culwin—'the humorous detached observer of the immensely muddled variety show of life'—is taken almost verbatim from Fullerton's report to his Harvard class secretary in 1910. (Lewis, *Biography* 288)

This last piece of evidence is the most conclusive tie between Fullerton and Culwin. However, the *roman-à-clef* approach to Wharton's work, as she warned, is a trap. Culwin's portrait may have allowed her to vent some of her disappointment with and anger towards Fullerton, but she most likely drew together a cluster of characteristics from many of the men around her and experimented in extrapolating the logical extreme to fit her literary purpose.[16]

David Holbrook who has explored the appearance of the "unsatisfactory male" throughout Wharton's work feels that "because of her strong attachment to her father," Wharton "saw men in general as being noncommittal, self-protective, unresponsive to women (even possibly homosexual) . . . ." (22). He argues that Wharton saw sexual intercourse as dangerous because she focused her erotic fantasies on her unattainable father or because she was indeed abused by her father. Her fear of intercourse led to her attraction to homosexual bachelors, who were safe. This, of course, leads to the conclusion that Wharton herself was an unsatisfactory female who, as the males she castigates, could never "come up with the goods" and achieve "a satisfactory coming to terms with sexual love . . . in the context of an on-going committed relationship" (200).[17] Does this also mean that some of her alleged distance from women was connected to her own same-sex desires? Her known disgust for lesbianism suggests that whatever such desires may have existed were readily and soundly repressed.[18] What is clear is that, for whatever reasons, Wharton maintained an uneasy sexuality along with her uneasy feminism. Clearly, she does show in her diary, her letters, her fiction a longing for a fully committed relationship with a man who could understand her. As Holbrook says,

> the message [from Wharton] is that the danger to the 'modern' independent intelligent woman, 'open' to the world, is the unsatisfactoriness of man—and his failure to begin to understand woman . . . . Edith Wharton's concentration at

> best is on being true to oneself, and seeking to relate to another in love, in such
> a way as to have one's true self confirmed . . . ." (61, 202)

Still the question arises whether Wharton's sense of flawed men and relationships which she infuses into her work is primarily a reflection of her
own personal limitations or a reflection of her social determinism (37).[19]

It is worth noting that the uncommitted bachelor appears in earlier
works prior to the onset of the Fullerton affair. As both Nevius and Wolff
have noticed, "'The Eyes' is a systematic flaying of the kind of man that
Selden [*House of Mirth*, 1905] had represented, a man who is aloof and
judgmental and who—without even allowing himself to be aware of his
own behavior—uses people, and in using them, destroys them" (Wolff,
Feast 156).[20] He is the type of man who avoids responsibility and commitment so that he can retain freedom and have social advantages (dinner
invitations and the opportunity to fraternize with other men's wives), despite his modest means. He uses his income not to set up a household, but
for his own aesthetic enjoyment (travel, book collecting). This bachelor
type appears in Wharton's work throughout her career. According to Judith
Sensibar, in *The Children* (1928), Wharton reveals the "erotic immaturity
of the perennial bachelor" in creating Martin Boyne.

> When [Wharton] began work on *The Children*, she was sixty-five. I posit that
> her maturity and the fact that James and Berry were dead gave her the distance
> needed to analyze and to come to terms with these friendships by exploring the
> sexual fantasies and actions of a character, who in his relations with others, bore
> strong resemblances to these men. The result is Wharton's revisionist reading
> of their composite fictional double. (575)

Sensibar also calls attention to the parallels among some of Wharton's
bachelor types with James's John Marcher ("The Beast in the Jungle,"
1903), and Eliot's Prufrock ("The Love Song of J. Alfred Prufrock," 1915)
(575-576). Perhaps throughout her career, Wharton developed from life a
critique of "the age's new Representative Man," a dry intellectual type
who withholds love from others and "sacrifices adult sexuality" in order to
promote his own "republic of the spirit," but who may at last have to face
the reality of a failed life (Sensibar 576). He is more than the artist *manqué*;
he is a person *manqué*.[21]

Andrew Culwin is a despicable character while Mary Boyne seems
pathetic, yet they are similar in that they have both chosen or accepted
"safe" roles. Patriarchal code dictates Mary Boyne's "safe" position.
Andrew Culwin chooses his role by default, in reaction to confining codes.

He retreats to a "safe" world where, free from commitment and responsibility (careers, wives, children), he can indulge his selfish desires. Both Mary Boyne and Andrew Culwin sacrifice self-knowledge and maturity by their unwillingness and inability to involve themselves in a larger sphere of influence and interaction. Although the two characters in general seem radically different, their flaws stem from the same source. Only freedom from rigid gender roles, and the freedom to forge their own personal identities while interacting fully with society, might have allowed them to develop satisfactory and moral life-styles.

"Afterward" and "The Eyes" critique both male and female gender roles fostered by American culture which, taken to their extreme, are debilitating and inherently immoral. The selflessness of Mary Boyne (victim) may be a more sympathetic posture than the selfish pose of Andrew Culwin (vampire), but both roles, submissive and aggressive, are, for Wharton, regressive. They represent individual and cultural failure. Although gender appears heavily involved in the creation of their different positions, Wharton shows in her fiction that the chauvinist patriarchy and the competitive capitalistic system offer both male and female the opportunity to play the victim or the aggressor. In *The Custom of the Country*, in order to emphasize her reservations about the brutal cultural system of power, politics, and economics, Wharton turns the gender tables: Ralph Marvell chooses ignorance, illusion, and submission while the uncharacteristic Undine Spragg aggressively manipulates the system to climb to the top. Wharton damns them both, killing one and leaving the other to be consumed by her compulsively greedy appetite. But the real villain becomes the social/cultural system based on the inequality of the sexes and classes fostering competition, greed, manipulation, domination, and the necessity of submission and ignorance.

"The Eyes" has been singled out as one of Wharton's finest stories. Lewis calls it "certainly one of the finest Edith Wharton ever wrote . . . a subtle study in human egotism at its most extreme and self deceiving" with "an intensity of concentration rarely achieved" (*Biography* 287, 288). Blake Nevius writes:

> Provided one can accept a necessity of the point of view—that of Culwin's obtuseness, his failure to relate cause and effect, as constituting the essential proof of his egoism—"The Eyes" ranks very close to the pinnacle of Edith Wharton's achievement in the short story. (97)

There is no question that it is a masterful tale. "Afterward," too, is a skillful tale leading to a horrifying moment of recognition. However, Lewis has called "Afterward" mere melodrama, and Douglas Robillard has referred to it as "a conventional tale of supernatural revenge," even though he points out the "careful and full characterization of Mary Boyne" (786, 787). One of Wharton's reviewers of *Ghosts* (1937), William Rose Benet, praised "The Eyes" and "A Bottle of Perrier," both masculine tales of domination (no women at all appear in "Perrier"), as the best tales in the volume.

> The present reviewer thinks that "The Eyes," owing to its psychological significance, and "A Bottle of Perrier, "because of its Arabian atmosphere, and perhaps also because of its perfectly reasonable and excessively grim explanation, are superior to the lady's tales of mere "fetches" and witches and letters from the dead. (W.R.B. 19)

Benet did not refer to "Afterward," but it is clear from his description of "the lady's tales" that he considers the ones primarily about men superior to "Bewitched," "All Souls," and "Pomegranate Seed" (the tales he is referring to), which all focus on women. "The Eyes," it seems, was early acclaimed as one of Wharton's best stories, not only because of its compact structure and psychological and moral validity, but because it is a male-centered story often reviewed by men. The story taps into male fears and fantasies and reflects conflicts for men that are still present in the patriarchal society. Moreover, early discussion of "The Eyes" is conceptually narrow. The primary focus on egotism overlooks the themes of gender entrapment, immaturity, homosexual panic, and domination/submission now acknowledged by critics. Early discussion of "Afterward" is also narrow, and this tale of a woman's plight in a patriarchal, capitalistic society, where men assume responsibility and women submissively go along, has only recently begun to be analyzed more fully. If placed in a broader social context, both stories can be read as skillful and incisive social critiques of companion problems in a society where domination and submission, immaturity and dependency, are for both men and women, terrifying possibilities. These stories deserve re-evaluation for greater complexity, and in the case of "Afterward," for higher praise.

Notes

1 Barbara White assesses Wharton's subtlety: "Wharton would never go very far to make sure her audience got the point . . . . If her theory of the short story is straight-forward, some might say simplistic, her practice is subtle and admits great complexity. She demands a good deal from her readers, and her attitude towards readers is again complex. We have already seen that Wharton considered reading a creative act and expected her audience to meet her halfway and fill in the gaps. But she was unwilling to do a lot to help" (24).

2 "The Triumph of Night" is discussed in chapter 3.

3 Lewis's actual comment was that "The Eyes" came from "far lower depths of her psyche" than "The Triumph of Night."

4 "The Jolly Corner" appeared several months before the publication of "The Eyes" and may have had some influence on Wharton's work.

5 All page references for "Afterward" and "The Eyes" are from the Scribner's edition of Wharton's ghost stories, 1973.

6 Wharton's fascination with the library as symbol not only came from literary tradition, but also from the many hours she spent in her father's library as a child. In *A Backward Glance*, she remembers vividly how the world first opened its knowledge to her in her father's library. It was here that she read books primarily written by men and discovered how the patriarchy thinks and speaks. She was an attentive student.

7 Kaye gives a convincing account of Wharton's awareness of the danger for women of male homosexuality by pointing out the "ubiquity of homosexually inclined men in Wharton's Paris circle" and also Wharton's likely "ambivalence . . . entangled with her feelings during and after her intense if attenuated affair with Morton Fullerton" who was bisexual (10). Kaye notes that "Although it is tempting to see Wharton as adopting the nerve-racked perspectives of the wives in ["Afterward" and "Pomegranate Seed"], we should be cautious about doing so. The conventions of gothic fiction, by definition hospitable to ambivalence, allow Wharton to express at once the confining terrors of the "feminine" home, the unstable state of modern marital relations, and the anguish of homosexual self denial" (17). Kaye claims that five of Wharton's ghost stories probe homosexual relations: "Afterward," "The Eyes," "The Triumph of Night," "A Bottle of Perrier," and "Pomegranate Seed." He does not mention "Miss Mary Pask."

8 These words, spoken by Alida Stair who originally told the Boynes about Lyng and its ghost, are also used at the beginning of the story. They make an effective

narrative hook. Wharton writes of her beginnings: "It is always a necessity to me that the note of inevitableness should be sounded at the very opening of the tale, and that my characters should go forward to their ineluctable doom like the 'murdered man' in 'The Pot of Basil'. From the first I know exactly what is going to happen to every one of them; their fate is settled beyond rescue, and I have but to watch and record" (*Backward Glance* 204).

9   Percy Lubbock (*Portrait of Edith Wharton*) writes that "she preferred the company of men (54). According to Louis Auchincloss (*Edith Wharton*), "Somebody once observed that Edith Wharton and Theodore Roosevelt were both 'self-made men'" (9). Supposedly, Wharton was pleased with this comment, the irony of which surely did not escape her. Wharton undoubtedly saw herself as different from the "normal" American woman, as a "man's woman" (*French Ways and Their Meaning* 119). Candace Waid (*Edith Wharton's Letters from the Underworld*) writes, " Wharton's description of the "'man's woman' . . . indicates the privileged position in relation to her sex that [she] reserves for women among men such as George Eliot and herself" (8). To acknowledge Wharton's male-centeredness is to acknowledge her efforts to develop a full life in relation to the dominant structure of society and language of which she longed to be a part. It does not mean that she disliked women or shunned the company of women. Indeed, she was close to many women with whom she spent time and corresponded. Sara Norton, through her long correspondence with Wharton, and Elisina Tyler, who shared Wharton's war work, are perhaps the best known, not to mention Wharton's long-time servants Elise DeVinck and Catherine Gross whom she saw on a daily basis. As a number of critics have pointed out, as Wharton aged, a theme that surfaces in her work suggests she came to see cooperation among women as a major factor in women's development. See Susan Goodman, *Edith Wharton's Women: Friends and Rivals*.

10 Olin-Ammentorp sees Wharton as "conservative (even reactionary), didactic, even preachy" and given to "large-scale oversimplifications and overgeneralizations" (18). She cites "multiple imbalances" in Wharton's essay on women which reinforce patriarchal code, including the superiority of men, the subservience of woman, and in general the rightness of hierarchical social structure. "The work as a whole is governed by rigid ideas of social structure, with Wharton apparently at the top of the social ladder" (17). Wharton, as a transitional woman, attempting to usurp power in the forbidden realm of maledom, certainly faced the confusing difficulty of trying to be a player according to established rules while breaking the ground for new rules. Weaving in and out of the prevailing social consciousness, she was sometimes immersed, sometimes detached.

11 Ammons writes in "Fairy-Tale Love and *The Reef*'" that "The fairy-tale fantasy of deliverance by a man appears to be but is not a dream of freedom for women. It is a glorification of the status quo: a culturally perpetuated myth of female liberation which in reality celebrates masculine dominance, proprietorship, and privilege."

12 Lewis writes that "The Letters" was a story connected to Fullerton. "That story, with another written a few months earlier, 'The Eyes,' suggests that she was definitely

making a reappraisal of Fullerton's character and his fitness to be her intimate companion . . . . Deering, indeed, is almost to a detail an ironic though tempered portrait of Morton Fullerton" (*Biography* 286, 287). Lizzy Deering does, however, accommodate herself to Deering's flaws. All page references for "The Letters" are from Lewis's *The Collected Short Stories of Edith Wharton*, vol. 2, 177-206.

13   Wharton refers to Mary Boyne as being "shortsighted" several times, a pun on Mary's nearsightedness and lack of insight.

14   This is the first of Wharton's ghost stories to have a first-person male narrator. In her study of Wharton's short stories, Barbara White notes "The observation . . . that a male point of view legitimates a narrative applies even more strongly to first-person narration: here the uncertain tones of the 'authoress' can be concealed by the 'authoritative' voice of a man" (63-64). In the next six ghost stories, the narrators or reflectors are all male. White says, however, that the most common explanation for Wharton's use of male narrators is to increase "the distance between the author and her material" (64). Only in the last three ghost stories does Wharton return to using a female narrator or reflector as she does in the first two tales. Out of Wharton's eighty-five short stories, only two, which happen to be ghost stories, have first-person female narrators, "The Lady's Maid's Bell" and "All Souls." In "All Souls," however, the gender is assumed by the reader and is not verified in the tale.

15   Wharton once remarked to Scribner's editor Burlingame "(*à propos* of some young woman in straitened circumstances, whose manuscript he had reluctantly had to refuse): 'How hard it must be to say 'no' in such cases!' But he answered quietly: 'Not as hard as you think, because if one isn't cruel at first one has to be so much crueller afterward'" (*Backward Glance* 146).

16   Barbara White suggests that Culwin might have also been inspired by the homoerotic James, "the Wharton intimate best known for his extraordinary eyes" or Wharton's father who incestuously may have had a taste for young flesh. George Frederic Jones had a library similar to the one Culwin works in, perhaps unrealized literary talents, "gastronomic enthusiasm," and "intensely blue eyes" like Culwin [*Backward Glance* 64, 58, 2] (67).

17   It is generally thought that she did have satisfying sexual experiences with Morton Fullerton in 1908 and 1909. In 1950, when Elisina Tyler, Wharton's long-time friend and executor of her estate, planned to write a memoir of her (it was never written), Morton Fullerton wrote to her to "seize the event, however delicate the problem, to destroy the myth of your heroine's frigidity." He said, in love, Wharton had "the courage of George Sand" and was "fearless, reckless even" (qtd. in Benstock, *Gifts* 225-226).

18   Shari Benstock notes that "In her adult life, Edith had only one lesbian friend, Vernon Lee, and she either did not recognize Lee's sexuality or turned a blind eye to it." Wharton met Lee in 1894 when she was a still sexually naive thirty-two years old. She may not have fully recognized Lee's sexuality although Benstock says Lee

"projected a male persona." The French novelist Paul Bourget introduced Wharton to the British art critic Viola Paget who, under the pseudonym of Vernon Lee, wrote books on Italian art and architecture; Lee also wrote ghost stories. Benstock notes that Wharton's homophobia did not surface until her Paris years when she pointedly avoided the lesbian community of poet Natalie Barney (*No Gifts from Chance* 76-77). Benstock writes that "Natalie Barney's 'private character' was, no doubt, too unorthodox and too public for Edith Wharton" (*Woman of the Left Bank* 87). Lewis notes "Edith Wharton made a point of steering clear of Natalie Clifford Barney . . . . Mme de Prevaux would remember that Edith looked upon . . . Barney as 'something—appalling'." Lewis also writes that Wharton was

> less discerning and less tolerant of the Sisterhood. Looking back, she suspected her girlhood friend Emelyn Washburn of what she called "degeneracy" . . . . The habit of several well-born Parisian ladies, like Anna de Noailles, of experimenting sexually in both directions also seems to have escaped her—or perhaps not interested her. When Radclyffe Hall's autobiographical novel about lesbian experience, *The Well of Loneliness*, was published in France—after having been banned in England and fiercely condemned in America—Edith Wharton dismissed it as "dull twaddle." (*Biography* 433-434)

19 Holbrook concludes that Wharton was probably an incest victim and had personal limitations from the experience; however, he also sees the cultural condition of the time was a hindrance and concern for Wharton. Joan Lidoff ("Narcissism in *The House of Mirth*") addresses the problem of determining how psyche and society drive individual fate. She writes:

> In *The House of Mirth*, Wharton transforms a personal psychic despair into a pessimistic social determinism, locating in society the forces of inevitable destruction of spirit that proceed from within. Ultimately, of course, there is a reciprocal relation between psyche and society. The narrative sensibility that creates the social world of this novel is itself shaped by development in society. Wharton shows Lily's destruction by the contradictions and limitations of needing to be independent and adult in a social context that neither equips nor permits her to be. In this, Lily [Bart], like many other heroines, acts out a cultural dilemma: when society provides no adult female role of active responsibility and initiative, women are confined to passive and childlike states and cannot mature. (537)

20 Wharton herself pointed out in a letter to Sara Norton that Selden is a "negative hero" (qtd. in Wolff, *Feast* 111). In "Wharton's 'Negative Hero' Revisited," Julie Olin-Ammentorp questions what this really means. She points out that Wharton was not discussing the novel, but rather the dramatization of *The House of Mirth*, and that her description may have been "more a technical description than a value judgment" in the sense that Selden is "an Anti-hero, a hero who does not act, who does not succeed as the novel's audience wishes him to succeed" (6, 8).

21 Some critics have accused Wharton of misandry. Ammons (*Edith Wharton's Argument with America*) notes that Wharton's contempt for men "plagued her work from the very beginning" (9). As one aspect of her work, her contempt for men, however, is mixed with respect for the male-dominated world of intellect and activity, her desire to participate in this world and function like a man (becoming male-identified), her desire for a male "soulmate," her heterosexual longings, and her compassion for men and women.

Three

"The Triumph of Night" and "Kerfol"

Non-involvement in human relationships represents, in reality, the most despicable kind of involvement.

Margaret McDowell,
"Edith Wharton's Ghost Stories"

Xingu and Other Stories, Wharton's sixth collection of short fiction, was published by Scribner's, October, 1916. In a letter to Gaillard Lapsley, December 21, 1916, Wharton writes, "I'm awfully glad you like the book, and every one seems to think it shows growth. But I don't deserve any of the coruscating things you say about it. *All* the stories except Coming Home were written before the war!" (*Letters* 385). Two ghost stories appear in the volume, both written during Wharton's "nightmare" period before her divorce in 1913 and the beginning of World War I in 1914. "The Triumph of Night" was written in 1910, but was first printed in *Scribner's Magazine*, August, 1914; "Kerfol" was written sometime between 1910 and 1914 and first printed in *Scribner's,* March, 1916.[1] Both of these ghost stories written during the period from 1910-1914 focus on the tyranny of immoral domination and regressive dependence and relate thematically to Wharton's other work from that time period. In its treatment of domination and dependence, "The Triumph of Night" echoes "The Eyes" and "Afterward"; in its connection to questionable American business practices, it has similarities to "Afterward" and *The Custom of the Country*. The main character, George Faxon, has regressive problems, as Ethan Frome did, which he confronts in a similar harsh and cold environment.

"The Triumph of Night" begins on an open railway platform "exposed to the full assault of nightfall and winter" (*Ghost Stories* 104).[2] The symbolic implications of "nightfall and winter" foreshadow the powers of darkness and the frozen state of immaturity that dominate the tale. The setting is Northridge Junction in New Hampshire. George Faxon, the registering consciousness of the tale and newly hired secretary for Mrs. Culme, awaits a sleigh to take him to her estate. The sleigh does not arrive, and Faxon finds himself alone and isolated, surveying the bleak scene. A blast of cold wind that has "traversed interminable leagues of frozen silence" sweeps over him from "snow fields and ice-hung forests" (104). Blake Nevius points out that the desolate New England landscape "roused [Wharton] to symbol-making activity" (129). Wharton found the cultural environment of New England and its resulting character "defined by emptiness . . . . In these barren settings [she] seems to have felt the full extent of negation, the sense of void which since St. Jean de Crèvecoeur has been seen as fundamental to experience in America" (Rose 425, 424). Like Starkfield in *Ethan Frome*, Northridge, an "exposed ledge over the valley" combed by the wind "with teeth of steel," is a "place uncommonly well named" (104). It is piteously cold and foreboding. As Wolff points out, for Wharton,

> Cold is an absence, a diminishment, a dwindling, and finally a death. Everything contracts in the cold . . . . This relentless constriction of place accompanies a slow shedding of adult personae and leads finally to a confrontation with the core of self that lives beneath these and that would emerge and engulf everything else should the supporting structure of the outside world be lost . . . . (*Feast* 171)

In this isolated setting, cut off from the outside world by the snowstorm, Faxon is about to confront horrors that will shake him to the core and expose the fundamental weakness of his character.

Temporarily rescued from the cold by young Frank Rainer, Faxon is whisked off in a sleigh to a contrasting scene, the palatial Overdale owned by business magnate John Lavington, Rainer's uncle. Here Faxon is assaulted by an overly warm, smothering atmosphere, Gothic in its oppressiveness. He has the "violent impression of warmth and light, of hothouse plants, hurrying servants, a vast spectacular oak hall like a stage setting . . . ." In spite of the opulence and luxury, Faxon finds the house "oddly cold and unwelcoming" (109). And he finds Lavington, a legendary millionaire, surprisingly "dry and stilted" and ordinary looking. Faxon "could only suppose that Mr. Lavington's intense personality—intensely negative, but intense all the same—must, in some occult way, have penetrated every corner of his dwelling" (109). Rainer, a pleasant, sincere young man for whom Faxon immediately feels a "sense of elderly brother concern" (106) idolizes his uncle and insists that his uncle has his best interests at heart: "My uncle has such an eye on me!" (107). Yet Rainer has tuberculosis, and his ill health is quickly clear to Faxon who observes the boy's spasms of coughing and emaciated, colorless hands that contrast with his healthy face. Rainer says Lavington tells him that the cold weather is good for him and that his biggest problem is only that he is bored.

Still something does not feel right to Faxon. Secrets lurk in the corridors of the seemingly protective and warming Overdale. Confined to the house because of the blizzard, on the occasion of Rainer's twenty-first birthday, Faxon confronts his first horror, although it is months later before he fully understands Lavington's evil plan to kill his nephew by neglect and inherit his money. Faxon sees a *doppelgänger* image twice, a ghostly double of Lavington, apparent only to him and not apparent to Rainer or to Lavington's lawyers, Balch and Grisben, who have arrived to complete Rainer's will. Faxon first observes the apparition standing next to Lavington's chair as the will is signed. It "turned on the boy a face of pale hostility" (112), and as Faxon looks away, the figure disappears. Faxon thinks he has seen an actual person who has exited noiselessly, but when the figure appears by Lavington's chair at the dining table, Faxon realizes that no one else perceives it. Again Lavington's "counterpart . . . fixed young Rainer with eyes of deadly menace" (118). Allan Gardiner Smith has raised the issue of whether the figure Faxon sees is a phantom or a hallucination. Referring to the debate over what the governess sees in *The Turn of the Screw*, he points out that this issue is irrelevant. What is relevant is why Faxon sees the double.

> Locally . . . within the terms of the story, the phantom is clearly an illustration of the actual malignity of Lavington, beneath his mask of ingratiation and benevolence, as he cheats his nephew out of his inheritance . . . . Hermeneutically, it suggests the vicious requirements of business practice beneath a bland mask, and it also belongs to a larger pattern in Edith Wharton's writing in which mature men are seen as tyrannical in respect of women and younger men. In none of these areas is the question of the apparition's reality of any weight—what matters is what it points to, material not repressed but suppressed in the overt recognitions of the group. (154)

Like the ghosts in Wharton's previous stories (Emma Saxon, Robert Elway, and Culwin's phantom eyes), the malevolent double of Lavington suggests suppressed knowledge, horrible knowledge, that will change people's lives when it finally surfaces.

Wharton suggests the nature of Lavington's evil through other images in the story. A key to understanding Lavington's cold, uncaring domination and manipulation of Rainer lies in a brief exchange between the boy and Faxon. Faxon notices the extraordinary fresh flower arrangements at

Overdale; there are flowers everywhere "not in senseless profusion" but "placed with conscious art" (109). Before dinner, he briefly visits one of Lavington's art galleries housing a French Impressionist collection. When Rainer says Lavington will love showing him all of his pictures after dinner, Faxon asks, "Does he really love things?" (113). Rainer replies, "Rather! Flowers and pictures especially . . . . I suppose you think his manner's cold; it seems so at first; but he's really awfully keen about things" (113-114). This key to Lavington's personality explains the malevolent double: Lavington is more interested in the acquisition of things than he is in caring for people whom he regards as objects to be controlled and used for his pleasure. When the Wall Street crash comes, Lavington, who has deliberately been leading Rainer to his death, does not hesitate to send the boy out in the cold to precipitate his demise and the transfer of his inheritance to cover financial losses. Here Wharton illuminates the "vicious requirements of business practices." In a comment to Grisben, Lavington reveals himself. Grisben points to the rumors of a crash as being "devilish close to facts." Lavington says, "What are facts? Just the way a thing happens to look in a given minute . . ." (114). Lavington is an artist of illusions, arranging an argument for Rainer's seeming health to bring about his death and a plan for his business affairs to cover his greed and corruption as artfully as arranging flowers or galleries of Impressionism. Lavington's portrait is part robber baron, part aesthete like Andrew Culwin, a man whose maniacal attempt to fulfill his selfish desires is at the expense of others and rationalized. Like Culwin, Lavington is a "dry" man who manipulates those who are younger and more naive for his own ends.[3]

Lavington's double, radiating greed and destruction, is not, however, the worst horror that Faxon encounters. Faxon responds to the evil he intuits by fleeing. He impulsively leaves Overdale without notice, running from one horror to another: his own inability to face a moral decision maturely. A nervous, rootless individual, Faxon has no life of his own. He is a loner, uncommitted to others, a man who relies on the wealthy for subservient secretarial positions. Not happy about his life which "had been mainly a series of resigned adaptations" (106), he is "unutterably sick of all strange houses, and of the prospect of perpetually treading other people's stairs" (109). He has "no personal life, no warm screen of private egotisms to shield him from exposure . . ." (121). "Private egotisms" suggest that Faxon does not see life in terms of any contribution he might make to others. His need for a "shield . . . from exposure" suggests that he does not see life within his control, but as a state of deprivation. He feels

deprived of a nurturing environment that would provide him with all he
needs as an infant is provided for.

The circumstances causing Faxon's emotional deprivation are not a
part of the story; however, the results of Faxon's life, whatever the circumstances, are that he sees himself as a victim and therefore lives a careful
life. He is another of Wharton's unsatisfactory men who elects a life of
non-involvement and "measures out [his] life with coffee spoons" (Eliot
5). When he arrives at Northridge Junction and finds no transportation
awaiting him, he observes drily that "the visitors who can least afford a
carriage are almost always those whom their hosts forget to send for" (104).
He decides to take a room in the inn at Northridge rather than hiring his
own sleigh because he fears if he hires his own sleigh, he will not be reim-
bursed for the cost. "What if . . . no one remembered to ask him what this
devotion to duty cost? That . . . was one of the contingencies he had ex-
pensively learned to look out for . . ." (104-105). Cautiously, painfully,
in what he perceives as his neglected, class-disadvantaged state, he delib-
erates on his course of action and chooses the safest alternative. The role
Faxon assumes as a deprived, cautious individual makes him a nervous
man:

> His own temperament hung on lightly quivering nerves, which yet, as he be-
> lieved, would never quite swing him beyond a normal sensibility . . . . That was
> what his rootless life had brought him to: for lack of a personal stake in things
> his sensibility was at the mercy of such trifles . . . . Yes; that, and the cold and
> fatigue, the absence of hope and haunting sense of starved aptitudes, all these
> had brought him to the perilous verge over which, once or twice before, his
> terrified brain had hung. (105,121)

In this desperate and despairing state, Faxon meets young Rainer who,
even in his ill health, represents the freshness of youth and untapped potential that Faxon has lost. He is immediately attracted to the young man
whose face is "full of morning freshness" (105) and whose smile is of
"such sweetness that Faxon felt, as never before, what Nature can achieve
when she deigns to match the face with the mind" (107). He instantly has
a caring attitude for Rainer which makes his later desertion of him all the
more shocking and disappointing.[4] Although Faxon becomes solicitous
about Rainer's health when he realizes the dire and immediate threats that
prey upon him, he is unable to assume moral responsibility and act
supportively.

The appearances of Lavington's apparitional double give Faxon the
awful sense of the threat to Rainer. But, just as important, Faxon's

responses to the double tell us a great deal about Faxon himself. The first appearance of the double causes him to feel "a strange weight of fatigue on all his limbs" (113), foreshadowing his moral inertia. Eager to forget the evil apparition after its disappearance, he is unprepared for the second sighting. "Faxon's first impulse was to look away, to look anywhere else" (117). Like Mary Boyne ("Afterward"), he would simply prefer to close his eyes and not see, not have to deal with the complications that contact with a greater reality beyond his own constricted world will bring. The apparition gives him a "sense of mortal isolation" (118), which lends him momentary awareness of his lack of connection with and commitment to others, but this painful knowledge does not change his conditioned response. He thinks, "I won't look up!" (119). He stares at his wine glass on the dinner table, a "merciful preoccupation which saved him, kept him from crying out, from losing his head, from slipping down into the bottomless blackness that gaped for him." In fear that his "last link with safety" will snap, he covers his eyes and "oblivion and reassurance seemed to fall on him." But when he opens his eyes again, he perceives once more the "monstrous vision . . . stamped on his pupils, a part of him forever, an indelible horror burnt into his body and brain" (120).

Even though he flees from the dinner table, Faxon cannot escape unwanted perceptions, nor does he escape responsibility. Smothered by the "abominable air" of the house, he plunges "into the purifying night. Resolutely he set his face for flight" (121). Driven to the point of decision, he questions why he has been singled out and, as he sees it, victimized.

> Why had he alone been chosen to see what he had seen? What business was it of his in God's name? Any of the others . . . might have exposed the horror and defeated it: but he, the one weaponless and defenceless spectator . . . he alone had been singled out as the victim of this dreadful initiation! (120)

As he flees, he begins to realize that he is "flying from a terror of his own creating," but his wanting to shun "other eyes until he should regain his balance" shows he is only worried about his own stability and how others see him; his thoughts do not deter his flight. He focuses not on the threat to Rainer, but the threat to himself. "Why else, in the name of any imaginable logic, human or devilish, should he, a stranger, be singled out for this experience? What could it mean to him, how was he related to it, what bearing had it on his case?" (121). Not until he finds that Rainer has followed him into oblivion does his focus shift. Squarely faced with Rainer's good will in pursuing him and Lavington's ill will in sending Rainer out into the freezing night, Faxon finally thinks of the boy's welfare. "Anxiety for the lad" becomes his main concern. Realizing that he is not crazy, Faxon begins to think that he is the "instrument singled out to warn and save." Although "overpowering reality" finally spurs him to positive action to preserve Rainer's well-being ("He couldn't let the boy go back!"), he soon finds that he is too late (125). Rainer makes it only to the lodge at Overdale where he dies. Faxon is left, literally, with the boy's blood on his hands.

Faxon's nervous sensibility cannot bear the shock; he has a nervous breakdown and faces "obliteration" (127). Five months later, in the warm climate and mellow atmosphere of the Malay Peninsula where he is being taken care of by a friend, Faxon accidentally faces the full extent of what has happened. Reading a collection of old newspapers, he finds that Rainer's will has left Lavington a large sum of money allowing him to rebuild his empire after the Wall Street crash. Only then does Faxon fully understand "what the warning meant" and that he might have exerted effort to change the course of events. "If he had not fled . . . dashed wildly into the night, he might have broken the spell of iniquity, the powers of darkness might not have prevailed!" The greatest horror finally for Faxon is the recognition of his moral failure, exacerbated by his fantasy that he could have been Rainer's savior. "That—that was what he had done! The powers of pity had singled him out to warn and save, and he had closed his ears to their call, and washed his hands of it, and fled" (128). Whatever he might have done to help Rainer, which may not have been as much as he imagines, Faxon, literally and figuratively, washed his hands of Rainer's blood.

The harsh winter of Northridge in which Faxon meets his doom evokes the isolating winter landscape of *Ethan Frome*, a work which Wharton was writing during the same period of time that she wrote "The Triumph of Night." George Faxon, like Ethan Frome, is a ruin of a man, because of his inability to assert himself as a mature individual. Both Frome and Faxon are unable to think clearly and formulate plans of positive action. They both prefer lack of awareness, passivity, and an infantile state of oblivion to the assumption of responsibility for their own fates and healthy commitment to others. Wolff makes the comment that we all harbor an Ethan Frome tendency:

> It is always tempting to cast aside the complexities and demands of adulthood. Within everyone of us there lurks a phantom self, not our "real" self, not the self that the world sees, but a seductive shade who calls us to passivity and dependency

in a sweet, soft voice. Here is the greatest danger . . . The horror of the void.
(*Feast* 174)

In writing *Ethan Frome* and "The Triumph of Night," Wharton was exploring the "electing of passivity and a life of regression" at a time when she was screwing up the courage to assert her own independence (*Feast* 177). In effect, she was trying to exorcise her personal demons of dependency and diminishment. Wharton's "nightmare" was the "terror of the desire to regress" (*Feast* 183). Wharton writes that *Ethan Frome* was for her a pivotal work. "It was not until I wrote 'Ethan Frome' that I suddenly felt the artisan's full control of his implements" (*Backward Glance* 209). She had also gained greater understanding and control of her life.

Ethan Frome and George Faxon both represent the "failure to transcend the ties of immaturity" (Rose 431). Wharton returned to this theme in *Summer*, the only work of fiction that she was writing during the early years of World War I. This book, which she called her "Hot Ethan" (Wolff, "Cold Ethan and 'Hot Ethan'" 231), is also set in the desolate New England landscape, but deceptively in the lushness of a budding and blossoming spring and summer. Charity Royall is not yet an adult, but an adolescent on the brink of adulthood. She is "determined to assert her independence" (*Summer* 126), but like Frome and Faxon, "Charity is incapable of the clarity of vision necessary to mature choice" (Rose 434). She loses her struggle for maturity and settles into a regressive, dependent life cared for by the father figure, lawyer Royall. Before she succumbs to her fate, she tries escape through a love affair with the socially incompatible Harney, becomes pregnant, and then in despair, like Frome with the futile sled ride, and Faxon in his futile running from Overdale, she turns to flight: "Suddenly it became clear that flight, and instant flight, was the only thing conceivable . . . " (*Summer* 157). She flees to the Mountain, the place of her origin, where, instead of a nurturing mother, she finds a dead woman who is a stranger to her. She also discovers a lawless, slovenly band of people who disgust her. Lawyer Royall paternally rescues her, marries her, and takes her home where—in dependent oblivion with little need to think clearly or assert herself—she will raise her child.

Charity sacrifices independence for security. Frome also forfeits independence and passion by electing to live his life with the safe and maternal Zeena after his mother dies. Faxon, too, forfeits maturity for safety. After his brief winter stay at Northridge, Faxon escapes into life in a warm and nurturing landscape where he is taken care of. Both Faxon and Frome finally face the horrors of their choices, as we suspect Charity will eventually face the horror of her "incestuous" life with a man over twice her age who has been her substitute father. *Ethan Frome, Summer*, and "The Triumph of Night" are linked thematically by their settings in New England and the symbolic nature of the locale; its "life-denying stasis" is the key to the souls of the ruined characters who inhabit it (Rose 436). As horror stories, these tales disclose the Gothic motifs of confinement, repression, regression, and entrapment. Patriarchal patterns of domination and submission ensnare victims who are further entrapped by the terrifying tendency of human nature to avoid conflict and growth and retreat to stultifying safety. Frome, Faxon, and Charity Royall lack the inner resources or the external opportunities or support to become mature individuals and assume moral responsibility beyond the mechanical level of daily duty left in their diminished lives.

Wharton's ghost stories begin to develop distinct patterns of negative gender roles and relationships. "The Triumph of Night" suggests two possible roles for the male, both failed models: the cruel dominator (Lavington) and the ineffectual shirker of responsibility (Faxon). Although no females appear in "The Triumph of Night," Faxon's sense of deprivation and desire to avoid responsibility and to retreat to a safe haven suggest a submissive dependency associated with femininity. *Ethan Frome* and *Summer* emphasize unhealthy dependency patterns in male/female relationships. In *Summer,* the role of the female is delineated as dependent, resigned, and repressed. In effect, Faxon, Frome, and Charity Royall, as motherless orphans, apparently lacking adequate parental nurturing, presented literally or figuratively, seek nurturing in regressive relationships. These negative patterns befit Wharton's mission: to reveal the "plague spots of society," or more specifically, the weaknesses of a culture that fosters domination and dependency as the accepted norm in human relations.

In "Kerfol," Wharton returns thematically to the horrors of domination and submission with a new vengeance. No other ghost story of hers contains such sustained cruelty and grisly detail. Reminiscent of Wharton's early supernatural tales with their focus on marital discord, "Kerfol" depicts an unhappy marriage and the suggestion of infidelity which result in tragedy. Revenge plays a part in the violent tale, but in this case, the lord of the manor does not prevail. Instead, the story depicts anger fully vented against patriarchal tradition and oppression.

Set in autumn in France, far from a New England winter, but in a "desert landscape" (*Ghost Stories* 80), the narrative structure of "Kerfol" resembles *Ethan Frome*. The narrator reveals the situation of the story and the nature of his character through three events: a visit to the house called Kerfol, the appearance of the ghost dogs, and the reading of the court records of Anne de Cornault's trial that investigates the violent death of her husband.

Intrigued by his friend de Lanrivain's description of Kerfol as the "most romantic house in Brittany," the narrator visits it because he is considering purchasing property and Kerfol is for sale. As he approaches the seventeenth-century house along the tree-lined avenue, he is sensitive to the nuances of environment which foreshadow the story of the house: "If ever I saw an avenue that unmistakably led to something it was the avenue of Kerfol" (80). Like the narrator approaching the house of Usher, he finds the "great blind house" an overwhelming presence. He confesses a "sense of irrelevance, of littleness, of futile bravado," in staring "into the face of such a past" (81). The weight of the past is the key to reading Kerfol. The narrator tells us: "One couldn't as much glance at that pile without feeling it a long accumulation of history . . . . Certainly no house had ever more completely and finally broken with the present." What the past of the house means puzzles him at first. He generalizes that his impression is perhaps only from "that sheer weight of many associated lives and deaths which gives a majesty to all old houses." He begins to want to know more about the house, "not to see more," for he is convinced "it was not a question of seeing—but to feel more: feel all the place had to communicate" (81).

Wharton gives clues about what the house communicates through imagery. The "dumb facade" does not speak, and the "long granite front" looks "like a fortress prison." "A few lean hydrangeas and geraniums pined in the flower beds, and the ancient house looked down on them indifferently" (83). The narrator sees the "whole place" as a "tomb": "it might have been its own funeral monument." The house communicates not a general past history, but a specific one of confinement, insensitivity, mute suffering, and death. The narrator finally suspects that "Kerfol suggests something more—a perspective of stern and cruel memories . . ." (81).

In many ghost stories, writers use symbols of the past to show the effect of history on the present. "Ghosts were a traditional medium of communication between the past and the present, the dead and the living, and thus the ghost story might be used to assert continuity . . ." (Briggs 111). This continuity might be positive. "The ghost as a link with a past from which we are afraid of being disinherited or disconnected had a particular appeal for a number of American writers" (Briggs 112). For Wharton, however, in "Kerfol," the ghostly evocation of the past is harshly negative. Wharton, along with other ghost story writers who show the sins of the fathers and mothers being visited upon the sons and daughters, was "inclined to identify tradition with one or another form of repression" (Wolff, *Feast* 263). Nevertheless, Wharton's attitudes towards tradition can be debated. In "Kerfol," the traditions of the past are oppressive, yet Wolff argues that in her later works, Wharton "began to formulate a new notion of tradition" as "the matrix within which personality is defined—a delicate fretwork of familiarities and understandings by which man's sense of self is confirmed and reconfirmed in his many daily encounters." Although some of Wharton's fiction manifests respect for "the force of tradition and civilization that permits us to establish that essential relation between ourselves and others" (Wolff, *Feast* 264), and in a Freudian sense, reflects the necessity of the curbing effects of civilization, "Kerfol" testifies to Wharton's continual argument with traditional social structures that cruelly oppress the individual. In particular, she deplores patriarchal habits that confine women to the status of mere objects to be bought and possessed and neglected.

The narrator next encounters five dogs that suggest impressions of past life at Kerfol. Although the narrator expects each dog to bark and snap at him, they are mute and maintain their distance from him. Remarkably, they "fall back on muffled paws" and make no sound (82). The narrator thinks they must be "horribly cowed to be so silent and inert." They do not look "hungry or ill-treated" as though they have been physically abused, but they seem psychologically subdued "as if they lived a long time with people who never spoke to them or looked at them: as though the silence of the place had gradually benumbed their busy inquisitive natures." To the narrator, "this strange passivity, this almost human lassitude, seemed . . . sadder than the misery of starved and beaten animals." With the dogs as with the house, the narrator's intuitions reveal to him a sense of the past. He thinks,

> I had an idea that their distance from me was as nothing as my remoteness from them. The impression they produced was that of having in common one memory so deep and dark that nothing that had happened since was worth either a growl or a wag.

Although he does not realize the dogs are ghosts, he comes close to comprehending their silent presence: "Do you know what you look like . . . . You look as if you'd seen a ghost . . ." (84).

These sad mute creatures provide a key to understanding the past of Kerfol and areas of Wharton's own past. The trial records later reveal that the dogs were the beloved pets of the childless Anne de Cornault. They were brutally strangled by her jealous husband (all but possibly one). According to Anne, they returned in supernatural revenge to kill him and, in effect, to protect her. The dogs, reminders of Yves de Cornault's cruelty and oppression, also represent Anne as a helpless victim of imprisonment and abuse. The use of the dogs to symbolize Anne's plight is a natural choice for Wharton because, throughout her life, she was very attached to her own pet dogs. Lewis says they were "among her main joys of being." At forty-two, Wharton wrote up a list of "ruling passions." "Dogs" appears second on the list after "Justice and Order" (Ozick 53, 54). At sixty-two, in a journal, Wharton writes:

> I am secretly afraid of animals—of all animals except dogs, and even some dogs. I think it is because of the usness in their eyes, with the underlying not-usness which belies it, and is so tragic a reminder of the lost age when we human beings branched off and left them; left them to eternal inarticulateness and slavery. (qtd. by Wolff, *Feast* 11)

"Inarticulateness and slavery" characterize the situation of Anne de Cornault and also Wharton's own perceived state of psychological deprivation that haunted her life. She writes:

> I always had a deep, instinctive understanding of animals, a yearning to hold them in my arms, a fierce desire to protect them against pain and cruelty. This feeling seemed to have its source in a curious sense of being, somehow, myself, an intermediate creature between human beings and animals, and nearer, on the whole, to the furry tribes than to homo sapiens. I felt that I knew things about them—their sensations, desires and sensibilities—that other bipeds could not guess; and this seemed to lay on me the obligation to defend them against the human oppressors. The feeling grew in intensity until it became a morbid preoccupation. (qtd. by Wolff, *Feast* 11)

Wolff connects Wharton's "morbid preoccupation" of nurturing and protecting her little dogs and her identification with them to the emotional deprivation she suffered in childhood, living under the shadow of the repressive social structure of Old New York, the unpredictably hot and cold attitudes of a non-affectionate mother, and over-attachment to her father.

> Edith Wharton would always carry with her this strange sense of kinship with animals, a sense of herself (like "them") as intolerably isolated . . . . When she

grew old enough to discover some creature smaller and more helpless than herself, she showered upon it the attention that this earliest self had craved and not
found. But nothing—not ever—would entirely compensate this sense of fundamental deprivation; and her modes of thinking, of formulating thoughts and
problems, of perceiving the world—all these were essentially formed by
Wharton's earliest sense of insufficiency. (*Feast* 11, 12) [5]

In "Kerfol," Anne de Cornault displaces her own unhappiness,
helplesssness, and grief over her isolation and childlessness by giving her
complete emotional attention to the helpless dogs. Dogs are also traditionally symbolic of fidelity, a subject which comes up in "Kerfol." At the
trial, Anne recounts an anecdote. One day she was asleep in her room and
awakened to find her husband smiling down at her. He thinks Anne looks
like his great-grandmother whose tomb in the chapel bears her marble effigy with her feet on a little dog. Anne, although chilled by the analogy to
the tomb, expresses the desire to have her effigy carved with her dog at her
feet. Her husband points out that the dog is "the emblem of fidelity" (94).
Anne asks him if he doubts her right to this emblem. He swears she shall
have her monument if she earns it. Anne swears to be faithful "if only for
the sake of having my little dog at my feet" (94). This revealing conversation not only emphasizes de Cornault's tyrannical possessiveness, but also
Anne's demeaning position of servitude as a faithful hound to its master, a
debasement traditional to the Cornault women. It also belies Anne's attitude towards Cornault and her marriage, a revelation that Yves de Cornault
surely did not miss. She will not be faithful, she says, because she is a
blindly loyal servant or because she loves him and is happy in her marriage, but because she wishes to find personal comfort, if not in life, in
death, by having her little dog at her feet on her tomb. If "Justice and
Order," not to mention love, are not available, she will at least have the
comfort of her little dog.

After his visit to Kerfol and his discovery from Madame de Lanrivain
that the dogs he saw are known as the ghosts of Kerfol, the narrator receives from the contemporary Hervé de Lanrivain a book that will satisfy
his curiosity about the house and its past. The book, 1702, written about a
hundred years after the events, contains "an almost literal transcription" of
the month-long trial of Anne de Cornault, who was tried for the murder of
her husband (86). As Browning's "yellow book" conveys the intricacies
of "A Roman murder-case" (*The Ring and the Book* 525-26), so *A History
of the Assizes of the Duchy of Brittany* promises to enlighten the narrator
about the strange death of Yves de Cornault. The narrator says that he first

thought of "translating the old record," but because it was "full of wearisome repetitions," he elected to try "to disentangle" its story in "simpler form." He claims to have often "reverted to the text" and that he has added nothing of his own (87). This latter claim demands further investigation for Wharton filters the story of Anne and Yves de Cornault through many layers of interpretation, producing a blurry and complex web of "truth."

In "Kerfol, as in writing *Ethan Frome*, Wharton drew upon precedents. "I make no claim for originality in following a method of which 'La Grande Bretêche' and 'The Ring and the Book' has set me magnificent example" (Modern Student's Library ed. ix). In Balzac's and Browning's work, what happened is a difficult matter to ascertain. "Truth," as a complex interaction and understanding of facts and feelings, is filtered through several consciousnesses. Another work that uses this method to highlight the multi-faceted aspect of truth is Brontë's *Wuthering Heights*.[6] Each of these works may have influenced "Kerfol," but an even more apt analogue for "Kerfol" (whether Wharton had it in mind or not) is Hawthorne's *Blithedale Romance*, a story filtered through one consciousness, which is ultimately about Coverdale, the narrator. Whatever the specific works, Wharton learned from literary tradition and used a method of focusing on the narrator as much as on the facts of the tale. Cynthia Griffin Wolff describes Wharton's technique:

> It is not the 'facts' themselves which are of primary importance in the end, but the collection of facts and . . . the impact of these facts upon the observer . . . . Not situation alone, not narrator alone, but each illuminating the other; the situation filtered through the larger categories of the narrator's consciousness . . . this is to be the subject of the work. In the end, such a method focuses our attention more clearly and precisely on the narrator than on anything else." (Wolff, *Feast* 163)

In "Kerfol," ultimately the narrator himself becomes the knot that ties the threads of the tale together. The book containing the court record is published long after the principals are all dead. Anne's testimony, the investigation pursued by the court, and the attitudes of the narrator are all interwoven and finally coalesce to present Wharton's themes.

Anne's de Cornault's testimony at the trial is problematical. She contradicts herself, and she attributes her husband's death to supernatural causes. Her husband, found dead at the head of narrow stairs leading to a courtyard at Kerfol, was "dreadfully scratched and gashed about the face and throat, as if with curious pointed weapons," which a doctor in the court testified appeared to be bites (90). Anne first testifies that she was asleep, heard her husband's cries, and found him at the head of the stairs. However, the court reveals flaws in her testimony. "Owing to the thickness of the walls and the length of the intervening passage," Anne could not have heard her husband from her room. Also, although the death occurred at midnight, she was dressed and her bed not slept in. This and other details (an open door, blood on Anne's dress, bloody handprints on the staircase walls) show that she had been at the courtyard door when her husband was killed. Two days later Hervé de Lanrivain, a young nobleman in the neighborhood, was "arrested for complicity" in the crime after several witnesses (supposedly disreputable ones) testified to seeing him climb the wall of the park the night of Yves de Cornault's death. The narrator points out that "One way of patching out incomplete proofs in those days was to put some sort of pressure, moral or physical, on the accused person." When Anne reappears in court, she seems "weak and wandering" (92) and changes her testimony. She admits Lanrivain was at the door, that she talked with him three times before her husband's death, and that he expressed pity for her isolated married life. She says she crept downstairs to warn Lanrivain, contradicting an earlier statement that she desired to run away (which the court had taken as an indication of infidelity). Graphically, she describes hearing her husband scream and the "noise of the pack when the wolf is thrown to them—gulping and lapping" (100). Anne swoons after this description, but upon her return to court, she tells the judge that she recognized the dogs as "my dead dogs" (101), alleging that the ghosts of her pets avenged her by killing her husband.[7]

Although Anne's testimony is confusing, her situation as garnered from other details indeed seems pitiable. Anne describes her married life as "extremely lonely: 'desolate' was the word she used." She was lonely and childless and talked of long, rainy days. She explains that Cornault left her alone frequently, never took her with him, had the servants constantly attend her, and although she says he never "struck or threatened her" or spoke harshly to her, many days he "did not speak at all" (93). He strangled a little dog that was a gift to her and subsequently three other little dogs that she befriended as substitutions for her lost pet. One other dog that she petted disappeared. She confesses that because of this cruelty, she was afraid for her life and wanted to ask Lanrivain to take her away. Only one other testimony corroborates Anne's own statements of unhappiness. One servant woman says she had surprised Anne "crying, and had heard her say that she was a woman accursed to have had no child and nothing in her life to call her own" (89). Ignoring the situation of her "desolate" marriage and its cruelties, the court quickly dismisses Anne's contradictory and unsupported statements. Although the mystery of Yves de Cornault's death is not satisfactorily solved, Anne is imprisoned, handed over "to the keeping of her husband's family, who shut her up in the keep of Kerfol, where she is said to have died many years later, a harmless madwoman" (101).

The portrait of Yves de Cornault that emerges from the trial record is unmistakably negative, yet this does not help Anne's case. The narrator describes Anne as an attractive young woman from the red crayon portrait owned by the contemporary Lanrivain. In contrast, Yves de Cornault is described as a 62-year-old "rich and powerful noble" without much physical or personal attractiveness. There is no mistaking his repulsiveness. The narrator describes him as being "short and broad" with a "swarthy face, legs slightly bowed from the saddle, a hanging nose and broad hands with black hairs on them."[8] Cornault was thought to have led a different life in his travels from the one he led at home. At Kerfol, he was known as a "stern and austere man" (87). The narrator speculates that he might have been free with the peasant women on his estate as nobles were wont to be in his day. After his first wife died and he married Anne, he became "less exacting with his tenants, less harsh to peasants and dependents, and less subject to fits of gloomy silence which had darkened his widowhood" (88). But at the trial, dependents at Kerfol

> were induced to say—with apparent sincerity [seemingly a contradiction] that during the year or two preceding his death their master had once more grown uncertain and irascible, and subject to fits of brooding silence . . . . This seemed to show that things had not been going well at Kerfol; though no one could be found to say that there had been any signs of open disagreement between husband and wife. (93)

From Anne's testimony we know Cornault strangled four dogs. The day he strangled the first dog with the bracelet he somehow retrieved from Lanrivain, the narrator says he hanged a peasant and nearly beat a young horse to death. The evening of his death, Cornault was "in his usual mood, between good and bad: you could never tell which" (95). According to all the accumulated details from the narrator's account, Yves de Cornault had few redeeming features. "Austere and stern," no less than cruel, seem apt descriptions for the man. Yet during the trial, the evidence, as interpreted by the court (and relayed by the narrator), justifies Yves de Cornault's behavior and condemns Anne.

Even deceased, Cornault holds power over Anne suggesting that in a patriarchal social order, power resides with the husband, and women are subjugated. In "Kerfol," the judge, the court, and also the narrator, all males, represent patriarchal control. The institutional deck is stacked against Anne at the trial, and she is debased and dehumanized by the proceedings. As for Cornault's possibly disreputable or immoral behavior when away from Kerfol, the narrator dismisses "these rumors" as "not particularly relevant." As for Cornault's relation to peasant women on the estate, he says "the evidence on this point was not worth much" (87). The narrator points out that "No one was found to say that Yves de Cornault had been unkind to his wife, and it was plain to see that he was content with his bargain" (88). The dependents of the noble Cornault family certainly would not admit that their master was unkind to his wife, and Cornault is thought to have behaved well because he was pleased with making a good "bargain." Anne is not seen as a marriage partner, but as an object purchased and possessed. Anne's father sold her to Cornault, an inappropriately old husband for the young woman, because of Cornault's power and privilege as a nobleman and because the father needed money, having "squandered his fortune at cards" (88). Further Anne's childlessness is seen not as a disadvantage to her, but to Cornault who did not get full value for his purchase. The narrator erroneously and prejudicially interprets Anne's tears over her childless state as "a natural enough feeling in a wife attached to her husband . . ." (89). He focuses on the grief that he perceives Cornault must have felt that she bore no son and, in effect, praises *him* for not reproaching *her,* instead showering her with gifts. The implication is that she alone is responsible for her childlessness and also that gifts rather than mutual understanding would appease her.

The rich gifts that Cornault purchased for Anne are trotted out at court so the judges and the public may admire his supposed taste and generosity. The story of the present of the little dog which cost a "long price" corroborates his generosity, but also suggests that Cornault measured all value in terms of possessions and money. "Anne's pleasure was so great that, to see her laugh and play with the little animal, her husband would doubtless have given twice the sum" (90). Also when Anne resisted being constantly watched by the servants, Cornault attested her value to him as a possession: "A man who has a treasure does not leave the key in the lock when he goes out" (93). Cornault has little respect for life in general; he values life in terms of advantages to his well-being, esteem, wealth and power. The narrator points out that the court laughed at Anne when she said she feared for her life because Cornault strangled her dog. "Another smile passed around the courtroom: in a day when any nobleman had a right to hang his peasants and most of them exercised it—pinching a pet animal's windpipe was nothing to make a fuss about" (94). The scene reveals the savageries accepted by patriarchal convention. Ultimately, Anne's attempt to present her case is futile. She is as helpless and mute as her dead dogs, although they or someone appears to have avenged her. Patriarchal bias systematically invalidates all evidence that might work in her favor.

The narrator's report and his speculations also support patriarchal practice and logic. According to his view, which he presents as the view of the court, Anne appears to be a hysterical female. When she describes the demise of dogs, the narrator tells us that her narrative was "not received without impatience and incredulous comment." The judges were surprised by the "puerility" of her tale which did not help her "in the eyes of the public." To them, her story ironically proved "that Yves de Cornault disliked dogs, and that his wife, to gratify her own fancy, persistently ignored this dislike." Her complaint was seen as a "trivial disagreement," no excuse for conversations with Lanrivain, and patently absurd (97). The narrator reports that her lawyer regretted letting her use the defense, was ashamed, and "would have sacrificed her without a scruple to save his professional reputation." The narrator says that most of the "dozing court" became tired of the case and only began to pay attention when Anne spoke of the titillating detail of receiving a message from her supposed lover. The narrator attributes any lack of feeling, even hatred, Cornault exhibited for his wife to legitimate cause, "his supposed dishonor" (98). Ultimately, it is Anne's unfortunate indiscretion in talking to Lanrivain, not proven murder or adultery, that condemns her. The court, not unsurprisingly, vindicates Cornault, without identifying his murderer, and upholds the prevailing views of the patriarchy and the indisputable rights of the noble class.

In the tale, Wharton shows ironically that the morality of the patriarchy and the ruling nobility receives Christian sanction. At the trial, a conspicuous Crucifix, mentioned several times, hangs over the heads of the judges, symbolically showing that Christianity validates patriarchal judgment. After possibly being tortured to change her testimony, Anne ironically vows "on her honor and the wounds of the Blessed Redeemer" to tell the court the truth (92). Although Yves de Cornault is a cruel man who hangs peasants and strangles helpless creatures, he is thought to be a religious man. He frequently brings his wife gifts with religious motifs that caution Anne to follow the rules of the faith and the faithful. Wharton underscores the double standard of gender and class privilege that exempts men and nobles from Christian moral law according to their whims and desires, and the hypocrisy of Christianity, with the story of the little golden dog. The dog was stolen by a sailor from a nobleman. However, the theft was reckoned "a perfectly permissible thing to do, since the pilgrim was a Christian and the nobleman a heathen doomed to hell-fire" (90). Thus male Christians emerge from the tale religiously just, even though from other perspectives, they can be judged morally wrong.

Wharton seems to be telling her tale to expose the hypocrisy of the social order, the ghost dogs symbolically representing protection for the abused Anne de Cornault as Emma Saxon represents protection for Mrs. Brympton in "The Lady's Maid's Bell." The dogs also seem to represent Anne's suppressed self, her legitimate anger and a desire for revenge. Are the dogs, however, literally to be taken as ghosts? Who killed Yves de Cornault? Is there a natural as well as a supernatural explanation? In her ghost stories, Wharton leaves loopholes or sometimes curious clues suggesting natural explanations, a technique that adds to the richness and ambiguity of each tale. In "Kerfol," surely one might suppose that Anne indeed killed her husband (with what weapons, one cannot be sure) or that the murder might have been committed by Hervé de Lanrivain.

Helen Killoran, following various clues in the story which might lead to natural explanations, suggests that the story is based on a Jansenist/ Jesuit longstanding quarrel and that the Jansenist Hervé de Lanrivain or Jansenist sympathizers, such as Anne or her father, may have killed Yves de Cornault. Killoran's evidence for "Kerfol" as a "historical murder mystery" ("Pascal" 12) is connected to Wharton's library of books on the Jansenist/Jesuit quarrels, the time of the tale coinciding with the time of the quarrels, the reference to Lanrivain joining the Jansenists, and the reference to Yves de Cornault's travels and gifts brought to Anne, which might be associated with the Jesuits' materialistic import business, the factor that angered the puritanical Jansenists in the first place. If indeed the Jansenist/ Jesuit quarrels were part of Wharton's artifice, her mastery of her craft is all the more admirable, a blending of romance and realism, to satisfy readers desiring the mysterious and metaphorical or the mere factual, and to satisfy her own yearnings to face life's hidden realities head on.

Finally, the narrator's role adds to the complexity of the tale and its revelations. The narrator pledges to summarize the trial records without distortion or embellishment: "I have said I would add nothing of my own to this bold statement of a strange case. . ." (88). However, it becomes less and less clear as he proceeds whether the responses and rationale of the court come from the court record or whether he is making his own inferences. It appears that by selection and emphasis, he presents his own interpretation of the case. Continually he refers to Anne as a "poor thing" or a "poor wretch," and at the end of his account, he concurs with the court that Anne is hysterical or mad. "I will try to keep as nearly as possible to Anne's own statements, though toward the end, poor thing . . ." (90). He interjects his own surmises to compensate for Anne's deficiencies. These language slips reveal that much of what he is telling are interpretations to fit his own biases. By the end of the account, this is blatant. "At this point, *I fancy* the drowsy courtroom beginning to wake up . . . . *As I read the case, I fancy,* there was no feeling for her left in him . . ." [added italics] (98). The narrator and the court have reached the same conclusion from similar biases, and the narrator fills in the gaps of the court's rationale with ease.

Who is the narrator, and why has Wharton chosen him to tell the tale? We know that the contemporary Lanrivain sent him to Kerfol because it was a "romantic" house, but also because it was the perfect place for a "solitary-minded devil" like the narrator. When he sees Kerfol, the narrator is dismayed with Lanrivain's assessment of his character and claims that under "his unsociable exterior" he had always had "secret yearnings for domesticity" (80). Therefore, he is "overwhelmed by the almost blasphemous frivolity of suggesting to any living being that Kerfol was the place for him" (81). What puts the narrator off about Kerfol? Ultimately Kerfol and its story reflect his own personality, values, and biases back to him, and they are disturbing. A well-to-do bachelor, the narrator is a solitary intellectual. His interest in the portraits of Anne de Cornault and Hervé de Lanrivain, his quick identification of the artists, his attentiveness to the architectural features of Kerfol show him to be an art connoisseur. He is an intuitive, sensitive man on the one hand, a man attuned to the nuances of the past, yet ultimately he shows himself to be blind to patriarchal and class biases which prevent him along with the court from fairly assessing Yves and Anne de Cornault. Finally, he lacks compassion. He has little understanding of Anne's real plight: he pities her inexplicable madness, not seeing that if she is mad, she has been driven mad by isolation and cruel treatment. He feels sorry for Anne, but like the court, he finds her story irrelevant and trivial. In the end, he even loses interest in her story.[9]

Wharton's conclusion of "Kerfol" is especially clever. After the narrator finishes Anne's story, he immediately forgets her. Also he never focuses on, debates, or questions the puzzling supernatural aspect of her tale which does not fit his rational bias. Instead he turns his attention to Hervé de Lanrivain, a minor figure in the tale, whom the contemporary Lanrivain refers to as "only a collateral" in the story (86). The narrator learns that Lanrivain was set free after the trial because of insufficient evidence and his family's influence. He went to Paris and became a Jansenist. The Jansenists were a heretical, intellectual, and puritanical religious brotherhood. The narrator confirms his own dry, intellectual, asexual (or perhaps homosexual) orientation by saying that he envies Lanrivain's fate. He envies him because "In the course of his life two great things had happened to him: he had loved romantically, and he must have talked with Pascal. . ." (102). Ironically, he envies Lanrivain for what seemed to be an unconsummated romance, simply the admiring of and sympathy for Anne de Cornault from afar. Unconsummated love is the ideal of the narrator who as an uncommitted bachelor and a "solitary" devil only deals with romance as a mode of thought, a Platonic ideal. Finally, he envies Lanrivain for a life spent in the company of other men safe from romantic attachment and marital commitment. The narrator also reveals his actual orientation when he equates romance with the intellectual satisfaction of conversation with the mathematician and philosopher Blaise Pascal. Again, as in much of Wharton's other fiction (for example, "The Eyes"), the intellectual bachelor character, trapped in rationalism, is blind to the rich texture of life. He unquestioningly accepts the patriarchy's biases and retreats to a "safe" environment to meet his own needs.

The ending of "Kerfol" seems abrupt and irrelevant without consideration of the narrator's personal tie to the story he has told. In *The Writing of Fiction*, Wharton comments on the conclusion of the short tale: "Obviously, as every subject contains its own dimensions, so is its conclusion *ab ovo*; and the failure to end a tale in accordance with its own deepest sense must deprive it of meaning" (51). Throughout "Kerfol," using irony, Wharton mocks patriarchal judgment. She also mocks the detached male who professes comprehension of life and tenderness towards others, but who actually has no genuine understanding of or compassion for human suffering, especially the suffering of women and other socially outcast inferiors who have little power in the patriarchy. These themes of "Kerfol" are implicit in the ending which discredits the narrator's reliability. As Barbara White points out, "Wharton's male narrators reflect her belief that men are the only legal inhabitants of the public sphere, but at the same time they take on other elements of her attitude towards men, such as her resentment of their tendency to patronize woman and detach themselves from human responsibility and connection" (63).

In "Kerfol," the concept of patriarchal power is systematically undermined by Wharton's method, by the filtering of information through many sources, especially the unreliable narrator, and through the use of imagery, symbolism, irony, and absences of information. Wharton focuses not on the tale of an adulteress, a mad woman, or a murderess, but the story of a society built on domination, submission, and detachment. "Kerfol" is a condemnation of this society whose moral structure is corrupt.

All four ghost stories from Wharton's "nightmare" period (1910-1914) focus on supposedly just moral stances that are blind facades, depicting injustice leading to suffering and increasingly to an association with death and violence. Wharton's personal horrors were undoubtedly channelled into the artistic stream of the horrors of societal injustice. In October 1913, having painfully dealt with her divorce, a verbal attack from her brother Harry, and a breach with Henry James, Wharton records a dream nightmare in her notebook:

> A pale demon with black hair came in, followed by four gnome-like creatures carrying a great black trunk. They set it down and opened it, and the Demon crying out: "Here's your year—here are all the horrors that have happened to you and that are still going to happen" dragged out a succession of limp black squirming things and threw them on the floor before me. They were not rags or creatures, not living or dead—they were Black Horrors, shapeless, and that seemed to writhe about as they fell at my feet, and yet were as inanimate as bits of stuff. But none of these comparisons occurred to me, for I *knew* what they were: the hideous, incredible things that had happened to me in this dreadful year, or were to happen to me before its close; and I stared, horror-struck, as the Demon dragged them out, one by one, more and more, till finally, flinging down a blacker, hatefuller one, he said laughing: "There—that's the last of them!" & the gnomes laughed too; but I, as I stared at the great black pile and the empty trunk, said to the Demon: "Are you sure it isn't a false bottom?" (qtd. by Lewis, *Biography* 355)

Unfortunately, Wharton's dream proved to be prophetic. With the promise of a new life after her divorce, Wharton tried to move past pain to new joy. Unlike Anne de Cornault who perished as a prisoner, Wharton "felt propelled out of her metaphorical prison and had begun to exercise what Henry James had called a fantastic freedom." She told Bernard Berenson that she was determined to eat the world "leaf by leaf" (Lewis, *Biography* 339).

But the world did not cooperate. Below the false bottom of the black box in her nightmare was more pain from the deaths of dear friends, including Henry James, and from the horrors of World War I. In 1916, Wharton writes to Sara Norton: "The sadness of things is beyond words, and hard work is the only escape from it" (qtd. in Lewis, *Biography* 384).

Notes

1   Pinning down the exact times that Wharton was working on a given piece is sometimes very difficult, partly because she frequently worked on several projects at once (Wolff, *Feast* 62).

2   All page references from "The Triumph of Night" and "Kerfol" are from the Scribner's edition of Wharton's ghost stories, 1973.

3   Carol Singley ("Gothic Borrowings and Innovations in Edith Wharton's 'Bottle of Perrier'") points out that Lavington has "stereotypically homosexual mannerisms" (278).

4   Faxon portrays his attitude towards Rainer as fatherly or big-brotherly, although Faxon's attraction to Rainer also has homoerotic overtones. Faxon, who seems bereft of maternal nurturing, might also be seen as a maternal figure.

5   Lev Raphael (*Edith Wharton's Prisoners of Shame*) alludes to Wharton's identification with dogs. He recalls her referring to herself in *A Backward Glance* as "a soft, anonymous morsel of humanity" and comments

> No wonder, then, that Wharton had such a deep and lifelong identification with small animals, particularly dogs. This affinity is very revealing in another way. Darwin was the first to observe that the dog is the most sociophilic of animals, and characteristically the most readily observed to display the head and eyes lowered in shame. Wharton describes herself as feeling in touch with the unexpressed feelings of small animals, and "possessed by a haunting consciousness of [their] sufferings longing to protect them against pain & cruelty." How, "safe and sheltered," then, was her childhood really, if she was drawn to the helpless and felt so herself? (19).

Raphael contends that Wharton's repressive childhood environment was fertile ground for her internalization of shame which led to a "deep and abiding sense of being defective, never quite good enough as a person" which became "the unconscious core of [her] personality" (8).

6   Helen Killoran ("Pascal, Brontë, and 'Kerfol': The Horrors of a Foolish Quartet") suggests allusions to *Wuthering Heights* in "Kerfol," noting that Cornault behaves like Heathcliff, imprisoning his wife and killing her dogs, and that the narrator resembles Lockwood who loses his way and finally reveals his own inadequacies. These comparisons have value in showing how Wharton was influenced by her reading and literary tradition, and in the Lockwood comparison, I think, value in pointing to Wharton's narrative techniques. However, Killoran's account of the narrator of "Kerfol" not following directions and never arriving at the actual Kerfol is based on

the unsupported assumption that Lanrivain had led him to expect certain features of the place.

7   Helen Killoran, citing the fact that the contemporary Mrs. Lanrivain says that "the women in Brittany drink dreadfully" claims that the lonely Anne was alcoholic. As further evidence, she cites Anne's "weak and wandering" appearance in court and Anne's swoon. This is possible; however, not easy to corroborate. Anne's behavior in court may be attributed to severe interrogation or torture, as implied by the narrator, or to her finally being overwhelmed by the weight of the evidence against her.

8   The narrator's physical description of Yves de Cornault comes from no clear source as does the description of Anne, which is from a crayon drawing. Surely, the description the narrator presents was not in the court record. It seems that Wharton offers the reader the description without sufficient textual support, blurring her narrative technique by the emphasis of her own bias. Helen Killoran connects Cornault with Heathcliff in *Wuthering Heights*, but the unattractive Cornault does not appear to be a "Heathcliffian Byronic hero" (15).

9   Candace Waid (*Edith Wharton's Letters from the Underworld*) concurs that Anne is a victim of the court, but she sees the narrator as a "sympathetic reader to Anne de Cornault's story" (188). She contends that "the power of 'Kerfol' emerges from the constant juxtaposition of the narrator's view of Anne de Cornault's speech and thoughts with the way that her words are apprehended by the listening authorities. Not only are her listeners hostile; they seem to come from another world." This other world is the "male point of view, a Baron's perspective." Waid then notes that the narrator "is to all appearances male" (187). I suggest that the narrator creates and corroborates the male point of view in the tale; he is an extension of this view. His seeming sympathy is surface pity, but not understanding compassion.

Four

"Bewitched" and "Miss Mary Pask"

[Wharton] was doing no more than adopting the Victorian habit . . . of distancing the most intense and private sexual feelings by projecting them in the various forms of fantasy. It is notable, for example, that the ghostly context permits a more direct acknowledgement of sexual experience than we normally find in the dramas of manners and the social life.

R.W.B. Lewis, Introduction,
The Collected Short Stories of Edith Wharton

Morbid dread always signifies repressed sexual wishes.

Sigmund Freud

Before World War I started, Wharton had a brief respite, a time filled with travel and spent with friends. Once the war began, she abandoned travel, except to the front, and, for the most part, her writing, except for journalistic efforts, and turned her attention to war relief. She founded a workshop for unemployed seamstresses, organized an American Hostel for Refugees and the Children of Flanders Rescue Committee, and worked with a committee helping to cure tubercular soldiers. In 1916, the French government recognized her as a Chevalier of the Legion of Honor, the first of several honors she received for her indefatigable war work. In spite of her efforts to help the unfortunate and cope with the pain and loss of war, she writes that the "weight of the war" was a "horrible inescapable oppression" (Lewis, *Biography* 383). Her only completed work of fiction from this period is *Summer* (1917).

After the war, she resumed her novel writing with vigor, producing *The Marne* (1918), *The Age of Innocence* (1920), *The Glimpses of the Moon* (1922), *A Son at the Front* (1923), *Old New York* (a collection of four novellas, 1924), *The Mother's Recompense* (1925), and she continued to write short stories. Her next volume of stories (after *Xingu*, 1916) did not appear until 1926, a volume called *Here and Beyond* brought out by her new publisher, Appleton. *Here and Beyond*, a collection of six tales, opens with four stories of the grotesque and the violent. Two of them are ghost stories, "Bewitched" and "Miss Mary Pask," first printed in the *Pictorial Review*, March and April, 1925.[1] The stories focus on women, but the fallible narrators of the tales are men. Both stories have strong erotic content.

In her own life, after her affair with Morton Fullerton, Wharton's sex life seems to have ceased abruptly. She apparently returned to the repression of sexual desire that characterized the twenty-seven years of her marriage. She spent a great deal of time with her bachelor friends, adding new friends during the war: Percy Lubbock, Geoffrey Scott, Robert d'Humières, André Gide, Eric Maclagan, Ronald Simmons. No evidence indicates any sexual relationships with these friends, all of whom were younger men. Nor is there any evidence that Wharton had a sexual liaison with Walter Berry, her friend and frequent companion until his death in 1927. Berry was, by all accounts, the primary relationship of her life. By 1913, Bernard Berenson writes to his wife, Mary: "Between him as sun and her writing as moon, her life oscillates. All else is meteoric drift" (qtd. in Lewis, *Biography* 351). But sexual passion was most likely a missing element of their relationship.[2]

At first glance, *Summer*, the story of Charity Royall's adolescent awakening to her sexuality and her passionate affair with Harney, seems an odd story to blossom out of Wharton's life in World-War-I Paris because Charity's story tells of sexual abandon and pleasure. However, locked into a daily grind of hard work and without the opportunity of actual sexual pleasure, Wharton lived with circumstances that predictably foster sexual fantasy. *Summer* caused many reviewers as well as Wharton's friend Sara Norton to exhibit "puritanical recoil"; Lewis notes that "a portion of the American literary press continued to bewail the fact, year after year, that one of the country's most highly regarded writers (and a well-bred woman at that) persistently delved into subjects that gave offense to the genteel" (*Biography* 398).

Another sexual fantasy that Wharton created during this time, written in 1918 or 1919 (Wolff, *Feast* Appendix),[3] but never published, is the erotic "Beatrice Palmato" fragment, the most explicitly sexual piece of her writing extant. "Beatrice Palmato," which Wolff writes was "evidently designed as a kind of ghost story," was to be the first story in *The Powers of Darkness*, a collection Wharton never completed (*Feast* 300). Compared to the subtly incestuous *Summer,* the "Beatrice Palmato" fragment is overtly incestuous, the graphic description of a father's seduction of his daughter. Wharton never finished the story beyond a plot synopsis and the fragment, and it appears from the synopsis that the incestuous fragment was not meant for inclusion in the story but was written as a background piece. Fortunately, Wharton chose not to destroy the piece. Whatever her motivation for writing and retaining the fragment, "Beatrice Palmato," like *Summer*, openly flaunts the sexual.[4]

"Bewitched" and "Miss Mary Pask," both written after 1919, are more subtly erotic than *Summer* and "Beatrice Palmato," focusing on sexual repression tied to isolation, loneliness, and discontent rather than on abandon and pleasure. Wharton recognized the female sexual dilemma in the patriarchy: sexual opportunity or the lack of it negatively controls the destiny of a woman. In *Summer* and "Beatrice Palmato," women choose sexual involvement and pleasure, yet these provide no escape from patriarchal tyranny. In making these tales incestuous, Wharton exposes the ultimate dominance of the patriarchy—authority of the father—in deciding the course of life for women. In *Summer*, sexually aggressive women who do not submit to male control are portrayed as outcasts; they are stigmatized as bad women, even though they may provide wanted pleasure for men. "Bewitched" reinforces this pattern.

Further, through "Bewitched" and "Miss Mary Pask," Wharton develops another pattern, women retaliating against patriarchal code by competition with and triumph over other women or through sexual abstention. They, too, pay a heavy price. Sexual inactivity may be safe and allow women more control over their lives, but they are sexually repressed and lose social standing being labelled as spinsters or frigid wives. Women in competition with more attractive or more sexually active women become witch-like and shrewish and lose opportunities for community and cooperation with other women. As Susan Goodman points out, in Wharton's fiction, "When women are competitive or cruel to each other, the blame clearly belongs to society" (*Edith Wharton's Women* 46).

Wharton's work also shows that the advantage of the sexual double standard for the male often does not keep the male from being sexually disadvantaged as he may vacillate between extremes of illicit sex or sexual repression. Finally these stories point to both men and women paying heavy prices in the sexual arena, for societal sexual codes and allied psychosexual development, do not promote fulfilling sexual and emotional relationships. Mutual needs are not acknowledged or fulfilled, and in the end, everyone loses.

"Bewitched" is set in familiar territory, the New England winter of *Ethan Frome* and "The Triumph of Night" where the harsh and cold environment represents constriction of life and personality. This setting reflects what Wolff refers to in relation to *Ethan Frome* as "a map of one portion of [Wharton's] mind, a systematic tracing of the contours of the child's desolation and the young woman's depression" (*Feast* 160). It may also draw on Wharton's dilemma as a middle-aged woman. Free of the earlier constraints of her marriage and the New York society through divorce and expatriation, she was still constrained by the demands of the war, the prudish societal codes that she had internalized, and her choice of the restrained Berry as a companion. More generally, the setting symbolizes the constraints of society on the individual and on the growth of adult relationships. Also, it reflects Wharton's impressions of the "derelict mountain villages of New England" (*Backward Glance* 293) during her years living at the Mount. Her New England settings, Wharton writes

> were the result of explorations among villages still bedrowsed in a decaying rural existence, and sad slow-speaking people living in conditions hardly changed since their forbears held those villages against the Indians . . . . The snow-bound villages of western Massachusetts were still grim places, morally and physically: insanity, incest and slow mental and moral starvation were hidden away behind the paintless wooden house-fronts of the long village streets, or in the isolated farm-houses on the neighboring hills; and Emily Brontë would have found as savage tragedies in our remoter valleys as on her Yorkshire moors. (*Backward Glance* 153, 293-294)

This grim estimate might be opposed by "the New Englanders who for years sought the reflection of local life in the rose-and-lavender pages of their favourite authoresses," writes Wharton, but she notes that they "had forgotten to look into Hawthorne's" where the sins of the fathers are visited upon the descendants (*Backward Glance* 294).

Isolation and repression are the dominant features of life in Wharton's fictional New England farm country. Her choice of place names in "Bewitched" captures the "mournful solitary air" that pervades the tale: Lonetop, North Ashmore, Cold Corners, Hemlock County (*Ghost Stories* 147).[5] Deacon Hibben says to Orin Bosworth about the Rutledge farm, "I never knew a place as seemed as far away from humanity. And yet it ain't so in miles." Bosworth replies: "Miles ain't the only distance" (147). Both physical and psychological isolation plague the inhabitants of the "unsocial region" (146). Wolff points out that Wharton was "interested in the effect of isolation upon the workings of man's emotional life" (*Feast* 163). The farms of Hemlock County with their hard work and bitterly cold winters are harsh places in which to live. Wharton's stories suggest that in this environment, people develop puritanical and rigid personalities and behaviors, influencing generation after generation. Few, if any, are able to counteract the stultifying effects of climate and habit that go hand in hand. The conditions are repressive, the people incommunicative. In "Bewitched," using a familiar technique, Wharton develops the repressive environment by absences, by what is not said. The tale proceeds with an "increasing air of constraint" (148).

Wharton uses the narrative voice of the limited omniscient point of view to remind the reader frequently that the people of Hemlock County are generally silent people. "A silence fell on the strangely assembled group" (152). "The three men stood for a moment; but not one of them spoke" (166). They "drove in silence" (160). The registering consciousness of the tale, Orrin Bosworth, is therefore somewhat atypical. At first, Bosworth offers hope and promise for a better environment. A young man with "standing in the county," he has had more "contact with the modern world" than the older men who accompany him to the Rutledge farm (157). He is the most "communicative of the three" men, and Wharton implies that he is more imaginative. The "situation" was "enough to excite the curiosity of a less imaginative man than Orrin Bosworth" (146). Yet through the horrors that he faces, Bosworth finds "the roots of the old life were still in him" (157), and that he, like the others, cannot escape their deadening effect. Bosworth witnesses events that allow him to unravel the supernatural mystery of Saul Rutledge and Ora Brand, but he succumbs to his fate: like Deacon Hibben and Sylvester Brand, the other two men who are summoned by Prudence Rutledge to the farm to hear her grievance and Saul Rutledge's reluctant testimony, he never speaks of what has happened. Conditioned by the defense mechanisms used by his friends and neighbors, he represses painful reality and suppresses information that the reader must finally infer.[6]

Prudence and Saul Rutledge claim that Rutledge is bewitched by the ghost of the woman whom he courted as a younger man. Bosworth and the others are at first quite skeptical about the story, yet Bosworth sees that something is sapping the life out of both Prudence and Saul. "A woman of cold manners and solitary character" in her late thirties or early forties, Prudence Rutledge is a prematurely dessicated figure with a white complexion, colorless lips, and "long thin hands . . . withered and wrinkled by hard work and cold." She seems rigid and bloodless like a "marble statue" (146, 149). Saul Rutledge is also a pathetic figure. Bosworth thinks he looks "like a drowned man fished out from under the ice" (151) with his "hollow face, so wan under the dark sunburn, so sucked and consumed by some hidden fever" (152). Indeed something seems to be sucking the life and blood out of both husband and wife. But is it a supernatural phenomenon as they suggest?

Both Prudence and Saul Rutledge claim supernatural events are at work, and legend in Hemlock County seems to corroborate their tale. Rutledge says that he is drawn regularly to the old shack on Lamer's Pond to meet the ghost of Ora Brand. He claims he has no control over the situation. Deacon Hibben asks him: "But if it's always there she draws you, man, haven't you the strength to keep away from the place?" Rutledge replies: "Ain't any use. She follers me. . ." (155). Mrs. Rutledge backs up what he says, repeating frequently: "I seen 'em (151) . . . . My husband's not lying, nor he ain't gone crazy. Don't I tell you I seen 'em?" (152). Mrs. Rutledge reminds the Deacon of the solution to the last case in the parish involving Lefferts Nash and Hannah Cory: "They drove a stake through her breast. That's what cured him" (156). Bosworth also remembers that a witch had been burned at North Ashmore. "Didn't the summer folk still drive over in jolly buckboard loads to see the meetinghouse where the trial had been held, the pond where they had ducked her and she had floated?" He also remembers "in a flash" that the witch who was burned "had the name of Brand" and he assumes it is the "same stock" as Sylvester Brand and his daughters (158).

Mrs. Rutledge draws on religious sanction to support her story and her demands, not an unexpected move in a household with an ominous Biblical text over the mantelpiece: "The Soul That Sinneth It Shall Die" (149). The Deacon present, the participants demur to his lead in handling the problem. Sylvester Brand notes: "The Deacon here—such things are more in his line . . . " (149). When Deacon Hibben suggests prayer, however, as a means of handling the problem, Mrs. Rutledge calls for the "old way; and it's the only way" to save her husband from the dead woman. She reads from Exodus as justification for the stern measure: "Thou shalt not suffer a witch to live" (156).

Saul and Prudence Rutledge's explanation of their problem, which at first seems incredible to Bosworth, Brand, and Deacon Hibben, takes on weight as the story proceeds. History and religion give the tale disturbing credibility. The dead Ora Brand is resurrected through mythical dimensions, through legends of witches and vampires who destructively prey on others. Although the three men investigating the situation intend to get the facts firsthand the next day at Lamer's Pond, Ora Brand looms in their minds as an uncanny fiend come back from the dead to draw the life out of Saul Rutledge, a bloodsucking vampire who feeds on him to preserve her own shadowy existence.

R.W.B. Lewis refers to "Bewitched" as "an artificial yarn which strives for effect by converting the figurative into the literal" (Introduction, *Collected Stories* xvii). Margaret McDowell writes: "I detect . . . a contrary tendency to the one he suggests, a converting—starkly yet subtly—of the literal into the figurative" ("Ghost Stories" 146). I agree with McDowell. The vampire myth is a key to the tale. According to Jackson, "The vampire myth is perhaps the highest symbolic representation of eroticism . . . a myth born out of extreme repression . . . . The fantasy of vampirism is generated at the moment of maximum social repression" (120). The figurative vampire provides the clue to the literal, but buried, story of the Rutledges, a story of sexual frustration and jealousy. Saul Rutledge is not having an affair with the dead Ora Brand, but with her very much alive younger sister, Venny Brand, Sylvester Brand's daughter who "ran wild on the slopes of Lonetop" (158). By sanction of the double standard that privileges men, Rutledge (like Brand who sometimes visits "the dives of Stotesbury") fulfills his unmet sexual needs in secret. Venny Brand's wildness is kept quiet as long as his needs are met, but when Mrs. Rutledge discovers the affair, Rutledge protects himself by casting Venny as the ghost of her dead sister. Casting Venny as a vampire excuses his behavior and also keeps others in the community from knowing the truth. This cover protects Rutledge, but not Venny, for once the secret is out that Rutledge is meeting someone at Lamer's Pond, whoever it is, human or not, will be a victim of societal reprisal. Thus Venny Brand's wildness is only acceptable when it feeds Rutledge's needs in secret. The secret out, the community labels her as a vampire because of her aggressive sexuality. In a patriarchal society, wild females, who are considered out of control and who no longer secretly meet men's needs, must be subdued to preserve the social order. As Jackson points out, the female vampire myth is "heavily misogynistic" (122).

Prudence Rutledge plays into the vampire tale as a means of stopping the affair. Ironically, this means that she reinforces the sexual double standard and misogyny in society and seals her own fate. She calls for the death of her rival by the tried-and-true method. As shocking and violent as her demands seem, even Deacon Hibben, the community's religious and moral leader, must concur with her because her solution has been developed by patriarchal code: errant female sexuality which surfaces and disrupts the social order must not be tolerated; it must be subdued. Prudence Rutledge, in effect, calls Saul Rutledge's bluff. No one can argue with her because she cleverly manipulates the code of masculine domination to meet her own ends. Out of jealousy and resentment, she insists on the traditional assertion of dominance to keep wild women in line; the phallic stake through the heart will assure her own revenge. Margaret McDowell notes: "Destructive women in [Wharton's] fiction gain power because they manipulate to their advantage the hypocrisy and pretense which characterized, in large part, the relations between the sexes in nineteenth-century and early twentieth-century American society" ("Feminism" 528).[7]

The community, represented by Bosworth, Brand, and Hibben, cooperates with Prudence Rutledge's incredible plan because puritanical repression of overt sexual knowledge contributes to patriarchal control. Ironically, no mention of sexual activity exists in the story. No one asks Saul Rutledge directly what he and Ora Brand do when they meet at the shack at Lamer's Pond; Prudence Rutledge makes no accusation of adultery. In the conversation at Rutledge farm, the supernatural becomes a euphemism for immoral sex. Deacon Hibben emphasizes to the group that what they discuss are "forbidden things" (156). "Think what you're saying!" he admonishes Rutledge. "It's against our religion!" (154). Yet the dry old man with his thin lips and rattling cough has a "glitter of curiosity in his eyes" about the situation (146). His eyes give off "red sparks" (151). His hands begin to quiver, and he begins to moisten his lips as the discussion proceeds. When Hibben and Bosworth prematurely arrive at Lamer's Pond, Bosworth, a bachelor, is aroused by thinking about what goes on there. "It gave him a curious agitated feeling to think that here in this icy solitude, in the tumble-down house . . . a dark mystery, too deep for thought, was being enacted" (161).

In the Old New York of Wharton's childhood and young womanhood, Wharton had gained firsthand familiarity with repressive social customs of "excessive strictness" (Wolff, *Feast* 309) which made the discussion of sexual matters absolute taboo. In her autobiography, she recalls her mother's hesitancy to speak of a cousin who had vanished:

> Vanished, that is, out of society, out of respectability, out of the safe daylight world of "nice people" and reputable doings . . . . My mother always darted away from George Alfred's name after pronouncing it, and it was not until I was grown up, and had acquired great courage and persistency, that one day I drove her to the wall by suddenly asking: "But, Mamma, *what did he do ?*" "Some

woman"—my mother muttered; and no one accustomed to the innocuous word as now used can imagine the shades of disapproval, scorn and yet excited curiosity that "some" could then connote on the lips of virtue. (*Backward Glance* 23, 24)

For Wharton, the mystery surrounding George Alfred's behavior planted seeds in her imagination that would grow in her work: "The vision of poor featureless unknown Alfred and his siren, lurking in some cranny of my imagination, hinted at regions perilous, dark and yet lit with mysterious fires . . . and the hint was useful—for a novelist" (*Backward Glance* 24-25).

Society's repression of sex provided grist for the writer's mill, but also grief for Wharton's married life. When she married, she was sexually ignorant. A few days before her wedding, she asked her mother "what being married was like." Her mother icily replied: "I never heard such a ridiculous question!" Wharton pleaded: "I'm afraid, Mamma—I want to know what will happen to me!" Her mother, after a silence, said with disgust: "You've seen enough pictures and statues in your life. Haven't you noticed that men are—made differently from women?" Wharton blankly replied, "Yes," but her mother, unable to carry on the conversation, ended it: "Well, then—? . . . . Then for heaven's sake don't ask me any more silly questions. You can't be as stupid as you pretend!" Wharton writes that her mother's failure to provide her with any sex education "did more than anything else to falsify and misdirect [her] whole life" ("Life and I" 1087-88).

In "Bewitched," the community's absence of discussion of sexual matters and the strict observance of the patriarchal code governing the acceptable practice of sex within society leads to a great deal of misdirection and sacrifice. Venny Brand's life is sacrificed. Sylvester Brand shoots his own daughter. Horrifyingly, there is some question about whether his action occurs spontaneously and ignorantly. When Prudence Rutledge reveals that Saul is bewitched and meeting someone at Lamer's Pond, Bosworth "whose eyes were on Sylvester Brand's face, fancied he saw a sort of inner flush darken the farmer's heavy leathern skin." Brand was also the first to want to leave when Mrs. Rutledge approached her subject, by saying "Bible mysteries" were not in his line, and he was the first to question Mrs. Rutledge when she implied a female was meeting Rutledge at the pond: "'Who do you mean by her?' he asked abruptly, as if roused out of some far-off musing" (149). If Brand suspects or even knows that Venny is involved with Rutledge, the tragedy of Venny Brand's death is compounded, for Brand yields to the community code which requires the husband to keep his wife in line, the father his daughter. He sacrifices his daughter (and himself) to uphold the community's repressive standards.[8]

Prudence and Saul Rutledge's marriage is also sacrificed to the community's conventions through isolation, lack of communication, and repression. After Bosworth, Brand, and Hibben agree to investigate what is happening at Lamer's Pond, and even after Deacon Hibben agrees that Prudence Rutledge's solution, death to the witch, is the only answer, Hibben still attributes Saul Rutledge's situation to an "ague of the mind." "It's his brain that's sick," he says. When Bosworth points out that "He ain't the first in Hemlock County," the Deacon agrees: "That's so . . . . It's a worm in the brain, solitude is" (160). The worm, a phallic symbol, and the brain, suggesting psychological difficulties, indicate that the tragedy is caused not by the sexually aggressive female/vampire, but the situation: an unhappy marriage in a solitary setting, breeding loneliness, lack of communication, sexual frustration, unbearable repression. Both Saul and Prudence Rutledge, locked in the prison of their marriage, their isolated farmstead, and their repressive community, have "worms in the brain" affecting their sexuality and emotional well-being.

Although Saul Rutledge escapes this prison temporarily through his affair with Venny Brand, there is no socially sanctioned escape for Prudence Rutledge. She must suffer quietly or become a vindictive shrew. She chooses the latter. We do not know enough of the Rutledges' lives beyond the negative circumstances of their life-style to judge just how each contributes to the failure of their marriage, but certainly Prudence Rutledge has suffered in the marriage as well as Saul. As a wife, however, with no societally condoned escape, she retaliates for her suffering. In avenging her unfulfilled life, she becomes the greatest horror of the tale. She is instrumental in bringing about Venny Brand's death to protect her position in a pitiful marriage. Her social position as wife is the only security she has, and she means to retain it. At Venny Brand's funeral, she appears in "a tall bonnet, lording it above the group" (166), thoroughly enjoying her victory. But it is a futile victory. "In the matter of human life," writes Wharton in *A Son at the Front*, "victories may be as ruinous as defeats" (392). By forcing the community to impose its codes on Venny Brand, Prudence Rutledge has protected her position, but sealed her fate in a repressive community and a loveless marriage. By conspiring in the spilling of Venny Brand's blood, she herself has become the bloodsucker who requires a victim to sustain her own life, but ironically, this single victim will offer little to sustain her for long.   She will sink back into a bloodless existence.

Wharton reinforces her themes in "Bewitched" with a succinct story-within-a-story, an allegory of the tragedy that occurs. As Bosworth listens to Prudence Rutledge insistently set up her argument which will lead to her hollow victory, he is reminded of another "bleak farm" where a great-aunt, "Cressidora Cheney, had been shut up for years in a cold clean room with iron bars to the window." Bosworth's mother suspected that the root of Aunt Cressidora's troubles lay in isolation and loneliness: "I do believe they keep Aunt Cressidora too lonesome." As a little boy, Bosworth took his lonely great-aunt a friend, "a canary in a little wooden cage." The boy thinks the canary will make her very happy. The aunt's face lights up when she sees the bird, and she instantly claims it. But the bird is startled and begins "to flutter and beat its wing distractedly." Aunt Cressidora shouts, "You she-devil, you!" and grabs the bird, wrings its neck, and plucks at its feathers. Bosworth's mother tells him: "You must never tell anybody that poor Auntie's crazy, or the men would come and take her down to the asylum at Starkfield, and the shame of it would kill us all." Bosworth remembers the scene "with its deep fringe of mystery, secrecy, and rumor" as he listens to Prudence Rutledge. "It seemed to relate to a great many other things below the surface of his thoughts. . . " (157-158). Again at Venny Brand's funeral, looking at Prudence Rutledge's "lowered lids" that look like "marble eyeballs" and her "bloodless . . . bony hands," he remembers Aunt Cressidora: "Bosworth had never seen such hands since he had seen old Aunt Cressidora strangle the canary bird because it fluttered" (166). Prudence Rutledge, like Aunt Cressidora, is crazed from isolation and loneliness. She takes revenge on a fellow female who, like the poor bird in the cage, is also locked in an isolated and repressed existence. She calls for the killing of the vampire ("she-devil") and literally brings about the death of Venny Brand (the bird) because Venny dares to try to "sing," to take pleasure within her limited circumstances. Prudence Rutledge's violent act, like Aunt Cressidora's killing of the bird, only buries her more deeply in her own solitary grave.[9]

In the final section of the story, Orrin Bosworth submits to his environment. His sister, Loretta, tells him that she hears that Venny Brand is dying of pneumonia. Although Bosworth appears to know this is not true, he has learned the code of the community and will not even speak or think of taboo subjects that threaten to disrupt the prevailing structure. He meets his sister's news with "listless eyes" (164). Echoing what he said in the beginning of the story about the destructive isolation of the environment he lives in, he thinks that "She seemed far off from him, miles away" (164). When Loretta brings up Sylvester Brand's plight as a man alone, Bosworth does not even respond. He changes the subject and leaves, burying himself in his daily chores. He walks out into the snow and cold representing the constricted, routine environment to which he has succumbed.

At Venny Brand's funeral, no one in North Ashmore speaks of what really happened. "Brand's face was the closed door of a vault, barred with wrinkles like bands of iron" (166). Prudence Rutledge tries to put the whole matter to rest by suggesting illogically to the Deacon that Ora, the alleged ghost, will sleep better in her grave now that she has company. Her brief moment of glory at the funeral is then eclipsed by her return to the habitual motions of everyday life. Descending from her fiendish throne to the pathetic position of the repressed and unhappy wife burying her frustrations in a repetitive round of tasks, she leaves the funeral to buy a box of soap. Thus the conclusion of "Bewitched" is another of Wharton's "ab ovo" endings that reinforce the ultimate horror of the story, of being forever imprisoned in a repressive environment with no means of expression or fulfillment.

"Miss Mary Pask," written in 1923, also tells a tale of sexual frustration, repression, and loneliness, but not within a marriage. This tale has two primary characters, the first-person narrator, another of Wharton's dry bachelors, and Mary Pask, an old maid.[10] As in "Kerfol," the narrator serves a prominent role, revealing his own weaknesses and vulnerabilities in response to Mary Pask. Both characters appear to have opted for celibate roles that allow individual autonomy and opportunity for artistic expression, yet they do not share an understanding of their choices. They view each other stereotypically, and they are both sexually repressed. Feelings of dread and anger color their encounter. Their story shows how social codes and resulting behavior thwart satisfying sexual and emotional relationships between men and women and also satisfying friendships among women. R.W.B. Lewis calls the story a "slender anecdote" ("Powers of Darkness" 644). Margaret McDowell, closer to the mark, calls the story "an extraordinary tour de force" and a "triumph of tone and atmosphere" ("Ghost Stories" 138).

Set in the coastal region of Brittany, France, where the narrator, a New York artist, has gone to paint waves, Wharton exaggerates the Gothic elements of the tale to the level of parody. The narrator arrives at Morgat near the *Baie des Trépassés* (Bay of the Dead) where "the sea fog shut down on us" (132). The oppressive atmosphere of "densest night, a wet blackness impenetrable to the glimmer of the lamp" envelops him and the boy who has driven him in a horse-drawn buggy from town out to Mary Pask's house where he will fulfill a long-neglected obligation, visiting the sister of a friend's wife. As the narrator approaches the house, the darkness grows "three times as thick" (132). The exaggerated details of setting reflect and mock the narrator's nervous, frantic, and self-imposed state of mind. He is plunging into a nightmare, largely of his own making. The sound of the sea also provides a clue to the narrator's state of mind and character. He hears the "endless modulations of the ocean's voice" nearby, which he senses as a "hungry voice," a demanding voice "asking and asking." "The sea whined down there as if it were feeding time, and the Furies, its keepers, had forgotten it" (133). The sensual sound of the sea, archetypically associated with the female/mother figure and with sexuality, is not at all a reassuring sound to him, but wild, demanding, and threatening, foreshadowing his discomforting encounter with Mary Pask.

From the beginning of the story, the narrator, an unpleasant character reminiscent of Andrew Culwin in "The Eyes," undermines his own reliability. He says he has an "enfeebled constitution," which may have come from a touch of fever in Egypt. His encounter with Mary Pask, whom he believes to be a ghost, further shakes his confidence in his health and his sanity. "There's nothing there, nothing whatever. It's your digestion, or your eyes, or some damned thing wrong with you somewhere," he thinks (135). His visit with Mary Pask leads to a "nervous collapse" and a rest cure in a Swiss sanatorium (130). When he much later dares to tell his tale to Grace Bridgeworth, Mary Pask's sister, he is still unsure of himself. He is afraid that, in telling his story, Grace "would just set me down as 'queer'—and enough people had done that already" (142). He asks her: "Do you suspect me of not being quite right yet?" (144).

The narrator is indeed "not quite right," but his problems are more fundamental than temporary emotional instability resulting from physical illness. He is self-centered and condescending. First, he insists that the boy drive him to Mary Pask's regardless of the intensity of the storm and the possibilities of an accident. Second, he visits Mary Pask as a favor to Grace Bridgeworth, yet he reveals that he does not think much of either of them; he endures them for the sake of his friend Horace, Grace's husband. He describes Mary Pask as a woman "like hundreds of other dowdy, old maids, cheerful derelicts content with their innumerable little substitutes for living" (130). He even patronizes Grace: "Even Grace would not have interested me particularly if she hadn't happened to marry one of my oldest friends . . . . She was a handsome, capable and rather dull woman, absorbed in her husband and children, and without an ounce of imagination" (131). Third, the narrator, as an artist, denigrates what he sees as Mary Pask's artistic pretensions. Grace Bridgeworth has told him that her sister refuses to join her in America because she is "too artistic"; however, the narrator finds this unbelievable owing to the "extremely elementary nature of her interest in art" (131). He refers disparagingly to her former "old-maidish flat decorated with art-tidies" and sardonically to her French house with its "bedraggled cushions, odds and ends of copper pots, and a jar holding a faded branch of some late-flowering shrub" as "A real Mary Pask 'interior'!" (131, 136).

The narrator also has a tendency to repress or ignore whatever disturbs or disrupts his view of the world and his sense of his place in it. This tendency, however, as a subconscious defense mechanism, is not under his control and works in mysterious ways, for example, in the case of his visit to Mary Pask, when his forgetting that he has heard she is dead inconveniently leads him to her door and the threatening encounter with her. Terrifyingly, his "smothered memory" that she is dead struggles "abruptly to the surface" of his "languid mind" (134). He notes: "Once before of late I had noticed this queer temporary blotting-out of some well-known fact" (135). When he escapes the frightening situation, he directs his energy towards re-repression. "The happenings of that night had to be overlaid with layer upon layer of time and forgetfulness before I could tolerate any return to them" (130). Ineffectual, like Ethan Frome and George Faxon, the narrator steadfastly avoids any assault on his narrowly drawn sphere of comfort. He also, in his repressive and regressive state, like Frome and Faxon, chooses flight as a means of conflict resolution.

The narrator's encounter with Mary Pask terrifies him because he mistakenly thinks she is a ghost, but also because he fears facing his own sexuality. Through a provocative mixture of death and sexual imagery, Wharton turns a woman, who is likely a virgin, into a vampire in the mind of the narrator. Mary Pask refers to herself as having died, which doctors thought had been the case before she was revived from a cataleptic trance. Since the narrator is missing the piece of information that she survived her "death," he becomes increasingly agitated and threatened in her presence. She speaks of how she has changed, how she has had so few visitors since her "death," and how she prefers the darkness to the light as "the dead naturally get used to it." Her comments are all punctuated with nervous laughter. She jokes: "It's such an age since I've seen a living being!" Her playful conversation with "confidential blinks," as she may think he knows the truth, is flirtatious (138).

To the narrator, her language is of the grave; yet her behavior is sexually suggestive. He thinks, "The horrible thing was that she still practiced the same arts, all the childish wiles of a clumsy capering coquetry" (137). Her appearance is also strangely suggestive. Her "changed and shriveled" hands with "blue under the yellowing fingernails" repulse him and confirm that she is dead, yet he envisions in his mind the way her hands used to be: "round, puffy, pink, yet prematurely old and useless;" her fingertips were once "so innocently and naturally pink" (136). In his mind's eye, he remembers her "pink" femininity in terms that suggest vaginal imagery. She beckons him with "one of those unburied hands" to sit on the sofa next to her. He reassures himself that the threat he feels is harmless: "Dead or alive, Mary Pask would never harm a fly" (138). Still he cannot bear to stay in her presence because he is horrified by his own ambivalent feelings of fear and arousal. When she blocks the door, he is desperate to leave. Mary Pask pleads with him to stay. Her plea is seductive: "Oh, stay with me, stay with me . . . just tonight . . . . It's so sweet and quiet here . . . . No one need know . . . no one will ever come and trouble us." When the candle goes out, the narrator feels himself to be on the brink of disaster: "My heart seemed to stop beating; I had to fetch up my breath with great heaves that covered me with sweat" (140). In sexual panic, he flees, leaving Mary Pask whimpering.[11]

In reality, Mary Pask is no vampire, although she may be something of a vamp. From the narrator's point of view, Mary Pask's retreat to the isolated Morgat, far away from her sister in New York who never comes to see her, results from jealousy and rivalry over her sister's marriage to Horace Bridgeworth. First, he wonders if Mary disliked Horace or then if "she may have liked him too much." He quickly dismisses the suspicion: "But that again became untenable (at least I supposed it did) when one knew Miss Pask: Miss Pask with her round flushed face, her innocent bulging eyes . . . and her vague and timid philanthropy. Aspire to Horace —!" (131). He insults Mary Pask for what is to him absurd fantasizing. Yet when he visits her, she confirms in his mind that she, like all women, conditioned by the society into thinking that a woman's place is in relationship to a man, is capable of such a fantasy: "And sometimes I sit here and think: 'If a man came along someday and took a fancy to you' . . . Well, such things *have* happened, you know, even after youth's gone . . . a man who'd has his troubles too" (140). Mary Pask appears to still long for and fantasize a relationship with a man. The narrator acknowledges her frustration: "Supposing something survived of Mary Pask—enough to cry out to me the unuttered loneliness of a lifetime, to express at last what the living woman had always had to keep dumb and hidden?" (141). To the narrator, what she has kept "dumb and hidden" is her poignant, unfulfilled longing. He is greatly threatened by her need, which echoes his own needs and vulnerability.

From Mary Pask's point of view, the story reads differently. Mary Pask may be a fellow [sic] artist, like the narrator, who has also chosen a solitary, celibate life, involuntarily assuming the societal role of lonely spinster which is, however, unfortunately, less attractive than the role of the free-wheeling bachelor. Jennice Thomas offers a convincing reading of the story from this point of view. If Mary Pask has chosen her life, the rift with her sister is because her sister has abandoned her for a man rather than that she covets her sister's husband. The price she pays for her life-style is great. She gains autonomy, but also isolation, loneliness, sexual repression. Her "spooking" of the narrator, says Thomas, is vengeance rising from "the buried power of female anger." Thomas argues that Wharton and her character use the supernatural to turn the tables of patriarchal power (112). Mary Pask sees the narrator's fear, guesses his plight, and takes advantage of the situation. Her comments to the narrator about her "death" are manipulative, in effect a vengeful practical joke.[12]

However, for the narrator, Mary Pask represents an odious and grotesque monster. "Old tales and legends floated through my mind; the Bride of Corinth, the medieval vampire—but what names to attach to the plaintive image of Mary Pask!" (141). What names indeed, and why? Curiously after his hysterical and insensitive flight, the narrator develops a certain tenderness in thinking about Mary Pask. He recalls her loneliness and frustrations, and he says: "The thought moved me curiously—in my weakness I lay and wept over it" (141). During his convalescence, he plans to return to Morgat to put flowers on her grave, although he doesn't. And he plans to speak to Grace about a proper gravestone. He continues to remember Mary Pask "more and more tenderly, but more intermittently . . . ." His tendency towards repression surfacing, he asks: "Ought I not to bury [the subject] in those deepest depths where the inexplicable and the unforgettable sleep together?" (142). After telling his story to Grace Bridgeworth and discovering that part of the mystery is solved for him (Mary Pask was not dead), the narrator represses the whole affair. Exasperated by Grace's desire to go over and over the tale, he says: "But though I sat and listened patiently I couldn't get up any real interest in what she said. I felt I should never again be interested in Mary Pask, or anything concerning her" (144). In effect, when the narrator learns that Mary Pask was *not* a vampire, but only the lonely old maid he expected in the first place, he has no more interest in her or the entire episode. As he points out, "The revelation of the dead Mary Pask . . . was so much more real to me than ever the living one had been" (142).

Virginia Blum looks at the erotic in three of Wharton's ghost stories ("Bewitched," "Miss Mary Pask," and "Pomegranate Seed") and finds a pattern: "The vampire woman is the fulfillment of the male dread of sexual depletion (and consumption)" (18). The vampire as a female aggressor is dangerous, yet she is also attractive and tempting. The danger of consummation (consumption) is mixed with the desire for sexual abandon and ultimate pleasure. In Bram Stoker's *Dracula,* Jonathan Harker, in a dreamlike state, finds himself beset by three vampire women in Dracula's castle. His initial dread slowly drains away, and he begins to succumb to their advances with a sense of intensely sweet sensual pleasure. But just as Harker closes his eyes in "langourous ecstasy," Dracula arrives and hurls the women away so that Harker will have the energy to aid him in carrying out his own seductive plans (48-49). The vampire woman may be taboo (representing aggressive sexuality and necrophilia), dangerous (energy-draining, putting the male in a submissive position), but she is nevertheless desirable.

Once the narrator finds that Mary Pask is not dead and dangerous, he buries his sexual needs awakened by the encounter. Freud's theory that the nineteenth-century man was unable to find sexual and emotional fulfillment in one woman pertains to the narrator's situation. Freud concluded that "loose women" are erotic objects for men who are fixated on the mother. The mother is perceived as two women, a virgin because she will not succumb to sexual relations with him and a whore because she has relations with the father. "Nice women" remind the man of the virgin mother to whom tender feelings are attached. Sensual feelings then are attached to bad women or whores (or vampires). Freud notes: "Where such men love they have no desire and where they desire they cannot love . . . . As soon as the sexual object fulfills the condition of being degraded, sensual feeling can have free play" ("Degradation" 177-178). Freud generalizes that "we shall not be able to deny that the behavior in love of the men of present-day civilization bears . . . the character of the psychically impotent type" ("Degradation" 180).

The narrator of "Miss Mary Pask" fits Freud's category. Margaret McDowell suggests that "it is really he who is the vampire, the one who, in his heedlessness, sucks the life from other people" (McDowell, "Ghost Stories" 138), or one might say in his denial of his own sexuality and sexual needs. In retrospect, he recalls Mary Pask, whom he previously thought of as a "dowdy old maid" tenderly. Although he bolts, he has been seduced by the projection of his own sexual desire on "innocent" Mary Pask. Most disturbing is that the narrator, ensconced in his own self-centered, celibate, sexually repressed world, shows fleeting sympathy for a woman who shares his plight, and he does not show any particular love for women or desire for personal commitment. When he is "seduced" out of his "psychically impotent" state, what occurs is that he cares "for a 'dead' woman to an extent that he finds impossible with the living . . . . The dead are far less terrifying than the living because they exact no commitment" (Blum 15). Unlike Saul Rutledge in "Bewitched," the narrator of "Mary Pask" does not acknowledge his own sexual needs or succumb to seduction. Neurotically locked in his celibacy, he cannot act at all from his sexual impulses towards women.[13]

This interpretation partly explains the psychology of the bachelor figure in Wharton's work. Whether apparently homosexual like Andrew Culwin or manifestly heterosexual like Lawrence Selden, Wharton's bachelor is unable to develop a successful sexual and emotional relationship with a woman. In "Miss Mary Pask," the narrator seems sexually repressed, incapable of any sexual relation. Wharton's bachelor type reflects some of the men around her, most notably Walter Berry and Henry James, but the type, as Freud noted, may be more general, a societal type characteristic of the times—as characteristic as the image of Mary Pask, the unmarried woman, who has voluntarily chosen autonomy or who has involuntarily not been chosen by a man and lives with sexual frustration. Both the bachelor and the old maid have diminished lives. Mary Pask intuitively recognizes the narrator as her counterpart: "A man who'd had his troubles too." Even in secrecy and isolation, the narrator cannot fully respond to the sound of what is really his own voice of repression and loneliness crying out. Later he weeps for Mary Pask—and for himself.

The individual tragedy that Wharton shows in the diminished lives of the narrator and Mary Pask points to an unbridgeable gulf between men and women in a society that operates by patriarchal law and locks individuals into rigid gender roles. If the narrator is an "unsatisfactory man" (Holbrook), Mary Pask is also an unsatisfactory woman. The conventional view of the spinster aside, her only way to avoid a rigid female role is to set herself apart in her own world where she may move more independently. But just as the man who sets himself apart, she, too, suffers diminishment. She is angry, sexually repressed, and develops a kind of psychological blindness. These "safe," independent, but unfulfilling gender roles lead to the lessening of any chances for equal and harmonious adult relationships between men and women. In "Miss Mary Pask" and "Bewitched," both men and women lose in the efforts to find satisfactory sexual and emotional fulfillment in conventional relationships or in unconventional arrangements.

> Ultimately, we confront Wharton's conviction that men and women in society cannot help but destroy each other. Lily Bart [*House of Mirth*] has a vision of "the disintegrating influences of the life about her. All the men and women she knew were like atoms whirling away from each other in some wild centrifugal dance . . ." and it is the steps of that infernal dance we see repeatedly retraced by the men and women of Edith Wharton's fiction. (Blum 26)

Notes

1   The other two stories are "The Young Gentlemen" and "The Seed of the Faith."

2   There is, of course, the possibility that they were having an affair which by necessity, at the time, would have had to have been kept secret; if so, it was a well kept secret. Critics generally conclude that the Berry-Wharton friendship was not a physically intimate one. In another story in *Here and Beyond*, "The Temperate Zone," Wharton provocatively writes the account of an affair between Emily Morland, a famous poet whose husband will not give her a divorce, and a younger man. Wharton writes:

> She simply let it be known to their few nearest friends that he and she belonged to each other as completely as a man and woman of complex minds and active interests can ever belong to each other when such life as they live together must be lived in secret. To a woman like Mrs. Morland the situation could not be other than difficult and unsatisfying . . . . Never once, in the short course of her love history, had she been able to declare her happiness openly, or to let it reveal itself in her conduct; and it seemed, as one considered her case, small solace to remember that some of her most moving verse was the expression of that very privation. (*Collected Stories* 2: 454)

Wharton's sentiments in this story may be representative of her feelings about her relationship with Berry or her former, younger lover, Morton Fullerton.

3   There is some dispute over when Wharton wrote the "Beatrice Palmato" fragment. I agree with Wolff's rationale (1977) for 1918 or 1919; however, Lewis in Wharton's biography (1975) suggests 1935. He continues to report this date in the notes of the more recently published collection of Wharton letters (1988).

4   The "Beatrice Palmato" fragment has contributed, along with the incest imagery in many of Wharton's works, to the idea that Wharton was a victim of father-daughter incest as a child.

5   All page references included for "Bewitched" and "Miss Mary Pask" are from the Scribner's edition of Wharton's ghost stories, 1973.

6   Kathy Fedorko in "'Forbidden Things': Gothic Confrontation with the Feminine in 'The Young Gentlemen' and 'Bewitched'" suggests that Orrin Bosworth is a more hopeful character than I see him. She writes, "Orrin faces [the] feminine/maternal part of himself and is an expanded, enriched male character compared to those in earlier Gothic stories" (8). Although initially in the story, Bosworth is characterized as imaginative, intuitive, and empathic, I think he shuts down by the end of the tale, conforming to the societal codes of behavior governing masculinity and sexuality.

7   Fedorko notes Prudence Rutledge's "constricted, phallic features." "Her 'small, narrow head' with hair 'passed tight and flat over the tips of her ears into a small braided coil at the nape' is 'perched on a long hollow neck with cord-like throat muscles.'" In effect, she becomes the embodiment of "the male power that keeps female power restrained" (7).

8   Barbara White (*Edith Wharton: A Study of the Short Fiction*) points out the comparison between the Palmato outline and the Brand family, alleging that the Brand family also has been "founded on incest or near incest" (104). Brand is portrayed as a violent, animalistic man and the women in the Brand family waste away and die. When Brand shoots Venny (with the phallic gun, as Fedorko notes), he may send a source of not only Rutledge's scandal, but his own, to the grave.

9   According to Susan Goodman (*Edith Wharton's Women: Friends and Rivals*), Wharton's view of women interacting, as shown by her work, fluctuates "between two paradoxical poles, one marking female competition and the other marking female cooperation" (9). Notably in the ghost stories, women are portrayed as alone and lonely or in competition with other women. They are not shown having the advantage of maternal nurturing or female companionship and support.

10 When Wharton wrote "Bewitched" is not known. However, "Miss Mary Pask" was written one morning in September, 1923, while she was recovering from the grippe. She reported this in a letter to Rutger Jewett, her editor at Appleton and also her agent. Arthur Vance, editor of the *Pictorial Review*, paid Wharton $1800 for the story (Lewis, *Biography* 456).

11 An alternative reading is that the narrator experiences homosexual panic. It is sometimes hard to tell with Wharton's bachelors whether they fear sexual involvement with a woman because they feel the pressure of involvement/commitment or because their sexual preference is homosexual. This may reflect Wharton's own difficulty in reading the men she associated with. Wharton's work raises serious questions about the relationship of psychosexual development and social codes affecting gender roles and sexual practice.

12 If Mary Pask begins to realize that the narrator thinks she is a ghost and takes advantage of his fear, then Wharton's story takes on a wry humor similar to a Twain tale. Wharton was a master of irony, which could be amusing or biting. From Wharton's perspective, what begins humorously may progress to a horrifying end. Barbara White notes,

> While . . . [Wharton's] stories have their dark aspects . . . and from one perspective the characters are caught in appalling situations, Wharton insists that we also see the broadly humorous side of their dilemmas. No story is finally tragic or comic, or finally any one thing, because Wharton really means what she says about "letting it reveal all its potentialities." If this characteristic makes her fiction cold and lacking in important messages, it might also be viewed as her strength, the source of her "original vision" as a short-story writer (26).

13   David Holbrook (*Edith Wharton and the Unsatisfactory Man*), in looking at Wharton's
     work (in particular referring to *The House of Mirth*), writes: "Are we to take it that
     Edith Wharton is telling us that her femininity can only fulfill itself in death, while
     the maleness she knows is unsatisfactory until it encounters the challenge of death—
     whereupon it is too late and becomes the final impotence?" Assessing how Wharton
     comes to this view, he relies on the incest theory which he supports: "For a girl
     whose all-possessing love has been for her father, love-in-death is the only solution"
     (925). Holbrook also echoes the Freudian view of men's psychosexual development
     when he looks at *The Reef*, suggesting that Darrow, who is sexually excited and
     seduced by Sophy, a loose woman, does not care for her, but rather cares for the
     proper Anna, to whom he is not as sexually attracted.

Five

"A Bottle of Perrier" and "Mr. Jones"

I had never known before how completely the dead may survive.

"The Moving Finger," 1901

We are sons of yesterday, not of morning. The past is our mortal mother, no dead thing. Our future constantly reflects her to the soul. Nor is it ever the new man of today which grasps his fortune, good or ill. We are pushed to it by the hundreds of days we have buried, eager ghosts. And if you have not the habit of taking counsel with them, you are but an instrument in their hands.

George Meredith, *Harry Richmond*
(Recorded in Edith Wharton's
Commonplace Book)[1]

From 1925-1930, Wharton wrote three novels, *Twilight Sleep* (1927), *The Children* (1928), and *Hudson River Bracketed* (1929) set in the post-war world. Many critics, thinking she best understood the pre-war world, have written that these are not her finest works because, as she grew older, she had lost touch with the new era. Although admired by the younger generation of writers (Sinclair Lewis dedicated *Babbitt* to her), she herself felt that they viewed her with some reservation. In a letter to F. Scott Fitzgerald (1925), who had sent her a copy of *The Great Gatsby*, she writes: "I am touched at your sending me a copy, for I feel that to your generation, which has taken such a flying leap into the future, I must represent the literary equivalent of tufted furniture and gas chandeliers" (*Letters* 481).[2] She might not have felt that she fully understood the effects of "a flying leap into the future"; however, she knew that the present and future generations must always come to terms with the past, that individuals grow out of a past of conscious and subconscious tenacity.

In *Hudson River Bracketed*, mid-westerner Vance Weston, the struggling young writer who becomes a mouthpiece for many of Wharton's ideas on the craft of writing, has an "impulse . . . to attach [himself] to a former age" (Lewis, *Biography* 472). Weston's attachment to the

Willows, a nineteenth-century mansion on the Hudson, and its library symbolize his desire to explore his heritage. Vance seeks a nurturing foundation for his own personal identity as a writer. Here Wharton views tradition
as a positive ground where new generations germinate. However, as pointed
out earlier, tradition for Wharton is double-edged. It can be positive and
nurturing, allowing the individual, like Vance (full name: Advance) to
progress in the new era, or it can be negative and oppressive, finally
destroying the individual and the advance of human civilization.[3]

In her eighth collection of short stories, *Certain People* (1930),
Wharton includes two stories which deal with the impact of tradition on
younger generations. Both stories are reprinted in *Ghosts*, although only
one is technically a ghost story. "Mr. Jones," first published in the *Ladies
Home Journal*, April 1928, is a ghost story of "indescribable cruelty, imprisonment and violence" (Lewis, *Biography* 522).[4] "A Bottle of Perrier"
first appeared in the *Saturday Evening Post*, March, 1926, as "A Bottle of
Evian." It is a "brooding murder mystery" (Lewis, *Biography* 522) and a
"particularly good example of the Poesque tale of terror" (Robillard 788).[5]
Both tales depict patriarchal tradition negatively affecting the lower
classes, young men, and women, subordinates linked by their inferior
positions within the culture.

The setting of "A Bottle of Perrier" does not immediately suggest traditions of western culture; on the contrary, it presents the opposite, the
"fairy tale" world (*Letters* 402) that Wharton encountered on her two trips
to North Africa "far from everything I know" (Lewis, *Biography* 360).[6]
When young Medford arrives in the desert at the "half Christian, half Arab
palace" occupied by his friend Almodham, who invited him for a visit, he
finds a peaceful oasis far away from "Western fret and fever" in a land
"full of spells" and "dreams" (*Ghost Stories* 511, 520).[7] The story captures a "queer sense of otherwhereness" (516), and "something vaporous
and insubstantial about the whole scene" (513). In this romantic spot with
no "time measures," Medford sinks into the pleasurable torpor of existing
from day to day (516). This lassitude proves to be dangerous, for the
"mystery of the sands" is a violent one (511). The mystery, however, is
not connected to the unfamiliar, primitive, sensual existence in the desert,
or to the treacherousness of the Arabs insisted upon as a reality by
Almodham's xenophobic servant, Gosling, but to the familiar, oppressive
effects of western hierarchical authority and insensitivity. Wharton drew
upon her brief sojourns in exotic lands to texture her setting, but the fore-
ground of her story deals with inherited, inescapable western modes of
thought which finally overshadow the landscape and the pulse of the land.

Medford, a young American archaeologist on vacation from work in Egypt, thinks his absent host's choice of abode a wise decision. The older British Henry Almodham, also an archaeologist, retired to his refuge twenty-five years before after "disappointing results" from an excavation. Medford, an analytical type, "puzzled out the essential lines of [Almodham's] character" at their single meeting the previous winter at Luxor:

> a nature saturnine, yet sentimental; chronic indolence alternating with spurts of highly intelligent activity; gnawing self-distrust soothed by intimate self-appreciation; a craving for complete solitude coupled with the inability to tolerate it for long.

Overall, Medford detects "an inertia, mental and moral, which life in this castle of romance must have fostered and excused" (514).

For all his astute analysis of Almodham's character and situation, Medford lacks self-awareness and fails to see himself in relationship to Almodham. Medford is readily seduced by Almodham's romantic world of dreams partly because he is "helplessly tired" from "malarial fever the previous summer" (512), but also because, as Almodham told his servant Gosling, he is "just my kind" (531). Medford finds in Almodham, a bachelor who prefers the cloistered aesthetic life of leisure and solitude, a self-reflection. Like Almodham, Medford is a dreamer. Once in the desert, he thinks, "How easy not to leave" (515). The "spell of inertia laid on him by the drowsy place" overcomes any draw he feels to return to the world of responsibility and commitment (519). "The midday heat lay heavy even on the shaded side of the court, and the sinews of his will were weakening" (520). The "mental and moral inertia" that Medford attributes to Almodham could clearly be his own fate. He realizes that Almodham would have to be "a scholar and a misogynist" to find his desert refuge appealing, and he admits that he is also "incurably both" (511). Medford remembers the night he met Almodham in Egypt on Colonel Swordsley's starlit terrace above the Nile and rode with Almodham back to Luxor in the moonlight. He casually refers to the presence of "two or three charming [nameless] women from the Winter Palace chattering and exclaiming" at Colonel Swordsley's dinner table (514), yet Almodham clearly interested him more than the women did. Wharton strongly "conveys the sense of a pressing, homoerotic attraction" between them (Singley, "Gothic Borrowings" 277).

Medford also detects "something, deeper, darker" in Almodham's character. Signs of danger surface in the dreamy desert environment, and

Medford's drowsiness shifts to alertness, finally to a greater awareness of his absent host: "his half-guessed selfishness and tyranny and his morbid self absorption" (527). Almodham's darker side represents the worst of western patriarchy. He is an indifferent, insensitive, dominating, elitist British aristocrat reflecting the tradition of British imperialism and colonialism. In short, Almodham, like Andrew Culwin ("The Eyes") and Lavington ("Triumph of Night"), two of Wharton's American characters of the same ilk, is an authoritarian dominator and oppressor.[8]

Wharton demonstrates Almodham's darker character through his relationship with his manservant. For almost twelve years, Almodham promises Gosling a holiday, an occasion which never occurs. Gosling, a "quick cosmopolitan manservant" from Malta, reveals his situation and its severity to Medford in bits and pieces (511). He says that he has "never been away once," although he wanted "to have 'ad a look at Wembley" [famous exhibition at Wembley near London, 1924] (517, 513). Apparently Almodham promised him a holiday "agine and agine," but says Gosling, "when he's here he needs me for himself; and when he's away he needs me to watch over the others" (518). According to Gosling, Almodham would never listen to his pleas "or only make believe to; say 'we'll see, now, Gosling, we'll see'; and no more 'eard of it" (523). Finally Gosling reveals that he was to sail for England the very morning news came that Medford would arrive. When Gosling asked Almodham, "And 'ow about my holiday?" Almodham with "stony eyes" deferred the trip to the next year. Gosling pleaded: "I told 'im . . . 'ow a man 'ad his rights after all, and my youth was going, and me that 'ad served him so well chained up 'ere like 'is watchdog." But Almodham laughed "sneering-like" and said: "Oh, Gosling, cut it out." Almodham's exploitation of Gosling to meet his selfish needs finally leads to his own demise. Gosling, driven to madness by Almodham's insensitivity, kills him and throws the body into the well.

When Medford arrives (not knowing his host is in the well, but growing suspicious of something wrong because of the stinking water that must be boiled) and hears Gosling's story about the "devilish long" time without a holiday, he expresses sympathy (517). Gosling begins to perceive Medford as different from Almodham. Medford tells Gosling: "When Mr. Almodham comes back I mean to put in a word for you. You shall have your holiday" (517). Gosling is surprised and appreciative: "You would, sir, you would?" And Medford is pleased to have appeased Gosling. "Medford felt that since his rash promise to secure a holiday for Gosling, he and Gosling were on terms of real friendship" (518). But

Medford, no different in many respects from Almodham, does not release the chains of servitude. He, too, depends on Gosling and sinks into the leisurely existence of the desert where all his needs are provided for, except for fresh water, the arriving caravan having lost the case of Perrier. Medford, happy with Gosling's "dog-like affection" (519), settles into Almodham's vacant throne, announcing to Gosling he may stay a year.

Gosling, becoming more and more nervous and confused, begins to realize that he has merely traded one dominating master for another. Medford notes that it "looked as if poor Gosling were on the edge of a breakdown" (528). Later Gosling mysteriously appears in Medford's room in the middle of the night.[9] When caught by Medford, who authoritatively brandishes a revolver and threatens to shoot him, he dubiously explains his presence. He says he planned to lock Medford in his room to keep him from riding off (to look for Almodham) with the treacherous Arab Selim (the head groom) who will surely murder him. "But you was different, sir. You said it, and I knew you meant it—about my 'oliday. So I'm going to lock you in" (523). Finally driven to desperation by Medford's continuing presence, Gosling, in conflict about his guest, tips his hand: he first tries to push Medford into the well and at the last moment pulls him back. Medford's authoritarian behavior and solicitous attitude, which seem contradictory, have confused Gosling, who half delirious, face wet with tears, says: "Oh God—and I 'ad you 'arf over! You know I did! And then—it was what you said about Wembley. So help me, sir, I felt you meant it, and it 'eld me back" (530). Medford's sympathy touches Gosling. Gosling wants to believe in him. But Medford, as Almodham's successor, upholds patriarchal authority and class privilege to subordinate Gosling's needs.

Carol Singley's reading of "A Bottle of Perrier" focuses on the relationship of Medford and Gosling, suggesting "new revisionary relations" that are "maternal" rather than paternal (272-273).[10] Gosling serves or mothers Medford, and Medford mothers Gosling, for both men are in compromised positions in relation to patriarchal power, Gosling as Almodham's oppressed servant and Medford as the younger man being seduced by Almodham. These "dispossessed males" begin to develop an intimacy to meet their own needs.[11]

> Wharton shows us that male power is dominating; homosexual or homoerotic relations reflect this imbalance of power and the necessary subjection of one individual to the other. In the mediating presence of the mother, however, or in the sympathetic bond between two disempowered males, the grip of the patriarchy may be seen momentarily to weaken, and a new configuration of human relations become possible. (27)[12]

Although Wharton hints at new possibilities, the patterns of the story show deeply engrained traditional behaviors. Ironically, as is often the case with oppression and submission, Gosling's habit of servitude chains him to Almodham as much as Almodham's domination victimizes him. Wharton stresses that Gosling, although finally driven to madness and murder, lives for twelve years as a loyal servant. He never deserts Almodham because he is not given a holiday. Even after killing Almodham, he does not flee for England. As long as Medford stays, Gosling keeps up the sham that Almodham will return rather than simply telling him that his host has left indefinitely and that he is leaving to go to England. Instead Gosling serves Medford as he did Almodham. Gosling pleases Medford with his "disciplined lips" (512), his respectful tone, his unfailing competence. Conditioned to servitude, dependent on the praise he receives for doing his job properly, Gosling is imprisoned by a habit of mind. His dedication to duty is reminiscent of many of Wharton's female characters devoted to their men and their positions as wives, comparable to the wife in "The Fullness of Life" and Mary Boyne in "Afterward."

Wharton's sensitive portrayal of Gosling's entrapment by an oppressor and his need to nurture and be nurtured is further complicated by the predicament that Medford shares: Gosling has internalized his master's behavior. Gosling, a white British citizen from Malta, lords his power over the subservient Arabs whom he frequently tells Medford are lying thieves. When Medford asks him why the other servants cannot take over to allow him to go on holiday, he replies with "careless contempt" that "they're just Arabs" (517). The disappearance of the case of Perrier after the arrival of a caravan upsets Gosling. Medford thinks Gosling is looking out for his welfare; Gosling thinks if Medford has his Perrier, he will not notice as quickly the putrifying state of the well. Gosling expresses his dissatisfaction in no uncertain terms with the Arabs assigned to bring the Perrier from the caravan. "Master of all the desert dialects," he curses "his subordinates in half a dozen" (526). Medford hears the hubbub and observes: "Gosling must have had a strong arm to subdue the shrill voices of his underlings. Now they had all broken loose, and it was Gosling's own voice—usually so discreet and measured—which dominated them" (525). The abused has become the abuser. Gosling's disrespect for and insensitivity towards the Arabs illustrates that dominance and abuse are learned behaviors that operate at every level in the hierarchy of a patriarchy.

Wharton does not miss the opportunity here to show the irony created by the contrast of abusive behaviors and religious postures as she did in

"Kerfol." In the part-Christian, part-Muslim world of Almodham's domain, Christianity supports the British male patriarchy. When Gosling shows contempt for the Arabs, he also shows contempt for their religion. He explains to Medford that the Arabs are not to be trusted because "It's 'ow their interests lie, of course, sir; and their religion, as they call it" (519). Their religion does not command Gosling's respect. Yet he, a Christian by cultural background, is ultimately exposed as the liar of the story. The chauvinistic representatives of Christianity in the story, not Islam, are ironically the murderers of body and spirit. As Carol Singley points out, it is the distrusted Selim who functions "as a kind of truth barometer" and whose words, having an ironic "biblical ring," are "faintly prophetic" ("Gothic Borrowings" 279).[13]

Wharton's desire for a change from the status quo and her sensitivity to those entrapped in old patterns permeate the tale. Gosling's and Medford's desires for maternal redemption reflect Wharton's own needs as a woman deprived of maternal nurturing in childhood. Wharton's sensitive portrayal of the vulnerable Medford reflects her situation as a female at the mercy of male power. Her sensitive portrayal of Gosling reflects her situation as a woman dependent on her servants for nurturing in order to be able to carry on her work.

Wharton's attachments to her own servants and their predominance in her life show how Wharton in her upperclass position developed a lasting and deep sensitivity to the predicaments of the servant class. As a child of a wealthy family in Old New York and as an adult who was the manager of several large households, Wharton was certainly familiar with servants; in fact, servants surrounded her for her entire life.[14] Not insensitive as an employer, she was compassionate and solicitous. Gaillard Lapsley writes that she "was possessed by a sense of compassion deeper and more authentic than I have ever seen in any other human being" (Lewis, *Biography* 388). Wharton, childless, estranged from her mother and older brother, and finally divorced, probably spent more time with her faithful servants than anyone else in her life. In a way, they became a substitute family. Cynthia Ozick writes that "Through her attachment to her servants, she became intimately bound to illiterate lives remote from her mentality, preoccupations, habitual perception—a second expatriation as deliberate as the more obvious one" (53).[15]

A number of Wharton's servants were with her for many years. She became very fond of them and was as committed to their well-being as they were to hers. Anna Bahlmann, Wharton's childhood governess and language teacher, later her secretary, was with her for more than forty years. Bahlmann told Mary Berenson: "The only object I have had in life has been to help Edith and spare her trouble and fatigue" (Lewis, *Biography* 382). Bahlmann died of cancer in 1915. In 1923, when Wharton's long-time chauffeur Charles Cook had a stroke and could not drive again, she was "sadly bereft," but committed to his care. She wrote: "Materially I can look after Cook for all his days" (qtd. in Lewis, *Biography* 449). In 1933, Wharton lost both her personal maid, Elise DeVinck, and her "Darling Gross." She wrote to Lapsley: "All my life goes with those two dying women." Catherine Gross, an Alsatian French-speaking woman whom Wharton always called "Gross" or "Grossie," joined her household in 1884. Lewis writes that Wharton "would grow fonder of her than almost anyone in her life" (*Biography* 514). Finally when Wharton herself died, her remaining servants mourned. Arthur White, an English butler with Cockney speech who may have provided the prototype for Gosling, joined the Wharton household in 1888. After Wharton's death, White wrote Berenson from the Pavillon Colombe: "I feel out of place here now and would like to vanish" (qtd. in Lewis, *Biography* 532).

A story told by Nicky Mariano, Bernard Berenson's secretary and companion, illustrates the importance of Wharton's servants to her and how Wharton insisted they be treated well by others. Mariano writes that she had met Wharton many times when she came to I Tatti (Berenson's home in Italy), but their relationship was only a polite, distant one. Then in 1926 at Naples, Wharton arrived with her friends on a yacht after a cruise in the Mediterranean. She invited the Berensons and Mariano to come visit at the boat.

> We found her and her party of friends in very good shape and delighted with all they had managed to see during their Mediterranean tour. I asked Edith how her maid Elise was and whether she had enjoyed the trip. I knew Elise well from her having accompanied Edith to I Tatti. My question made Edith's face suddenly light up and she begged me to go down to the cabin deck and to have a little chat with Elise. From then on I became aware of a complete change in Edith's manner to me. There was a warmth, a tone of intimacy that I had never heard before. A gesture that was natural to me had let down the drawbridge leading into the fortress of her small intimate circle. (Mariano 172)

Margaret McDowell praises "A Bottle of Perrier" as a story illustrating Wharton's "almost uncanny—and certainly distinctive—ability to secure atmospheric effects and to fuse them with psychic tension . . . . The suspense and sudden reversals generate authentic power" ("Ghost Stories"

144). I agree. A great part of the appeal of the story does lie in its intense Gothic atmosphere and the building of suspense. A "sense of peril" begins to close in on Medford, and the "impenetrableness of the mystery" makes him resolve to stay at Almodham's palace when his host does not arrive (523, 525). Medford's terror increases as he begins to suspect that Almodham did not leave, but is hiding somewhere in the rambling dwelling. On the evening Gosling confesses to the murder of Almodham, Medford fancies he can "almost feel Almodham reaching out long ghostly arms from somewhere above in the darkness" (529). In Poe fashion, Wharton adds humorous irony to the scene. When Medford confronts Gosling with his suspicion that Almodham "walks" in the court late at night, Gosling cowers in "ashen terror," fearful that Medford has indeed seen the ghost of his master (530). The story also evokes the macabre. Medford experiences a "slight shrinking of the flesh" from the stinking well water: "Something sick and viscous, half smell and half substance, seemed to have clung to his skin since the morning bath, and the idea of having to drink that water again was nauseating" (525). And the exotic background of the desert with its feeling of "raw violence" (Wharton in Lewis, *Biography* 404) enhances the mood of the tale.

After praising Wharton for the "atmospheric" strengths of the story, McDowell adds that "Mrs. Wharton's customary depth and subtlety are mostly in abeyance here." She calls the story a contrived literary exercise rather than a story capturing a moment "of significant experience given permanent form and perennial fascination" ("Ghost Stories" 144). On the contrary, I see the "significant experience" of the tale as a perennial and important one. The literal scum of the well symbolizes a pervasive, clinging problem: patriarchal authority and elitist insensitivity passed from level to level in the hierarchy and from generation to generation. However, Wharton's message is subtle and, for many readers, lacks a dramatic moment of epiphany beyond the "who-dun-it" confession. As Medford and Gosling stare "at each other without speaking and face the ghastly truth," it is not clear if Almodham's inheritor, the young Medford, has learned anything about himself (531). The final touch of awareness that accosts Andrew Culwin ("The Eyes") as he looks in the mirror is missing for Medford. For some readers, no final moment may appear to tie the threads of the tale together showing the significance of the experience for the survivors.

Carol Singley and Monika Elbert have read this final scene as hopeful. Emphasizing that Medford and Gosling have developed a bond which prevented Gosling from killing Medford, they point out that, at the end of the tale, the two men are standing above the female space of the well where male power is dead and decaying. As Singley points out, however, they "are still physically, psychologically, and socially stranded in a foreign land." What new structures of sexuality, race, and class might emerge from their experience? "Can one imagine a sexuality that is not a function of power relations or sustain an intimacy that transcends barriers of class and race?" Singley notes that Gosling's "near-insane state" and the question of morality in murdering the father figure suggest the "risks of changing the existing order" ("Gothic Borrowings" 287). Elbert points out that the light of the moon representing "the dark feminine realm" which at the end of the story "suddenly illuminates the sky and reveals the secret of male bonding . . . foreshadows a spark of hope in the otherwise desolate landscape" (22).[16] But it seems likely Gosling's and Medford's temporary bonding will dissolve the next day in the bright light of the sun when they face the alternatives. Does Medford betray Gosling and turn him in to authority, reinforcing the patriarchy? Do Medford and Gosling hide out at Almodham's indefinitely, caring for each other, perhaps developing their own homoerotic attachment? If so, they insure their own isolation, suggesting a frustrating, transitional period before the blending of the paternal and the maternal evolves. Or do they both flee, ironically escaping back into the open arms of the all encompassing father (Western patriarchy)? The alternatives look grim.

"A Bottle of Perrier" develops the theme of oppression and revenge frequently seen in Wharton's work. Her first short story, "Mrs. Manstey's View," published in *Scribner's*, July 1891, depicts a woman's life blocked off by insensitive interference. Mrs. Manstey, for whom looking out the window of her apartment has become the last of her meager life's pleasures, tries to burn down the apartment house renovation next door which threatens to block her view. Her adversary is a vague, impersonal, indifferent authority; she attempts futile revenge. "Mrs. Manstey's View" was Wharton's first attempt at defying what was yet for her a nameless enemy. A subversive statement, it tells of a woman in an inferior and limited position in the patriarchal society who wishes to rise up against the choking of her individuality and creative expression. Some critics have not connected this earliest tale with Wharton's life. Lewis writes: "Like several other of Edith Wharton's earliest stories, this one has no obvious bearing on the life she was leading" (*Biography* 61). But I see the story relevant to Wharton's inner life and also the first in a long line of tales dealing with oppressive authority and revenge. Most of these stories depict patriarchal authority dominating weaker adversaries and squelching rebellion.[17]

In "Mr. Jones," rebellion by the younger generation results in murderous revenge by the patriarchy. In a broad sense, "Mr. Jones" fits the Romantic mode of American fiction (Emerson, Melville, James, Fitzgerald) or European fiction (Stendhal, Balzac, Thackeray, George Eliot) where characters are trapped and destroyed by a fallen or evil world. Gary Lindberg points out that Wharton frequently taps into a pattern in which "tentative entry of the free candidate into a world where laws and assumptions are inherited, complex, alien" leads to disaster. "What is at stake is how much exposure a character can endure before losing either his integrity or personal energy by which he can impress his character upon others" (33). In Wharton's work, the "free candidate" is pitted against patriarchal codes and the weight of repressive tradition.

In fantasy, undesirable tradition is often projected on to "the other," a ghost or monster, who represents not only the conventions of the past, but also unconscious repression of that past. Rosemary Jackson writes:

> Themes of the other, the "not-I," deal with problems generated by desire, by the *unconscious* . . . . Ideology—roughly speaking, the imaginary ways in which men [sic] experience the real world, those ways in which men's relation to the world is lived through various systems of meaning such as religion, family, law, moral codes, education, culture, etc.—is not something simply handed down from one conscious mind to another, but is profoundly unconscious. (52, 51, 61)

In "Mr. Jones," Wharton's "other" is the ghostly Mr. Jones himself who represents rigid societal conventions. The younger generation is represented by Lady Jane Lynke who inherits the ancestral Bells where "Mr. Jones still rules" (*Ghost Stories* 183).[18] Lady Jane struggles in vain against repressive tradition to become a New Woman. Mr. Jones, however, is insidious; he is not seen or barely seen, representing the strong, invisible, unconscious hold of the past upon the present.

The story takes place in twentieth-century England near the sleepy fictional village of Thudeney-Blazes in Kent. Arriving for a brief visit to the ancestral home called Bells, Lady Jane, the new owner, holds her breath and gazes at the first glimpse of the house. It resembles "an aged cedar spreading immemorial red branches" as though her family tree is reaching out to place her in her rightful position (170). First she visits the chapel and the family vaults where she longs to hear the "marble lips" speak and comment on the old house and the lives lived there to which she was about to add another chapter, subdued and humdrum beside some of those earlier annals, yet probably freer and more varied than the unchronicled lives of the great-aunts and great-grandmothers buried there so completely that they must have hardly known when they passed from their beds to their graves. (175)

Lady Jane's arrival immediately sets up a tension between the past and the present. The house personified seems to feel a jolt; when she rings the bell, "a flurried echo . . . seemed to ask what in the world was happening" (172). Lady Jane is not the kind of woman the house is accustomed to. At thirty-five, she has led "an active, independent and decided life." Leaving home at an early age, she lived in London alone, studied abroad, travelled in the tropics, and became a writer, author of "two or three books about cities usually dealt with sentimentally" (171). Upon her arrival at Bells, unfamiliar, but sentimental, feelings and behavior assault Lady Jane. She immediately falls in love with the house and impulsively dedicates herself to it. "'I shall never leave it,' she ejaculated, her heart swelling as if she had taken the vow to a lover" (171). In the chapel, she vows "to the dead to carry on their trust." When she goes to ring the bell, she thinks: "' I ought to have brought someone with me' . . . an odd admission for a young woman who, when she was doing her books of travel, had prided herself on forcing singlehanded the most closely guarded doors." However, as she looked back," these "seemed easy and accessible compared to Bells" (172). When she is told by the maid that a Mr. Jones, the caretaker, will not permit her to see the house, instead of declaring herself as the new owner, she timidly backs off. "Lady Jane stood and gazed up at the inexorable face of her own home." Afterwards, she admits to her friends, who receive the story of her rebuff with "mingled mirth and incredulity," that she thinks she was afraid (173). They jolly her into laughing at the incident, "yet she knew it was true she had been afraid" (174).

What does the independent young woman fear? To what in her impetuousness has she pledged herself? Unconsciously, she is being drawn back into the patriarchal world of the conventional woman which she left behind when she became the unconventional, unmarried traveller and writer. This New Woman, not young by traditional standards of spinsterhood, confronts her ancestral past, and remarkably decides to give up everything else for Bells.

Her previous plans and ambitions—except such as might fit in with living there—had fallen from her like a discarded garment, and things she had hardly thought about or had shrugged away with the hasty subversiveness of youth,

were already quietly laying hands on her; all the lives from which her life had
issued, with what they bore of example or admonishment.

A part of her pities her women ancestors "piled up like dead leaves, layers
and layers of them, to preserve something forever budding underneath."
But although she is conscious of much of the deprivation of the past, even
intuitively seeing the house as "sometimes no doubt a prison," she finds
herself mesmerized, acquiescing to tradition. A part of her responds strongly
to Bells: "She was satisfied to carry on such a trust" (175).

As a foil to Lady Jane, Wharton creates a traditional woman of the
past, Juliana Portallo who, in 1817, married "Peregrine Vincent Theobald
Lynke, Baron Clouds, fifteenth Viscount Thudeney of Bells, Lord of the
Manors of Thudeney, Thudeney-Blazes, Upper Lynke, Lynke-Linnet and
so forth." The weighty list of titles suggests the Viscount's power and
significance as well as the encrusted layers of social hierarchy. When
Lady Jane visits the family vaults, she sees the "tedious enumerations" of
the Viscount's titles on his sarcophagus while, in contrast, she discovers
the Viscountess almost by accident. Underneath the copious notes on the
Viscount "in small cramped characters, as if crowded as an afterthought
into an insufficient space" were the words "Also His Wife" (171). Later
Lady Jane learns that the nameless, and thus insignificant, wife has a portrait that hangs in Bells. A curious portrait of a "sad-faced" woman, the
Viscountess looks out from it "dumbly, inexpressively, in a stare of frozen
beauty." At first, Lady Jane thinks the Viscountess has been painted as an
"inconsolable widow" (184). However, according to the inscription on
the portrait, she was painted one year after her marriage, ten years before
her husband's death. Lady Jane concludes correctly: "She must have
been inconsolable before his death, then." The Viscountess, painted in the
blue parlor by the desk in front of the window, stands against a "melancholy" background. The window frames "snow-laden paths and hedges in
icy perspective." The "wintry desolation" (185) of the scene and the "frozen beauty" of the Viscountess suggest archetypal reverberations, symbolic patterns frequently used by Wharton, foreshadowing yet another
thwarted personality, stunted by the lack of opportunity for growth.

The wretched story of Juliana Portallo surfaces in documents hidden
by Mr. Jones. According to the marriage settlements, she was the daughter
of a wealthy merchant and banker, and she was literally deaf and dumb.
Her dowry to the Viscount was substantial "and this explains the marriage" (193). Various letters reveal "a dirty record altogether" of the Viscount. A gambler and a womanizer who "seems to have been always

disporting himself abroad" (192), he left the Viscountess in the care of a Mr. Jones. In a poignant letter dated 1826, she reveals her wretched state. Also figuratively deaf and dumb, she lives in isolation, virtually imprisoned by Mr. Jones. She writes:

> I . . . fail to conceive how anything in my state obliges that close seclusion in which Mr. Jones persists—and by your express orders, so he declares—in confining me . . . . To sit in this great house alone, day after day, month after month, deprived of your company, and debarred also from any intercourse but that of the servants you have chosen to put about me, is a fate more cruel than I deserve and more painful than I can bear. (192-193)

She pleads for the opportunity to make the acquaintance of a few friends and neighbors for companionship. Juliana's request never honored, she remains all her days "speechless, soundless, alone" at Bells (193).

Wharton creates for the Viscountess Thudeney the most pitiable state of existence she can imagine, capturing the traditional plight of women in a patriarchy. Juliana Portallo, like Anne de Barrigan de Cornault ("Kerfol"), is literally sold, in this case, to a young rake. The marriage offers a tremendous "bargain" for him; his empty coffers are filled. In a marriage based on the concept of bargaining for and taking possession of goods, Juliana is chattel. After the transaction, in her condition, she becomes worthless, her deafness and muteness symbolizing her lack of worth, power, and voice. She is locked in her own world (a woman's world) by her husband, the patriarchal heir, and his minion, Mr. Jones, who, like Gosling ("A Bottle of Perrier"), though a lowly servant, but still a male member of the patriarchy, is allowed to mimic the privileges of class. Juliana Portallo's beauty, expression, and potentiality are frozen by insensitive treatment.

As Juliana Portallo, Viscountess of Thudeney, reflects the wretchedness of the condition of the traditional woman, so Mr. Jones reflects the patriarchy and its iron rule. When the modern Lady Jane arrives at Bells, she finds Mr. Jones nominally in charge, but she does not meet him. Mrs. Clemm, the housekeeper, the medium for Mr. Jones' oracles, establishes right away that "Everything came to depend on him" (178). From pantry boy to footman to butler, Mr. Jones advanced to his position as master of Bells and guardian of tradition. The mystery surrounding Mr. Jones stems from his invisibility and his seemingly great age. Mrs. Clemm maintains that he is her great-uncle, an explanation which she considers logically acceptable. However, Stramer, a friend of Lady Jane's, remembers being turned away from Bells by the orders of a Mr. Jones thirty years before, and a Mr. Jones was clearly Juliana Portallo's jailer. Both Mrs. Clemm and her niece, Georgiana, the maid, know that Mr. Jones is "in his grave in the churchyard—these years and years he is" (196), but because of his hold on them, Mrs. Clemm ambiguously states his condition: "Well, my lady, he's more dead than living, too . . . if I may say so . . . . He's between life and death, as it were . . . . He'd know you, my lady; but you wouldn't know him . . . . I mean, for what he is: he's in no state for you to see him" (174, 178). To Mrs. Clemm and Georgiana, Mr. Jones's will represents law, a law that cannot be defied; it is as impossible for these women to express their rights and fight patriarchal control as it was for Juliana Portallo physically to speak. Georgiana explains why her aunt, Mrs. Clemm, obeyed Mr. Jones: "She always had to do what he told her to . . . because you couldn't ever answer him back" (196).

Mr. Jones's hold on the household, the female servants, and Lady Jane is not direct and conscious. His control is subliminal illustrated by Lady Jane's two brief sightings of him in the blue parlor. The images she sees quickly vanish. First, "What she saw, or thought she saw, was simply an old man with bent shoulders turning away from the citron wood desk. Almost before she had received the impression there was no one there" (181). She finds herself shivering after the sighting, recalling "the uneasy feeling which had come over her" when she first visited Bells (181). She is not sure what she is seeing, but the image affects her because it embodies repressed tradition that has an unconscious hold on her in spite of her independent status. The second time she sees "an old man at the desk," she addresses the image as "Mr. Jones," but again there was "no one there" (189). Intuitively she feels Mr. Jones's presence, but she cannot consciously unravel the mystery—his age, his position, his location in the house—and she cannot grasp his significance or the nature of his power. Again Wharton uses the technique of "absences" as a powerful statement of the underlying order of things, an order that is unjust and immoral.

Lady Jane's response to the enigma of Mr. Jones is ambivalent, partly obedient to tradition and partly defiant. She is not consciously aware of her ambivalence. When she invites her friend, Edward Stramer, to come and work on his novel at Bells and keep her company, she promises no one will bother him, "Not even Mr. Jones. As she wrote she felt an absurd impulse to blot the words out. 'He might not like it,' she thought; and the 'he' did not refer to Stramer" (182). Like the dead Juliana and the living servants, Lady Jane fears offending Mr. Jones, but she does not understand why she is afraid. When Stramer playfully pops into the blue parlor in an attempt to surprise Mr. Jones, Lady Jane is again fearful. "It was stupid, but Lady Jane's heart gave a jerk; she hoped the challenge would not evoke the shadowy figure she had half seen the other day" (185). She even tells Stramer not to try the drawers of the desk, intuitively realizing that Stramer may be trespassing on Mr. Jones's territory. "'Oh, don't!' [she] exclaimed. The words slipped out unawares" (186). A part of her fears the consequences of breaking patriarchal law. Her female sense of propriety in a male-dominated culture imprisons her, affecting her thoughts and behavior.

However, another part of her realizes the absurdity of the patriarchal hold on women. She becomes increasingly defiant of her circumstances: a household where an invisible man rules and where she is not allowed to use the blue parlor (the best spot in the house) or gain access to the family archives (a source of knowledge) because of his dictatorial pronouncements. Like a child, she defers to a tyrannical parent, but as an adult, she begins to rebel. She finally insists to Georgiana that she will have the fire in the blue parlor despite Mr. Jones's warning that the chimney does not draw and that the area appears to be his domain. When Mrs. Clemm objects, Lady Jane perseveres, "That will do, Mrs. Clemm. I want the fire in the blue parlor" (183), before, again, she acquiesces to Mr. Jones. When the key to the muniments room where the archives are kept cannot be found and the summoned locksmith suspiciously loses a tool and leaves, Lady Jane threatens to break the lock. "I'll break in that door myself if I have to" (188). Finally, she crosses the boundary of safety. In response to Mrs. Clemm's continual acceptance of mysterious authority ("There's a great many things in old houses that nobody knows about"), Lady Jane replies: "There shall be as few as possible in mine." She then proceeds to scale the patriarchal stronghold by searching Mr. Jones's desk. Mrs. Clemm, always the obedient and respectful servant, even foregoes appropriate manners of class to uphold patriarchal convention. She admonishes her mistress: "No, my lady—no—no. You won't do that." Lady Jane does it anyway, but not without "a slightly shaking hand" (191).

The modern woman's independence and defiance are not, however, triumphant. Wharton realistically declares the battle between the sexes and the generations a battle won by tradition. The overpowering strength of the patriarchy and the upholding of its view of women and women's unempowered position in the society is assured in the tale with the finality of death. The ghost of Mr. Jones strangles Mrs. Clemm because she did not prevent Lady Jane from overstepping the boundary. Georgiana blames Lady Jane: "You hadn't ought to have meddled with his papers, my lady . . . . That's what he punished her for" (196). Mr. Jones takes revenge, showing that a woman who moves beyond her predetermined role in the society must suffer dire consequences. In her attempts to be the New Woman and the rightful head of her own household, Lady Jane finds herself enmeshed in conflict with the law of the ages. As the story concludes, Georgiana flings "her arms above her head," straightens "herself to full height" and falls "in a swoon" (196), exactly what Anne de Cornault ("Kerfol") does after she gives her futile testimony at her trial. In defeat, Georgiana and Anne resort to the conventional female's plea for mercy, the submissive swoon.

In an earlier story, "The House of the Dead Hand" (1904), Wharton created a situation similar to the one at Bells.[19] In a Gothic setting, a tapestried apartment in an old Italian palace with a marble woman's hand drooping above the doorway, Wharton placed three characters, a mother and daughter virtually kept prisoner by their husband/father Doctor Lombard. The father persuades the daughter to spend an inheritance on a famous Leonardo painting which, it is clear, is more a treasure to him than to the daughter. He keeps the painting and his women locked up. After Lombard's death, the daughter, whose suitor is a desirable Count, has the opportunity to sell the Leonardo to pay her dowry and to escape her oppressive environment, yet remarkably, she does not, eventually losing her suitor who marries someone else. While Lombard is alive, the Count explains the situation to Wyant, a young man who visits Lombard to see the famous Leonardo and whom Sybilla, the daughter, asks to help her. "She has no one to advise her; the mother is an idiot; the father is terrible; she is in his power, it is my belief he would kill her if she resisted him" (521). Wyant does not help Sybilla and appeases himself by arguing: "She isn't walled in; she can get out if she wants to" (526). Years after Lombard's death, however, Sybilla explains to Wyant her dilemma: "I was free— perfectly free— or I thought I was till I tried . . . to disobey him—to sell the picture. Then I found it was impossible. I tried again and again, but he was always in the room with me." Even Wyant feels that "the room seemed full of a third presence." Sybilla says, " I can't lock him out; I can never lock him out now." Both Lynette Carpenter and Barbara White have pointed out the "emphasis on male power" (Carpenter 63) and the sexual/incest imagery, "keys, locks, secret doors, and velvet folds" and Lombard depicted as a vampire (White 40), in "The House of the Dead Hand." Rescue does not seem to be a possibility. Wyant is detached and ineffectual in the situation because he does not "see" the problem; he is not a ghost-seer. Maternal redemption is not in evidence either as the mother is "an idiot."[20]

Lady Jane, like Sybilla Lombard and Juliana Portallo, has no maternal or female support in her bid for independence. In "Mr. Jones," Lady Jane's family "were all in the north and impossible to dislodge." Her sisters are too busy to visit; her mother writes, "Why not come to us? What can you have to do all alone in that empty house at this time of the year?" Therefore, Lady Jane invites for company Edward Stramer, a bachelor novelist whose help she finally enlists. Stramer, who appears to spend his life availing himself of the hospitality of his well-to-do friends, is another of Wharton's intellectual bachelors, representative men of the new age, who have been presented in earlier work in an unflattering light, but Stramer is a sympathetic and hopeful character.[21] Although he finds the Mr. Jones's situation silly and intolerable, he does not belittle Lady Jane for not having control of her household, nor does he try to take control. He is supportive in trying to puzzle out the mystery. Stramer and Lady Jane represent gender roles in transition. They lead unconventional lives and are unmarried, independent, creative. They have not chosen the roles of husband or wife or assumed responsibility for regular jobs or children. As friends (there is no suggestion they are lovers), they both tackle the intellectual challenge of Bells as equals. However, the challenge is more an emotional one for Lady Jane who is the register of the tale and a female vulnerable to the conflicts revolving around the status of women in a male-dominated society.

Stramer's and Lady Jane's experimentation with new roles and directions available to men and women in the twentieth century remind one of Wharton's life. Wharton, like Lady Jane, was independent, unmarried, and also a travel writer who "prided herself on forcing singlehanded the most closely guarded doors" (172). In the 1920s and 1930s, she managed two impressive households, the Pavillon Colombe north of Paris at St. Brice-sous-Fôret and Ste. Claire Chateau near Hyères on the Cote d'Azure, and enjoyed the friendships of many intelligent, artistic bachelor friends who visited her. The external similarities lead to internal ones. Lady Jane struggles with conflicts familiar to Wharton. The unconscious pull of past tradition and conventionality was strong and attractive for Wharton, but finally in many ways reprehensible. In "Mr. Jones," through creative expression, Wharton speaks out for the Viscountess and all female ancestors as well as the transitional woman, realistically showing the difficult struggle against the strength of the conventions of patriarchal society, subversively bringing out its insensitive attitudes and cruel behavior.[22]

In "The House of the Dead Hand," Lynette Carpenter explores "men's power over language with their power to control women's lives" and to wield authority over younger men. She points out how language is clearly a "male preserve." Lombard mocks his wife with ironical comments she obviously does not understand. Wyant, as a literalist and younger man, cannot find the words to describe the Leonardo painting. Lombard programs Sybilla, who parrots his ideas on the meaning and beauty of the Leonardo.[23] Lombard controls by the power of language, power which Sybilla attempts to usurp when she writes letters to her Count. However, her use of language is surreptitious and weak; it is always uncertain if the letters will be delivered.

The theme of a woman trying to steal patriarchal language to create a language of her own is the very theme implied in Wharton's own efforts to write her ghost stories. In "Mr. Jones," Wharton mimics her own process when she portrays the deaf and dumb Juliana Portallo attempting to gain control over her own life by writing to the Viscount. Lady Jane enters this power struggle. When she arrives at Bells, a writer herself, she is unable to enter the locked room where the family archives are kept. Mr. Jones has the key. When she threatens to break the lock, Mrs. Clemm produces the key, but Juliana's letters are missing. Lady Jane finally rifles Mr. Jones's desk to find the letters which give Juliana's own story of her imprisonment and her attempt to write her way out of patriarchal space.[24]

Margaret McDowell notes that Wharton was "preoccupied with the problems of women in a changing society over a period of some fifty years" ("Feminism" 523). "She subtly juxtaposes women whose behavior is traditional with those whose behavior challenges social expectations" (521). McDowell also highlights "Wharton's concern with the social pressures placed upon women, the rigid expectations of others with respect to them, and the complex choices which confront them" (523). In spite of these perceptions, McDowell finds little depth in "Mr. Jones" which she thinks "fails because Mr. Jones's motives for suppressing the family history are trivial, his implication in the destinies of the family does not run deep, and little of significance results from his relationship to the present owner and her friends" ("Ghost Stories" 144).[25] To the contrary, Mr. Jones, as the symbolic keeper of patriarchal law, has good reason for suppressing family history that might offend Lady Jane. What he and Lady Jane's ancestors represent are closely allied to her destiny. The heritage of the past weighs heavily on the shaping of the present, creating the conflicts which Lady Jane must resolve. However, Lady Jane Lynke must compromise, as Wharton did: given the conventions of a society which dictates roles for women, Lady Jane and Wharton, must come to terms with inherited restrictions that affect opportunities for independence, freedom, and creativity. Both "Mr. Jones" and "A Bottle of Perrier" depict a battle between the old and new orders with the old order affecting the new at an unconscious level. The older generation enslaves the new, both men and women, in tradition and convention.

Notes

1   I am indebted to Cynthia Wolff, *A Feast of Words*, 189, for the idea of using this quote as an epigraph.

2   Wharton's perception contrasts with how she is viewed today. Monika Elbert in "T.S. Eliot and Wharton's Modernist Gothic" has compared "A Bottle of Perrier" with T.S. Eliot's *The Waste Land* (1922) and called them both "Modernist-Gothic in describing the fragmentation of the modern mind and the possible solutions for healing and integration in some distant past" (19). Garry M. Leonard in "The Paradox of Desire: Jacques Lacan and Edith Wharton" has pointed out that "one reason Wharton's reputation has grown throughout the Twentieth Century is that she examines, with amazing subtlety, the difficulty—perhaps the impossibility—of discovering and maintaining an identity." He continues that he sees "Wharton's work as 'eerily modern' because of the way she intuits problematics of 'identity' that have only recently been put into concrete discourse by thinkers such as Michel Foucault and Jacques Lacan" (13).

3   In "Convention in the Fiction of Edith Wharton," Mary Suzanne Schriber writes that

>   the predominant impression Wharton's fiction conveys is that convention, while useful and even necessary, restricts human possibilities . . . . Wharton's far-reaching complex critique of the operations of social tradition, particularly in the lives of women, suggests that unless individuals are alert to its power and influence, it will substitute itself for a direct apprehension of life and then for life itself.

4   Barbara White (*Edith Wharton: A Study of the Short Fiction*) reports from her research at the Beinecke Library that the story was originally titled "The Parasite" (40).

5   Lewis notes that, to Bernard Berenson's consternation, Wharton wrote "A Bottle of Perrier" in a single day (*Biography* 522).

6   In 1914, Wharton visited Tunisia and Algeria. Her account of her visit to Morocco in 1917 appears in her book *In Morocco* published by Scribner's in 1920.

7   All page references for "A Bottle of Perrier" are from Lewis, *The Collected Short Stories of Edith Wharton*, vol. 2, 511-531.

8   Wharton's view of patriarchal control varies when seen through national lenses. American patriarchal control is frequently associated with capitalism and business practices; British control with colonialism and class; the French patriarchy associated with class and religious convention.

9   The inspiration for writing this incident and the description of it probably draw upon
     an actual experience that Wharton had in North Africa in 1914. At Timgad in Alge-
     ria, Wharton retired for the night and was awakened by a noise in her room. Lewis
     reports: "As she groped for matches beside the bed, she touched the hand of a man
     bending down over her" (*Biography* 360). Wharton sprang up, scuffled with the
     man, escaped, and ran into the hallway of her hotel screaming. The intruder disap-
     peared. After a futile search of her room, everyone went back to bed. Wharton wrote
     Berenson: "Don't let *anybody* talk to me about being frightened who hasn't known
     that sensation" [awakening to find a strange man]. "I would rather have given him
     my cheque book than gone through that minute when I touched him. Brrr!" Wharton
     reported that the man was small and strong, and she thought he was not an Arab. She
     was glad to leave the hotel in Timgad: "The whole atmosphere of the place was
     indescribably sinister . . . " (*Letters* 318-19).

10   Singley ("Gothic Borrowings and Innovations in Edith Wharton's 'A Bottle of
     Perrier'") reads "Perrier" as a female Gothic narrative. She writes

>   By this I mean that it is a text in the gothic mode written by a woman, with
>   the by-now familiar elements: a young, feminine innocent [Medford]; a
>   mysterious castle; and threatening enigmatic male forces. The female gothic
>   is, like all gothic, concerned with fear, but at the root of the female gothic
>   are two concerns. The first is a preoccupation with the self as seen or
>   desired by the male other. The second is a complex, ambivalent relation-
>   ship with the mother, in which essential issues of longing for, and need of
>   separation from, the mother are intertwined. (271-72)

     Candace Waid (*Edith Wharton's Letters from the Underworld*) reads "Perrier" as a
     "barely encoded psychosexual struggle between men and women" (179). She sees
     the house with its "crimsoned shutters," the well and water, as the "landscape of the
     female body" (180). Gosling functions as a traditional, repressed female who be-
     comes a female revenge figure (182).

11   Singley shows that Wharton's names in "A Bottle of Perrier" suggest her themes:
     Almodham means "the very black one"; Gosling, "young goose"; Medford, "one
     who crosses or negotiates a middle way" ("Gothic Borrowings" 279).

12   By all accounts, Wharton had a "distaste for homosexuality." As Singley notes, she
     saw it simply as another "version of the familiar power struggles between the sexes"
     as one individual becomes the seducer/dominator and the other becomes the passive
     victim ("Gothic Borrowings" 278).

13   Singley notes that Selim means "sound, safe, healthy, perfect, whole, faultless"
     ("Gothic Borrowings" 279).

14   Cynthia Ozick ("Justice (Again) to Edith Wharton") describes her households as
     veritable hives of activity. "She had a household staff consisting of maids ('house-
     maids' and 'chambermaids'—there appears to be a difference), a chief gardener

and several under-gardeners, cook, housekeeper, major-domo, chauffeur, personal maid, 'travelling' maid, secretary, 'general agent,' footmen . . . . Her solitude was the congested solitude of a monarch . . . ." (52).

15 Still by class and wealth, Wharton was a first-class citizen who employed her servants to meet her physical and emotional needs. She herself occupied the position at the top of the hierarchy. Julie Olin-Ammentorp ("Challenge to Feminist Criticism") writes,

> It appears she never questioned the right to ask a dozen individuals to run her household . . . . She saw no problem in preventing others from developing their potential so that she might develop her own. At the bottom of this is a certain classcism that is, or one would hope, inimical to feminism in the 1980s" (242).

16 Elbert emphasizes that both Wharton and T.S. Eliot were searching for new meaning and a new order in the modern world by trying "to find some connection between an anarchic present and a coherent mythologized past." She says Wharton was looking for some "mythological past" which might redeem us (19). "The maternal myth of fertility" might lead to a "higher understanding of self" (23).

17 Evelyn Fracasso ("Images of Imprisonment in Two Tales of Edith Wharton") writes that "Mrs. Manstey's View" demonstrates "Wharton's 'obsession' with imprisonment and the techniques she employs to portray her captive protagonists" (319). Fracasso notes, among other techniques, Wharton's irony and symbolic settings and imagery, in particular, the use of enclosed space.

18 All page references for "Mr. Jones" are from the Scribner's edition of Wharton's ghost stories, 1973.

19 "The House of the Dead Hand" was written in 1898, but published in the *Atlantic Monthly* in 1904. All references to "The House of the Dead Hand" are from Lewis, *The Collected Stories of Edith Wharton*, vol. 1, 507-529.

20 Wharton's depiction of women's psychological enslavement and acceptance appears in another early story that functions like a ghost story. "The Angel at the Grave" (*Scribner's*, 1901) features Paulina Anson, the intelligent granddaughter of the brilliant philosopher and celebrity, Orestes Anson, who gives up her own life and freedom to become high priestess at the altar of her grandfather's fading memory. Paulina learns too late that the very "foundations of her consciousness" have been molded to enslave her to a fruitless life of sacrifice ministering to the preservation of patriarchal authority and law.

> The discovery came to Paulina suddenly. She looked up one evening from her reading and it stood before her like a ghost. It had entered her life with stealthy steps, creeping close before she was aware of it. She sat in the library, among the carefully-tended books and portraits; and it seemed to her that she had been walled alive into a tomb hung with the effigies of

dead ideas. She felt a desperate longing to escape into the outer air, where people toiled, and living sympathies went hand in hand. It was the sense of wasted labor that oppressed her; of two lives consumed in that ruthless process that uses generations of effort to build a single cell. There was a dreary parallel between her grandfather's fruitless toil and her own unprofitable sacrifice. Each in turn had kept vigil by a corpse. (*Collected Stories* 1:253)

However, this moment of recognition does not change things for Paulina. Isolated, aging, lonely, and dispirited, she ends up responding to a new call of the cause. A young man, George Corby, arrives at Anson House and asks her to help him write an article on Orestes Anson. Anson's fame has diminished over the years in spite of Paulina's futile ministrations, but Corby hopes to revive Anson's work and reputation. In agreeing to help Corby, an act which awakens her former belief in her grandfather and his ideas, Paulina resumes the vicarious female role for which her consciousness has been conditioned. Pathetically, "she looked as though youth had touched her on the lips" (258).

21   Stramer, as a laudable New Man, may represent Wharton's relationship with Walter Berry later in her life and the qualities about him that she most admired.

22   Elaine Showalter ("Death of the Lady (Novelist): Wharton's *The House of Mirth* ") discusses Lily Bart and Selden in terms that have some relevance to Lady Jane and Stramer. Showalter points out that Lily never gives up the "hope of continuity, rootedness and relatedness . . . as the central meaning of life." Yet she and Selden struggle to find a "republic of the spirit." Selden's "failed effort to define himself as the New Man parallels Lily's futile effort to become a New Woman." Finally, Showalter says Wharton shows that "Real change . . . must come from outside the dominant class structures" (142). Lady Jane and Stramer in their unconventionality, cooperation, and boldness have progressed towards some still-not-fully-definable future more than the defeated Lily and Selden.

23   Wharton's deadly, but humorous, irony makes these three pawns of Lombard look ridiculous and silly.

24   Candace Waid addresses Juliana's attempt to try to write her way out of prison in "Mr. Jones." She sees the discovery of Juliana's words "which are read after death by a sympathetic reader [Lady Jane]" as a "reassuring motif."

25   Lewis found the story "inept" (*Biography* 81).

Six

"Pomegranate Seed" and "All Souls"

Traditions that have lost their meaning are the hardest to destroy.

"Autres Temps," 1911

In 1930, Edith Wharton was 68 years old. She had survived the loss of her beloved Walter Berry in 1927 and her own flirtation with death the winter of 1929 when she almost succumbed to pneumonia. An ardent gardener, but as she aged, only a sometime traveller, her life became more and more focused around her homes, the Pavillon Colombe in summers and Ste. Claire in winters. She was still vigorously producing and selling work in the last decade of her life. Her all-time bestseller and moneymaker, *The Children*, had been published in 1928. In the 1930s, she produced a sequel to the story of Vance Weston's artistic career, *The Gods Arrive* (1932); an autobiography, *A Backward Glance* (1934); three more volumes of short stories; and a promising, but uncompleted final novel, *The Buccaneers* (published posthumously in 1938). Interestingly, as a member of an older generation of writers, she was still working ahead of her time, struggling for artistic autonomy and battling public prudishness. *The Gods Arrive* was turned down by several periodicals because of Halo Tarrant's out-of-wedlock pregnancy; "The Joy in the House" was turned down because of Christine Ansley's flight to Europe with a lover, leaving her husband and child; and "Duration," though purchased by the *Woman's Home Companion*, was withheld from publication presumably because of the fierce revenge of the matriarchal Martha Little (Lewis in *Letters* 509).

Wharton wrote her last two ghost stories in the 1930s. At the end of 1930, she was writing "Pomegranate Seed," published in April, 1931, in the *Saturday Evening Post*.[1] It later appeared in *The World Over* (1936), which also included the well-known "Roman Fever." According to Wolff, these two pieces "can take their place among Wharton's best" (*Feast* 396). Lewis calls "Pomegranate Seed" a "first-class ghost story" (*Biography* 495). Wharton's last completed story before her death on August 11, 1937, was "All Souls," which is a "ghost story of sorts" (Lewis, *Biography* 523).

She sent it to her agent in February, 1937, and it was published posthumously in *Ghosts* . Lewis acclaims this "climactic ghost story" ("Powers of Darkness" 645) as "a highly superior one" (*Biography* 523).[2]

Both of Wharton's final ghost stories avoid the overt Gothic touches evident in many of her earlier stories: the dark mansion on the Hudson in "The Lady's Maid's Bell"; the mysterious Italian villa and the statue with the grotesque expression in "The Duchess at Prayer"; the romantic fortress-like house in "Kerfol"; the stormy night at the Bay of the Dead in "Miss Mary Pask"; the historic Bells with its portrait of the Viscountess whose expression seems changed when Lady Jane challenges Mr. Jones in "Mr. Jones"; and so on. Still, subtle Gothic vestiges remain: Charlotte Ashby of "Pomegranate Seed" hesitates on the threshold of her home as though she might be entering a House of Usher; Elsie Ashby's absent portrait looms in the mind's eye. In "All Souls," Sara Clayburn's modernized eighteenth-century Connecticut home is still linked by legend and superstition to a dark past. The claustral Gothic atmosphere remains in both tales: Sara Clayburn nearly suffocates in the silence of Whitegates, and Charlotte Ashby's world closes in on her.

Nevertheless, a striking feature of both stories is modernity. In "Afterward," Wharton introduced a perfectly modern-looking man in a business suit as a ghost to contrast with the Tudor background of Lyng. For Wharton, the Gothic or exotic was not a prerequisite for the eerie. In her last stories, she seems to want to prove the point. When Charlotte Ashby hesitates on her own doorstep, it is clear the "old-fashioned marble-flagged vestibule" is part of the modern "soulless roar of New York" and its "devouring blaze of lights . . . congested traffic . . . skyscrapers, advertisements, telephones, wireless, airplanes, movies, motors, and all the rest of the twentieth century" (200, 205).[3] Sara Clayburn's home is "open, airy, high-ceilinged, with electricity, central heating and all the modern appliances" (252). No dismal passages, winding stairs, or brooding portraits appear at Whitegates. In the preface to *Ghosts*, Wharton writes: "What the ghost really needs is not echoing passages and hidden doors behind tapestry, but only continuity and silence." She explains:

> Mr. Osbert Sitwell informed us the other day that ghosts went out when electricity came in; but surely this is to misapprehend the nature of the ghostly. What drives ghosts away is not the aspidistra or the electric cooker: I can imagine them more wistfully haunting a mean house in a dull street than the battlemented castle with its boring stage properties. (3)

In the exposition section of "All Souls," Wharton confirms her view by having her narrator allude to Mr. Sitwell and his silly notion:

> I read the other day in a book by a fashionable essayist that ghosts went out when the electric light came in. What nonsense! The writer, though he is fond of dabbling, in a literary way, in the supernatural, hasn't even reached the threshold of his subject. As between turreted castles patrolled by headless victims with clanking chains, and the comfortable suburban house with a refrigerator and central heating where you feel, as soon as you're in it, *that there's something wrong*, give me the latter for sending a chill down the spine! (252)

Wharton also shifted away from her prerequisite ghost-seer, no longer creating narrators or registers with weak constitutions debilitated by illness (Hartley, Faxon, the narrator of Miss Mary Pask, Medford). In the last three stories, she created strong characters: Lady Jane Lynke, Charlotte Ashby, and Sara Clayburn, all robust modern women. In "All Souls," the narrator points out: "And, by the way, haven't you noticed that it's generally not the high-strung and imaginative who see ghosts, but the calm matter-of-fact people who don't believe in them, and are sure they wouldn't mind if they did see one?" (253).

As in "Mr. Jones," both of Wharton's last ghost stories depict New Women struggling with internalized conventions. Charlotte Ashby and Sara Clayburn face horrors that lie not without, but within: their own unresolvable internal conflicts with gender roles, patriarchal control, and sexuality. They both wrestle with doubles represented by ghostly women who threaten their independence, freedom, and happiness. In "Pomegranate Seed," Charlotte Ashby wages a battle against her husband's dead first wife to save her relationship with her husband, while in "All Souls," Sara Clayburn succumbs to the spell of a "fetch" or witch whose powers seem to cast her into a state of dependency, abandonment, and loneliness.

In "Pomegranate Seed," Charlotte, second wife of Kenneth Ashby and stepmother of his children, assumes the traditional roles of wife and mother with forthrightness and efficiency. A confident and "sophisticated woman" (203), she observes proprieties, but like her mother-in-law (which may explain Kenneth Ashby's attraction to her), she has "a fearless tongue" (217). She contrasts boldly with the silent, suffering traditional women Wharton portrays in earlier stories, such as the mute Juliana Portallo ("Mr. Jones") or the ineffectual Anne de Cornault ("Kerfol"). Yet Charlotte Ashby's life in modern New York City still traditionally revolves around her home and her husband. The key conventional characteristic she exhibits is her dependence on Kenneth Ashby as the center of her life. She exults in her almost year-old marriage and her closeness to her husband. She prefers being with Kenneth, or she prefers being alone, even to the company of friends, because when alone "it was another way of being with Kenneth thinking over what he had said when they parted in the morning, imagining what he would say when he sprang up the stairs, and found her by herself and caught her to him" (201).

As the story proceeds, Charlotte's independent self and her tendency to give Kenneth "a little liberty for a change" from the situation he had with his first wife are in conflict with her need for dependency and her ferocious desire to preserve her new position as wife and loved one (202). On the one hand, she shies away from "the feeling he had given her at times of being too eagerly dependent on her, too searchingly close to her, as if there were not enough air between her soul and his" (217), but on the other hand, she fights with all her power to keep his love and confidence and to strengthen their ties: "It was as if Kenneth's love had penetrated to the secret she hardly acknowledged to her own heart—her passionate need to feel herself the sovereign even of his past" (204). She assertively demands knowledge of the mysterious letters which arrive periodically on the hall table and upset Kenneth, yet she is "ashamed of her persistence" and fearful of losing his love (218). She insists to Kenneth that "sooner or later the question must be settled between us. Someone is trying to separate us, and I don't care what it costs me to find out who it is. If it costs me your love, I don't care! If I can't have your confidence I don't want anything from you." Later she reflects on her words: "Think of telling him I didn't care if my insistence cost me his love! The lying rubbish!" She starts to follow him and "unsay the meaningless words," but she angrily asserts herself again when she realizes that he "had had his way after all; he had eluded all attacks on his secret, and now he was shut up alone in his room, reading that other woman's letters" (213). Torn between "a little liberty" and her strong need for dependency and love, Charlotte becomes increasingly distraught.

Charlotte Ashby, as a woman in conflict, is a transitional woman, an ambivalent woman. Margaret McDowell sees Charlotte negatively: egotistical, jealous, distrustful, possessive, cowardly ("Ghost Stories" 139). These characteristics describe Charlotte at points in the story, but the key to Charlotte's complexity lies in the conflict and tension of the story. Carol J. Singley and Susan Elizabeth Sweeney see Charlotte as a "typically passive woman . . . stereotypically feminine and compliant" but also as a "potential usurper of texts [the letters] and the power they represent"

("Forbidden Reading" 178, 184).[4] She is "poised 'on the threshold'; suspended between two realms of gender expectations" (178). Margaret Murray also speaks to Charlotte's assertive/passive, male/female duality seeing her as both the "accomplished" woman and the "powerless" woman (320).

In the plot, a third party, the writer of the mysterious letters, precipitates Charlotte's conflict with her husband and her internal conflicts and ambivalence. Lois Cuddy points out:

> In so much of Wharton's work, there is never a conflict between two characters. There is always a third person to complicate choices, to create trouble, to suggest ethical alternatives, or to act as a catalyst for the decisions that further limit the protagonist within roles determined by the conventions of the culture. (21)

In "Pomegranate Seed," Charlotte Ashby conjectures at first that the intruding letter-writer is female, possibly a client of her lawyer husband, but later she feels sure that Kenneth is involved with another woman. By the end of the story, with the help of her mother-in-law, she identifies the third person as the ghost of Kenneth's first wife, Elsie Ashby. Little information is given about Elsie Ashby in the story. Charlotte remembers her as a "distant, self-centered woman, whom she had known very slightly" (200). Friends warn her against marrying the widower Ashby because he adored his first wife and she dominated him. The implication is that the dependent ties between the two will not easily be broken, not even by death, and that Charlotte is walking into a difficult situation. Friends tell her "Whatever you venture to do, he'll mentally compare with what Elsie would have done in your place." His nearest friends report that "only his absorbing professional interests had kept him from suicide after Elsie's death" (204).[5]

Psychologically, the ghost of Elsie Ashby, whose haunting presence pervades the story, emanates from latent, unresolved conflicts plaguing Charlotte and Kenneth. Elsie sends Kenneth messages from the underworld to keep him from forgetting her and finally to summon him to her. Emblem of the traditional woman in a dependent relationship, she has the power to manipulate Kenneth; like Prudence Rutledge in "Bewitched," she will hold onto her man at all costs like a demon from hell. In life and death, Kenneth's and Elsie's relationship, unhealthy in its closeness, drains the life out of Kenneth who, although he suffers, cannot reveal or exorcise his misery. Kenneth is addicted to the traditional male/female relationship in the patriarchal society based on ownership and domination (male), and dependency and manipulation (female). Like Saul Rutledge ("Bewitched") and the narrator of "Miss Mary Pask," he is also drawn to the ghostly female for eroticism. Charlotte catches Kenneth kissing one of Elsie's letters. Elsie, the shrewish wife, becomes the forbidden woman and exerts an erotic pull stronger for Kenneth than his desire for the satisfying sexual relationship with his new wife.[6]

For Charlotte, Elsie Ashby, her rival, also represents her double, the woman she partly is, but whom she needs to leave behind in order to build a healthy new life.[7] Wharton illustrates the difficulty of Charlotte's divorcing herself from Elsie by the use of a favorite technique, architectural imagery to reveal the soul. When Charlotte marries Kenneth, he tells her that he cannot afford to have the house completely redone, but encourages her to make whatever changes she chooses to suit her. "She made as few as possible" (204). Charlotte takes over Elsie's drawing room, a room she had seen once years ago and thought it was just the drawing room she would like to have. Content to live basically with the old style, Charlotte changes "neither furniture nor hangings," making only "minor modifications" (200). Part of Charlotte covets the position that Elsie Ashby had in her relationship with Kenneth; part of her wishes to modify the house and relationship to move towards "a little liberty for a change."

Elsie Ashby, like Charlotte, is an ambiguous character. As Charlotte's double, Elsie, is also defined by ambivalent possibilities, created by the tensions of the text. In part, Elsie represents the powerless woman like Anne de Cornault ("Kerfol") and Juliana Portallo ("Mr. Jones") whose desperate and futile attempts to tell their stories come too late from the grave to the eyes of sympathetic readers. As a powerless woman trying to find voice, Elsie mimics Wharton's own attempts to appropriate male language and prerogatives and to communicate women's struggles in her fiction, but Elsie also represents traditional women who negatively use manipulation to gain a "dead" victory. Elsie is not Charlotte's ally, but her competitor who will use what power she can exert to regain her position. Her efforts are pathetic and pitiable, but successful. As a female intruder, she is deadly and desirable. As Wershoven notes, "In whatever form she appears and whatever world she enters, the intruder's function remains basically the same; she disrupts the society she has entered, usually by representing an attractive yet dangerous alternative to it" (24). But who is actually the intruder here? Elsie who intrudes on Kenneth's new marriage, or Charlotte who comes into Kenneth's established world after Elsie's death? Charlotte, too, qualifies as the intruder, more in line with Wershoven's concept because she offers the alternative for a new, more open relationship.[8]

Kenneth Ashby becomes the pawn in the struggle between Elsie and Charlotte, between the past and the present, between the mysterious supernatural realm of the unconscious and a conscious future. Torn between the old way of living and progression towards a new path, he resists change. Except for his discreetly moving Elsie's dominating portrait from his library to the nursery to watch over the children, the house stays the same for him. Kenneth is stuck in the old ways. Transition to a new role and a new style of relationship is not a possibility for him. He tells Charlotte to make the changes she needs, but he presumes that they will be minor. He says "that he knew every woman had her own views about furniture and all sorts of household arrangements a man would never notice" (204). In other words, as long as she makes no major changes, only ones he will never notice, Charlotte may do as she pleases.

Kenneth claims the prerogatives of his patriarchal biases. His general attitude towards women is condescending; he tells Charlotte that " women . . . were nearly always tiresome as clients" (203). When Charlotte presses him to reveal the writer of the letters, she sees a "line of anger she had never seen before come out between his eyes," and he adopts the "cool and faintly ironic tone of the prosecuting lawyer making a point." Charlotte observes that when he is upset by her discussion of the letters and her assertive approach, he rapidly regains self control: "His profession [and gender socialization] had trained him to rapid mastery of face and voice" (209). Disdainful of Charlotte's assault on what he considers to be his private business, "Her husband . . . submitted to her cross-questioning with a sort of contemptuous composure, as though he were humoring an unreasonable child" (210). He continues to condescend: "It's not easy to prove anything to a woman who's once taken an idea into her head" (211). When Charlotte, like Lady Jane Lynke ("Mr. Jones"), persists in demanding suppressed knowledge, pushing beyond the bounds of patriarchal propriety, Kenneth stonewalls or evades her to preserve his sanctuary of power. First, he quits arguing and refuses to answer her; he withdraws into himself. Charlotte sees him "change into a stranger, a mysterious incomprehensible being whom no argument or entreaty could reach," although she is "aware in him of no hostility, or even impatience, but of a remoteness, an inaccessibility" (212). Then, he simply evades her. He says he has a "blinding headache" and leaves the room (213). When they dine later, he ignores their earlier difficulties by totally changing the subject, incredibly rambling on "about municipal politics, aviation, an exhibition of modern French painting, the health of an old aunt, and the installing of the automatic telephone." Aghast, Charlotte finds his ability to "make conversation with an assumption of ease" in the face of their problem "more oppressive than silence" (215). After dinner, he dismisses her suggestion for a holiday, saying he cannot go away. In effect, he will not change.

Despite his patronizing tactics, Kenneth's control crumbles in the face of his need for the old way. He holds Charlotte's hands with the "clutch of a man who felt himself slipping over a precipice" and uncharacteristically cries (218). Charlotte conjectures that the woman letter writer will not give him permission to leave for the holiday she has suggested, that he is completely in "bondage" to an "old entanglement" (217, 203). True, Kenneth Ashby is in bondage to the unspoken conventions which dictate his own role as a male/husband and also his wife's rightful role. The pattern even controls his sexual response. He begins to pull away from Charlotte towards Elsie, eventually disappearing, presumably to join his more "traditional" wife, whose plight and techniques Charlotte ironically begins to mirror.

Charlotte's conduct vacillates. At first, she is submissive (a traditional woman). Although concerned by the arrival of the series of gray envelopes and the change that comes over Kenneth, she dismisses her uneasy premonitions. As she becomes more uncomfortable, she considers subversive action, holding the most recent letter over a tea kettle to open and read it. The repressive atmosphere of a proper patriarchal environment, where the woman knows only what the man chooses to tell her, leads her to consider this possibility; the prevailing ethics prevent her from using it. She ponders the "alternative . . . question her husband; but to do that seemed even more difficult" (206). Thinking as a submissive, conventional woman, Charlotte considers direct action impossible. Finally, she resorts to spying.

When she, in hiding, sees Kenneth kiss one of the letters, she is spurred to confrontation and behaves like a New Woman. By nature "forthright and simple" (214), she becomes direct in her efforts to find out what is going on "even if it is another woman" (209). But when she attempts to openly defy patriarchal prerogative, she faces condescension, aloofness, and evasion. When Kenneth does not meet her halfway, Charlotte, whose position as wife is threatened, begins to fight for survival with traditionally feminine weapons. Forgetting her concern about Kenneth, she reverts to manipulation, which is not subtle or appealing. Becoming competitive and destructive, she experiences a momentary illusion of success. In the end, she fails, driving Kenneth away. He disappears.

Wharton uses competitive or agonistic imagery to show how Charlotte becomes her husband's enemy. When Kenneth resists her questioning, Charlotte turns panicky, beginning to feel as if "she had run a hard race and missed the goal." Although feeling "excluded, ignored, blotted out of his life," she takes "heart; perhaps after all she had not spent her last shaft" (212). She tries sympathy to no avail. She tries sarcasm. She threatens. No longer compassionate but impatient and calculating, she weighs her advantages and moves in for the kill. He pulls his last punch: he leaves the room, and she begins to drown in doubt and remorse. Later when she proposes a holiday as an escape from their difficulties and he refuses to go, she begs him to see her side of the case, "to see what I'm suffering." She persists, expressing sympathy for his suffering, but by then,"making him suffer even more than she suffered . . . no longer restrained her." She feels that the "struggle was a losing one . . . . A sense of defeat swept over her" (218). Finally Kenneth breaks down and capitulates. Relieved, she feels she "had fought through the weary fight and the victory was hers—at least for the moment" (219).

Charlotte's victory is a momentary and hollow one, but she luxuriates in Kenneth's acquiescence and seeming dependence on her. The next day she vainly admires herself in her mirror. "It made her feel young again to have scored such a victory." Her hair "waved electrically above her head, like the palms of victory." She thinks:

> Ah, well, some women knew how to manage men, and some didn't—and only the fair—she gaily paraphrased—deserve the brave! Certainly she was looking very pretty . . . . After all she had a right to claim victory, since her husband was doing what she wanted, not what the other woman exacted of him . . . . Nothing mattered now but that she had won the day, that her husband was still hers and not another woman's. (220, 221)[9]

Overconfident, she feels "that nothing could ever again come between Kenneth and herself" (222). Like Prudence Rutledge ("Bewitched") and like her double, Elsie, Charlotte has dug a deep hole for herself through the use of feminine deceit.[10] Abandoning compassion, embracing manipulation, Charlotte maneuvers herself into a position of power, but she becomes a possessive shrew with illusions of success. In a forthright way, Charlotte rises above her repressive environment temporarily, by trying to speak directly to Kenneth about the problem. Faced with no corresponding efforts at communication, she resorts to the old "feminine wiles," and in doing so degrades herself and insures her ultimate defeat and unhappiness.

Wharton portrays Charlotte, the New Woman, as actually a transitional woman similar to Lady Jane Lynke ("Mr. Jones"). Admirable in their assertiveness, Charlotte and Lady Jane both appear pushy and demanding in their attempts to scale the patriarchal stronghold. They both are usurpers, attempting to "read" the text of their lives. Doomed to a choice between silence and ignorance or rebuke and reprisal, they turn to sneaky methods. Lady Jane "burglarizes" Mrs. Jones' desk; Charlotte spies on Kenneth. Lady Jane's assault ends with her "theft," and Mrs. Clemm suffers the brunt of revenge. However, Charlotte, driven to desperation, persists with worse tactics. Adopting Prudence Rutledge's ("Bewitched") and Elsie Ashby's techniques of manipulation, the last resort of the traditional woman, she fights fire with fire, getting burned in the process. Becoming witch, shrew, vampire, succubus herself—she ironically attempts to drain the life out of her husband to save her own.

In an early story, "The Moving Finger" (1901), which strongly resembles "Pomegranate Seed," Wharton already voices doubts about the traditional relationship. "The Moving Finger" is the story of a man whose first wife dies. Their relationship is described as a traditional, dependent one: "Mrs. Grancy's niche was her husband's life . . . . Grancy's life was a sedulously cultivated enclosure, his wife was the flower he had planted in its midst—the embowering tree, rather, which gave him rest and shade at its foot and the wind of dreams in its upper branches." The security of their life is, however, plagued by suffocating closeness: the narrator writes, "We had seen him sinking under the leaden embrace of her affection like a swimmer in a drowning clutch" (*Collected Stories*, 1:301).[11] The second Mrs. Grancy "opened fresh vistas, reclaimed whole areas of activity that had run to waste under the harsh husbandry of privation" (302). Yet when the second Mrs. Grancy dies, it becomes clear that she, too, had been an "enveloping medium" as her portrait becomes an "unappeasable ghost," dominating Grancy's life to the extent that he has Claydon the painter, a friend, periodically modify the portrait so that she and Grancy appear to age together. Finally, the face in the portrait tells Grancy he is dying; in effect, the wife calls him to her. The painter, Claydon, who inherits the portrait after Grancy's death, restores the painting to its youthful freshness, revealing his desire to "own" the beautiful Mrs. Grancy. Grancy's relationships with his wives, Claydon's pleased ownership of the portrait, and the power of women, in the case of the second wife, even after death, suggest the desire for the traditional relationship (the soulmate) which results in domination, dependency, and manipulation. What appears initially as the greatest good ultimately destroys the soul. It is also interesting that the perfect mate is finally dead, suggesting that traditional relationships lead not to vibrancy, but to death in life.

In "Pomegranate Seed," the struggle between Charlotte and Elsie as doubles and opposites, the one trying to sustain life and failing, the other mired in death, is further delineated by the portrait of Kenneth Ashby's mother. Two-thirds of the way through the story, Kenneth Ashby disappears, and the balance of the story depicts Charlotte and her mother-in-law trying to figure out what to do. The mother-in-law becomes a foil for Charlotte's ambivalence. Seemingly concerned about convention and propriety, Mrs. Ashby is shocked when Charlotte wants to open the final letter awaiting Kenneth. "I don't believe any good ever came of a woman's opening her husband's letter behind his back." Accustomed to the repressive conventional environment of male/female relations, she at first will not admit that she recognizes the writing on the letter, even though her response to the envelope unnerves her. "Charlotte noticed that the letter shook in her usually firm hand" (225). Charlotte asks her directly four times if she recognizes the writing, and she does not answer directly, for the information Charlotte asks for is taboo, the unspeakable. Finally, Charlotte intuits the truth when Mrs. Ashby peers at the blank space where Elsie's portrait once hung. At first, open communication is not any more possible between the two women than between Charlotte and Kenneth because it disrupts the order of things; it brings dangerous knowledge to the surface. Charlotte finds herself reflecting on "what depths of the unknown may lurk under the clearest and most candid lineaments." Then Mrs. Ashby enters the struggle between the unconscious pull of the past and a more conscious present. Charlotte observes,

> She had never seen her mother-in-law's features express any but simple and sound emotions—cordiality, amusement, a kindly sympathy; now and again a wholesome flash of anger. Now they seemed to wear a look of fear and hatred, of incredulous dismay and almost cringing defiance. It was as if the spirits warring within her had distorted her face to their own likeness. (228)

The warring spirits observed by Charlotte echo what Kenneth Ashby observed earlier when he said he did not want to go on a holiday and leave the children with his mother (even though they had left the children with her for their honeymoon). Kenneth said of his mother, "She isn't always judicious . . . . And sometimes talks before them without thinking" (217).

Together the ambivalent Charlotte and her ambivalent mother-in-law are a team, trying to solve the mystery and to take some control over their

lives. Mrs. Ashby becomes a nurturing mother figure, a woman in cooperation, not competition with Charlotte. As Susan Goodman points out, "Very
seldom do men and women in Wharton's fiction find the right word to say
to each other . . . and for this reason women's relationships with other women
are crucial" (143). We can see in the developing relationship between
Charlotte and Mrs. Ashby what Goodman observes in Wharton's work:

> Mothers need to nurture and spiritually mentor their daughters, and women need
> to direct their energies inward. If one behaves with honesty and openness, other
> women can be a source of help . . . . Only then can there be a 'new' woman and
> a new world." (66)

The image of the two women working together is a hopeful image. However, whether the image is sustained until the end of the story is questionable. Singley and Sweeney confirm that "a daughter may gain power with
her connection with the maternal," but posit that Mrs. Ashby "lead[s] Charlotte back to a traditional feminine dependence on male authority" when
she suggests calling the police (194). Nonetheless, Mrs. Ashby's suggestion is a bold and confident one, realistically based. Taking ownership of
the problem along with Charlotte, she says "We must do everything—
everything." "Heroically," she claims "Kenneth himself will" resurface to
give an explanation. But her confidence is undercut by Charlotte, who
ironically, as the younger woman with more presumed potential to change,
takes the weaker position. Charlotte stands "up slowly and stiffly" with
"joints as cramped as an old woman's." With resignation, she asks, "Exactly as if we thought it could do any good to do anything?" The strong
Mrs. Ashby "resolutely" responds yes, and Charlotte acts (230). Ambivalence plagues the situation until the end where resigned "dismay"
and hopeful "defiance" still war.

The portrait of Charlotte Ashby and her mother-in-law as potentially
New Women, caught between dismay and defiance, calls to mind societal
attitudes of Wharton's time towards the independent woman, attitudes which
unfortunately still persist. The independent woman was generally seen to
be pushy, demanding, and unattractive. She was not lady-like. A usurper
of masculine tradition, she was thought to be unattractively mannish. If
she crossed the border between assertiveness and aggressiveness, using
manipulative ploys to gain ground, she was easily labeled witch or shrew.
Even if she avoided manipulation, the old labels were handy to deflate her
defiance of the patriarchy.[12] Wharton suffered her share of negative response to her independence. "The more successful Wharton became in

her vocation—and the more she thrived upon that success—the more difficult her position as a woman became" (Wolff, *Feast* 257). Percy Lubbock writes that "she had a very feminine consciousness and a very masculine mind . . . and she liked to be talked to as a man" (54). She was both applauded and criticized for her "masculine" mind. On the one hand, it was good that she could think and talk like a man; her work could be no good if she wrote like a mere woman. On the other hand, her ability to win critical acclaim in the male-dominated literary community made her femininity suspect.

Ambivalent societal attitudes towards the independent woman contributed to Wharton's ambivalence about feminism. Covertly harboring feminist ideas, Wharton was not active in women's reform. Confusing for us, she also occasionally made conservative remarks about the woman's role in society. She said she was not sure that women giving up the "household arts" for "the acquiring of university degrees" was a boon to civilization. "Cold storage, deplorable as it is, has done far less harm to the home than the Higher Education" (*Backward Glance* 60). To Mary Berenson, who sent her a book by her daughter Ray Strachy on the role and status of women in the contemporary society, she wrote "women were made for pleasure and procreation" (Lewis, *Biography* 483). These statements have usually been reported without considering Wharton's seriousness about the genuine problem of maintaining home life and individual achievement, or without any sense of irony which Wharton may have intended, so that to some, Wharton does not seem feminist at all. However, her work realistically reveals the dilemmas created by the departure from traditional gender roles. She depicts both the traditional and progressive role models positively and negatively. Margaret McDowell sums up Wharton's position: "For Wharton a woman must exist as a conventionally feminine presence in order to be seen sympathetically as a 'new woman'" ("Wharton's Feminism" 524). In other words, the best of the old and new must blend. Few of Wharton's characters, however, master this blend. Perhaps she herself exemplifies what could be accomplished by a representative New Woman in her time. And yet, her example suggests sacrifices in a society not ready for her: she traded off intellectual and economic independence against divorce, sexual repression, and loneliness.

Societal ambivalence towards the independent woman and Wharton's own ambivalence over changing gender roles in the society contribute to her view of the complexity of modern relationships, in particular the modern marriage. The traditional male/female relationship based on ownership and domination, dependency and manipulation, does not seem to work, but what will take the place of the old pattern? Wharton's work, by default, shows that she sides with open communication, honesty, and trust as prerequisites to change. Her characters, unwilling or unable to communicate and confront truth, suffer in repressive environments. In almost every instance, Wharton's ghosts suggest suppressed or repressed knowledge that individuals must confront for personal growth and that couples must acknowledge for healthy relations.

In "Pomegranate Seed," through the use of absences in her texts, Wharton suggests repressed knowledge and suppressed communication. The absent first wife, Elsie Ashby, sends messages in faint, unreadable handwriting. The pages of the letters appear to be almost blank. When Charlotte Ashby dares to speak openly and attribute the letters to a ghost (guardian of the past), her mother-in-law admonishes her. The subject is taboo. She replies:

> Why shouldn't I say it, even when the bare walls cry it out? What difference does it make if her letters are illegible to you and me? If even you see her face on a blank wall, why shouldn't [Kenneth] read her writing on this blank paper? Don't you see that she's everywhere in this house, and closer to him because to everyone else she's becomes invisible?" (229)

The crux of Kenneth's and Charlotte's rocky relationship lies in interpreting absent handwriting, an absent portrait, absent explanations, finally an absent husband and especially the ghost, the absent wife, who represents invisible patriarchal conventions and their unconscious hold on the lives of Kenneth and Charlotte. The series of haunting absences reflect internal conflict between an invisible, debilitating past and a vital, progressive present and future. In a repressive environment where social text cannot be read and where communication is absent, men and women are trapped in debilitating patterns of ignorance, silence, and stasis. Relationships can only fail. Caught in a web of unexamined conventions, Kenneth and Charlotte "seemed both to have reached the end of their arguments and to be helplessly facing each other across a baffling waste of incomprehension" (212).

Wharton's difficulties in personally trying a "new" style relationship emerge from her correspondence with Morton Fullerton, revealing patterns of behavior and thought that appear in "Pomegranate Seed." Wharton was frequently exasperated by Fullerton's "hot and cold" behavior. He showered her with attention sometimes and then disappeared. He wrote frequently or not at all. Wharton writes to him:

> I never expected to tell you this, but under the weight of this silence I don't
> know what to say or leave unsaid . . . . My reason rejects the idea that a man like
> you, who has felt a warm sympathy for a woman like me, can suddenly, from
> one day to another, without any act or word on her part, lose even a friendly
> regard for her & discard the mere outward signs of consideration by which friend-
> ship speaks. And so I am almost driven to conclude that your silence has an-
> other meaning. (qtd. in Gribben 31)

At first patient and reasonable, she asks for communication rather than
silence, the talking over of their respective goals and positions in the relationship. She is shocked by the lack of response. "But this incomprehensible silence, the sense of your utter indifference to everything that concerns
me, has stunned me" (Gribben 32). Wharton sometimes sounds panicky
and possessive and even combative, although she never loses sight of herself and Fullerton as independent individuals whose needs must be re-
spected or of open communication as the key to defining their roles and
their relationship.

> What you wish, apparently, is to take of my life the inmost & uttermost that a
> woman—a woman like me—can give, for an hour, now & then, when it suits
> you; & when the hour is over, to leave me out of your mind & out of your
> life . . . . I think I am worth more than that, or worth, perhaps I had better say,
> something quite different. (qtd. in Gribben 33)

She suggests that a simple postcard

> addressed by you would be a message in itself! . . . And if a woman asks these
> signs, it is not necessarily because she is 'sentimental,' or jealous, or wishes to
> dominate a man, or restrict his freedom; but because these are the ways in which
> the heart speaks, & because, when two people are separated, there are no other
> ways available. (qtd. in Gribben 33)

Fullerton persisted in his behaviors with sporadic silence and the maintaining of his version of the male prerogative, the double standard. Finally,
their relationship failed. Wharton was not sure whether the experience
was worth the difficulties. "I said once that my life was better before I
knew you. That is not so, for it is good to have lived once *in the round*, for
ever so short a time." She found it difficult to go from "being my own
comrade" to intimacy with Fullerton and back again to her lonely state:
"When one is a lonely-hearted and remembering creature, as I am, it is a
misfortune to love too late & as completely as I have loved you. Everything else grows so ghostly afterward" (qtd. in Gribben 54).[13]

Connections between Wharton's personal struggles and "Pomegranate
Seed" are perhaps easier to see than the connection between the story and

the myth referred to by the title.[14] In a cover letter to Rutger Jewett that accompanied the revised manuscript of the story, Wharton explains the title's significance for the benefit of Loring Schuyler, editor of the *Ladies Home Journal,* who had apparently seen the manuscript, but not understood. Wharton writes:

> As for the title, Mr. Schuyler must refresh his classical mythology. When Persephone left the under-world to re-visit her mother, Demeter, her husband, Hades, lord of the infernal regions, gave her a pomegranate seed to eat, because he knew that if he did so she would never be able to remain among the living, but would be drawn back to the company of the dead. (*Letters* 532-533)

Critics have labored over the relationship between the myth and the story, producing tentative and conflicting interpretations. Lewis and McDowell agree that Elsie Ashby reflects Hades; Kenneth, Persephone; Charlotte, Demeter. Elsie Ashby does not want her former husband to "remain among the living," or with Charlotte, but to return to her, "the company of the dead." Lewis thinks the connection of the myth "with Mrs. Wharton's tale is superficially slender, especially since the Persephone story is usually interpreted as a seasonal myth—the annual return of winter darkness and sterility, the annual rebirth of nature in the spring" (Introduction, *Collected Stories* xvi). Sterility and rebirth are core symbols in Wharton's story depicting two life-styles, two states of mind.

But what is the pomegranate seed and how does the eating of the seed determine sterility or rebirth? McDowell speculates that the

> "seed" could be the letters which Kenneth kisses as if to consume them; he is unfaithful in thought to Charlotte and is captive to the underworld. Or perhaps the "seed" is the seed of jealousy in Charlotte which she is not able . . . to control; and by consuming this seed she may condemn her husband to the power of one who dwells in the spirit world. Or perhaps, as R.W.B. Lewis suggests, the "'seed' may be Kenneth's own perfidy to his wife's memory." ("Ghost Stories" 140)

Another possibility is that the pomegranate seed which Kenneth Ashby as Persephone has consumed is a "seed of thought," the ideology of patriarchal conventions that governs him and causes him to leave Charlotte. Charlotte, the potentially New Woman, allied with the female and maternal, offers rebirth through a relationship with new vitality, but in the end, Kenneth returns to Elsie, the traditional woman who can only offer a dead relationship, a sterile existence. When Kenneth meets and marries Charlotte, they are initially very happy. Friends say he looks years younger to which Charlotte replies, "I suppose I've got him out of his groove" (203). Kenneth speaks "frankly of his great love for his first wife" to Charlotte, but also confesses "that from the beginning he had hoped the future held new gifts for him" (204). Charlotte, as the Demeter figure, offers potential salvation in moving towards a new way of life; however, Kenneth, having consumed the "seed" of convention given to him by Elsie, the guardian of the old way of life, returns to the dead past. The pomegranate seed comes from the "underworld" of invisible, unconscious convention, destroying possibilities for growth.

The problem with this interpretation or any of the interpretations which peg Charlotte as one character and Kenneth as another is that they put too much faith in Charlotte's ability to change the relationship, for she, too, is struggling with the conventions of the past. Margaret McDowell, describes Charlotte "as at best a Demeter figure manqué, lacking the force, vitality, and persuasive presence of the goddess and imagination to save her captive husband from demonic powers . . . . Neither she nor Kenneth are up to the spiritual demands of the situation" ("Ghost Stories"139). Margaret P. Murray suggests that "In slaying the ghost of her ambivalence regarding her own gender, [Wharton] was able to create an omnipotent women: Charlotte-Elsie, who is Aphrodite-Persephone" (320). Is Charlotte the woman who is forging a new path or the woman who herself is drawn into the underworld? She is the ambivalent woman, a combination of the two. Singley and Sweeney suggest

> The story's title . . . evokes many more questions for Wharton's reader than it answers. And yet this ambiguity is appropriate; indeed, it might be the real reason that Wharton alluded to the Perspehone-Demeter myth to begin with . . . . Persephone . . . is ultimately the very figure of ambivalence, forever poised on the threshold between masculine power and feminine propriety. ("Forbidden Reading" 192)

Finally, Charlotte represents the internal conflicts with which Wharton herself struggled in trying to find the integrity of individual separateness and fulfillment, and connectedness with others.[15]

Lewis writes that Freudian and Jungian analyses suggest strong sexual motifs in mythology. He connects the Persephone myth and "Pomegranate Seed" to the "sexual struggles and yearnings as in the cycle of nature" (Introduction, *Collected Stories* xvi). If we take the pomegranate seed to be the unconscious conventions that affect gender roles and relationships, it assumes a new meaning for Wharton's story in sexual terms. Kenneth's consumption of the pomegranate seed binds him to sexual perversion:

sexual desire tied to the forbidden (necrophilia; dominance-submission; bondage; sadomasochism) represented by Elsie (a vampire).[16] On the other hand, Charlotte, as a living woman, not a phantom, may offer a healthy, rejuvenating sexual relationship. Thus the consumption of the pomegranate seed threatens Kenneth and Charlotte in another way. Those who consume the seed and allow patriarchal conventions to become a part of themselves face diminished prospects for sexuality. Wharton seems adamant in desiring healthy new roles and relationships, requiring men and women to give up the consumption of traditional assumptions and fantasies that control behavior. For rebirth, men and women must "grow up" and give up the tyrannizing myths of the past to create a new future.

In "All Souls," Wharton focuses on conflicts suffered by a single woman rather than a couple, but the narrator's superstitious interpretation of events in the story suggests the control of the myths of the past over the present as seen in "Pomegranate Seed." As the narrator points out, "All Souls" is not "exactly a ghost story" (253). The supernatural being that impinges upon the life of Sara Clayburn is a "'fetch' or perhaps a living woman inhabited by a witch" (273). The appearance of the fetch, the other woman or double like Elsie Ashby, signals the beginning of an inner journey for Sara: she crosses the threshold of consciousness to the land of her disturbing unconscious fears and desires where she struggles with internal conflicts revolving around gender, sexuality, aging, and finally the inevitable encounter with death.

The setting of "All Souls" echoes Wharton's earlier work. Whitegates is a comfortable upper-class home in the "cheerful and populous" Connecticut Valley, but when the early snow (the last day of October, All Souls' Eve) begins to blanket the area and the house, "muffling the outer world in layers on layers of thick white velvet," the New England scene begins to resemble the frozen wastelands of Starkfield and Northridge and Cold Corners [*Ethan Frome*, "The Triumph of Night," "Bewitched"] (274, 259).[17] The bleak environment reflects Sara Clayburn's constricted life and personality, Whitegates itself representing Sara Clayburn's internal dilemma. In "The Fullness of Life," Wharton used the image of the house and its rooms as a path to the woman's soul. Sara, whom the narrator describes as "very much like her house" (252), literally, or perhaps only in a feverish fantasy or dream, walks through her house; figuratively, she moves into the inner recesses of herself, a self she reluctantly explores. Normally, her dwelling is "in irreproachable order" (263); she nonetheless realizes that "she had never thought of [her house] as a big house, but now, in [the] snowy wintry light, it seemed immense, and full of ominous corners around which one dared not look" (261). Not physical danger, but repressed fears and desires await her.[18]

The narrator, a cousin,[19] describes Sara Clayburn, a widow probably in her early sixties, as an independent woman, "a muscular, resolute figure" with a "quick imperious nature" (253, 255). Living a well regulated life, up early, she always observes daily rituals. "She was not the kind of woman to nibble on a poached egg on a tray when she was alone, but always came down to the dining room and had what she called a civilized meal" (263). She is "authoritative" and obstinate. When her husband died, people expected her to leave Whitegates and move to an apartment in New York or Boston where she had relatives, but she did not. The narrator tells us: "Sara Clayburn seldom did what other people expected, and in this case she did exactly the contrary . . . ." A proud woman who outlives the "fat Presley boy," would-be heir to Whitegates, she shows up at his funeral "in correct mourning, with a faint smile under her veil" (253).

Although not young, Sara is a New Woman of sorts. An experienced manager of her household, she has additional independence thrust upon her by widowhood. Allan Gardiner Smith suggests that in assuming her position as a widow, Sara Clayburn, in effect, inherits "an authoritarian male position in relation to the house and servants." "Masquerading as a male," she maintains "compulsive control over the household" (151). Her "authoritative" behavior suggests that she oversteps the boundaries of what is properly feminine. Yet she has little choice in a society that dictates that a woman who assumes independence sacrifices femininity. Sara may not have the easy flexibility and gentleness of conventional femininity, but Wharton makes her character admirable. "She had always been regarded as a plucky woman; and had so regarded herself" ("Ghost Stories" 259).

Sara's encounter with the fetch is the catalyst for understanding the traditionally feminine and submissive side of her nature. Her independence may have an unattractive edge, but her submissive side is presented as less appealing. On All Souls' Eve, Sara goes out for a late afternoon walk and meets a "stranger," a "middle-aged, plain and rather pale" woman who in a voice "foreign" to the Connecticut Valley announces her intention of going to the house "to see one of the girls" (254-255). Half an hour later, the usually "light-footed" Sara slips on a frozen puddle and fractures her ankle, rendering her "suddenly helpless" and confined to bed by her doctor (254). Her servants, on whom she is dependent, curiously disappear during the night and the next day, not reappearing and resuming their chores until the following day. Strangely, they do not even acknowledge that they have been absent. Sara, terrified to be left alone, finds herself with no telephone, electricity, heat, with only interminable silence and pain. Layer after layer, her independent self strips away, revealing the frightened, lonely, and powerless old woman inside. After her experience, recognizing her dependency and fear of being left alone again, she behaves uncharacteristically and does not even question the servants about their absence. The following year, again All Souls' Eve, Sara, out on a walk, meets the same strange woman approaching the house. This second instance makes her angry. Thinking the appearance of the woman an evil omen, Sara orders her to leave, but the woman laughs at her, passes behind the hemlocks (symbol of poison), and virtually disappears. Sara, "deathly frightened," flees to her cousin's apartment in New York, arriving unnerved. Her cousin, the narrator, reports: "I had never seen her as unquestioning and submissive . . . . She was not the woman to let herself be undressed and put to bed like a baby; but she submitted without a word, as though aware that she had reached the end of her tether" (269). In telling her cousin what happened, Sara looked at her "like a frightened child" (271).

The fetch represents Sara's double, the regressive part of her personality which she fears. Regressive dependency is the same passive tendency that Ethan Frome and George Faxon ("Triumph of Night") struggle with. Not by nature exclusively reserved for women, in the patriarchy, dependency and submission typify the inherited condition of women. When Sara Clayburn's independence is undermined by the regressive state she enters when she is abandoned, she recognizes that her independent stance is something of a sham; she is more dependent on her servants and her reassuring daily rituals than she thought she was. The fetch reveals the horror of Sara's genuine position in the socioeconomic divisions of the patriarchy. Her dependency and submissiveness brought on by her injury and her abandonment by her servants suggest that her "compulsive control" is an attempt to overcompensate for her fear of being a weak and powerless female.

What most terrifies Sara is her vulnerability. She and her cousin, the narrator of the tale and a potentially New Woman, connect her exposed vulnerability to the appearances of the strange woman whom they believe to have supernatural powers. Her cousin posits, as does Sara, that the strange woman involves some ominous cause/effect relationship. The cousin theorizes that the woman arrives to arrange a meeting of a coven, whose powers are channeled through Agnes, Sara's maid from the Isle of Skye in the Hebrides, an area "full of the supernatural." She says that Sara herself regarded "Agnes as the—perhaps unconscious—at any rate irresponsible—channel through which communications from the other side of the veil reached the submissive household at Whitegates" (273). Sara and her household indeed do become submissive after the appearance of the woman. The apparition suggests submission and also represents Sara's repressed sexuality.

Widowed, old, alone, Sara's active sex life is a matter of the past. But the appearance of the fetch (the "bad" woman) unlocks repressed erotic feelings and desires. The fetch's mission may be to summon the servants to an orgy. The cousin speculates:

> Such a messenger might well have been delegated by the powers who rule in these matters to summon Agnes and her fellow servants to a midnight 'Coven' in some neighboring solitude. To learn what happens at Covens, and the reason of the irresistible fascination they exercise over the timorous and superstitious, one need only address oneself to the immense body of literature dealing with these mysterious rites. Anyone who has once felt the faintest curiosity to assist at a Coven apparently soon finds the curiosity increase to desire, the desire to an uncontrollable longing which, when the opportunity presents itself, breaks down all inhibition; for those who have once taken part in a Coven will move heaven and earth to take part again. (273)

Not explicit about the "irresistible fascination" or the "uncontrollable longing," the cousin alludes to the "history of witchcraft" for elucidation. As Lewis directly states: "Edith Wharton knew well enough that a coven was an exercise in witchcraft which usually led to the wildest erotic activities." He attributes Sara Clayburn's terrors to her "intuitive moral and psychological *reaction* to the coven" (Introduction, *Collected Stories* xvii). In other words, Sara Clayburn reacts negatively to the idea of sexual abandon and to the witch (the loose woman) as she has been conditioned to react. However, another part of her terror stems from the "irresistible fascination" that draws her. Still capable of sexual desire, she feels jealous of whatever conspiracy and fulfillment her missing servants may have engaged in. Afraid of, but fascinated by "disturbing some unseen confabulation on which beings of flesh-and-blood had better not intrude" (261), she compulsively explores her house in an attempt to find out what is going on. "No matter what it cost her in physical suffering, she must find out what was happening belowstairs . . ." (259). As she proceeds, she becomes almost hysterical in her quest. "'I must find that out, I must find that out,' she repeated to her self in a sort of meaningless sing-song" (262). A "man's voice," sexually suggestive, speaking in a "language unknown to her . . . passionately earnest, almost threatening" waits for her. Her terror "surmounted by the urgent desire to know what was going on, so close to her yet unseen," she discovers that the voice is coming from a "portable wireless" and then faints (264).[20]

Sara's ordeal assumes symbolic erotic significance similar to dream scenes in tales by Irving, Poe, or Hawthorne.[21] There are clues that Sara's experience lies within a fantasy or dream, the product of a feverish imagination. Lying in her bed awake the night after her injury, waiting for the time when the servants will appear and care for her, Sara imagines the furniture regrouping itself "after goodness knows what secret displacements during the night." She fancies she sees a table slipping back into place. "'It knows Agnes is coming, and it's afraid,' she thought whimsically." Not a typical thought for Sara Clayburn, "Her bad night must have made her imaginative for such nonsense as that about the furniture had never occurred to her before . . . " (257). Also after she explores the house and faints, the "memory of what happened next" was "indistinct," (264) suggesting not fully conscious perception. In addition, the narrator reminds us that no other "single witness" exists "except Sara Clayburn herself" (252). When the doctor arrives the day after Sara's supposed abandonment, Sara herself "understood that her mind was confused by fever" (267). Whether she actually was alone or not, the significance of her experience resides in the surfacing of her unconscious fears and desires. Sara's journey lies below; she ventures "belowstairs" or into the unconscious recesses of her mind.

Along with her fears of vulnerability and dependency and her unfulfilled sexual needs, other repressions surface. Sara is getting old, and as she ages and approaches death, she faces the reality of loneliness and the natural fears of abandonment and annihilation. Her house is in a "remote and lonely" location; her husband is dead; she is childless (253). Her family consists primarily of her servants, many of whom, like the usually faithful Agnes, have been with her for a long time. Sara scoffs at the doctor's suggestion to send up a nurse to keep her company during her convalescence. "Lonely? With my old servants? You forget how many winters I've spent along with them. Two of them were with me in my mother-in-law's time" (256). But when her servants desert her, "Her sense of loneliness" grows "more acute." She feels "utterly alone" (262). When her servants reappear, she wants to press her case, to accuse them of their neglect, to find out why they have conspired against her. But she fears upsetting them. Sure that Agnes is lying, she finds the horror of her distrust is "nothing to the horror of being left alone in [the] empty house" (266). When the servants return, "efficient, devoted, respectful and respectable," Sara represses her need to speak, hoping that all will be as it was before and that she will not ever be left alone again (268).[22]

Sara's fear of abandonment is compounded by a greater fear, the fear of permanently being cut off from life through death, the "cessation of all life and movement." She feels oppressed by the silence of the house and "the cold continuity of the snow . . . still falling steadily outside." What lays "a chill on her" is the "feeling that there was no limit to [the] silence, no outer margin, nothing beyond it" (262). The silence has a "peculiar quality," folding "down on her like a pall." What "emerged now and then for her was a dim shape of fear, the fear that she might lie there alone and untended till she died of cold . . ." (265). Sara's vulnerable, helpless condition brings to her conscious mind the fear of death.

Sara Clayburn's situation strikingly resembles Wharton's own life when she wrote "All Souls." At age 75, Wharton, an independent old woman, husbandless and childless, lived alone in a large household staffed by servants. After Walter Berry's death in 1927, she began to feel increasingly isolated and alone. She wrote to John Hugh Smith: "I perceive that I, who thought I loved solitude, was never for one moment alone—& a great desert lies ahead of me" (*Letters* 504). In 1933, her maid, Elise DeVinck, and her housekeeper, Catherine Gross, who had been with her for many years, both died. She wrote Mary Berenson: "The strain on my heart-strings (I mean the metaphorical ones) is severe, for since Walter's death I've been incurably lonely *inside*, & these two faithful women kept the hearth-fire going" (*Letters* 561). In April, 1937, Wharton, always attached to her little dogs, lost her Pekinese companion, Linky. She told William R. Tyler the next day: "I wish she could have outlasted me, for I feel for the very first time in my life, quite utterly alone and lonely" (*Letters* 606).

Leon Edel ponders why Wharton would have written "All Souls," "this strange fantasy . . . . What does this story really say?" ("Literary Psychology" 462). He notes that Wharton had a heart condition from which she died six months after writing the tale, implying perhaps an "unconscious announcement of impending death" (460). Edel also writes that Wharton "was perhaps the most servanted writer in our literary annals" and suggests that having been so well attended throughout her life that "she never knew what it meant to fend for oneself" (461-462). Thus she would, like

Sara Clayburn, fear abandonment as she grew older and weaker. Apt in recognizing Wharton's servanted state, Edel overstates the case. Although dependent on servant care, Wharton was a woman who showed great for- titude throughout her life, especially during World War I, and who used the freedom afforded by her servants' ministrations to do a prodigious amount of work. She once wrote to Berenson asking him to understand some of her special needs and demands. "Don't be hard on me or think me uncertain or capricious." She comments that he had a wife to care for him; she did not. She had full responsibility for "household, cheque book, pub- lishers, servants' questions, business letters, proofs—and my work!" (Lewis, *Biography* 351).

Edel also speculates that her "final fantasy may contain remote as well as immediate personal data." He cites her lonely childhood when she "was more aware . . . of servants than of parents" ("Literary Psychology" 463). Another experience in her past which Wharton may have drawn on to sketch the isolation at Whitegates is the experience she had at Mrs. Humphry Ward's country house, Stocks, in England where she had gone for an ill- timed summer vacation just preceding World War I. When the war began in August, 1914, she was unable to return to Paris, and all communication with France was cut off. Stocks did not even have a telephone. She soon moved into the "Wards' other house" in London, for as she wrote to Berenson, "this loneliness in which I sit inactive seems to make things worse" (*Letters* 337). Wharton must have felt an incredible loneliness cut off from her usual life at "this historic moment" (Lewis, *Biography* 367). Whatever well-springs of the past might have contributed to "All Souls," Wharton's old age with the loss and sorrow of the advancing years would have been sufficient for her to project her own fears of regression, aban- donment, and death onto Sara Clayburn. Wharton wrote: "When I am dressing, I find myself wondering who is the ugly old woman using my glass" (Lubbock 210).

The incongruity of a public self and a private self is a major theme of Wharton's ghost stories. When an undesirable denied self surfaces through circumstances, the repressed "ghost" self creates as much horror as an externalized ghostly projection. "All Souls" uses the "fetch" as a catalyst, but the greatest impact of the tale lies in Sara Clayburn's awakening hor- ror in response to her denied self. In 1928, Wharton published "After Holbein," a story included in the 1930 collection *Certain People*. "After Holbein" has been referred to as a ghost story yet no externalized ghostly figure appears. The main character struggles with his "ghost" self which he becomes aware of but manages to re-repress until he dies. Like Sara Clayburn, "Anson Warley . . . dodged his double . . . ." (*Collected Stories* 2:533).[23] He is at times aware of his "dual personality," his public, man-about-town "remarkable" self and his "small poor creature, chattering with cold inside" (532). Warley, a man drawn to ideas and the heights of scholarship and creativity finds "the view from there was vast and glorious" but "icy." Finding "the place too lonely," he immerses himself in a continual round of entertainments and distractions, becoming, as he sees himself, the witty, fashionable, desired guest at innumerable New York society dinner parties (533). He becomes aware that his personalities merge: "Finally he made the bitter discovery that he and the creature had become one . . . ." (532). Wharton is clear that, in this case, Warley has "murdered" the better part of himself. As he ages, "the two distinct Anson Warleys" have long since disappeared, the "lesser" part of himself having "made away with the other" (534).

The story then is a look at the results of repression, of living the lie. Anson Warley pushes himself to go out regularly to continue to validate his identity as the highly desired dinner guest much to the dismay of his manservant, Filmore, who recognizes how old and weak Warley has become and who attempts unsuccessfully to "mother" him. The crux of the tale lies in the clever pairing of Anson Warley with Evelina Jaspar, a Mrs. Astor type whose identity has been built on entertaining desired guests. In a humorous, yet poignant scene, reminiscent of the tragicomedy of Anton Chekhov, Anson Warley becomes Mrs. Jaspar's only guest at an imaginary dinner party. The two are aided in creating their fantasy by Mrs. Jaspar's servants who dutifully help her to maintain her pretense, even though in reality, the gilt china is now the blue and white crockery from the servants' quarters, the orchids on the table are wadded-up newspapers in a bowl, and the fine wine is water. Contriving the meeting of the two characters, Wharton creates a "queer coincidence" with Warley forgetting where he is going and stopping at Mrs. Jaspar's "lit-up" house on the very evening that she suddenly adds Warley to her pretend guest list (545). It is "almost uncanny" (546). The reality is that the two pathetic old people live in the past, nursing their fading identities which have surely, but inadequately, sustained their unintegrated selves. As Anson Warley leaves Mrs. Jaspar's, he steps forward "to where a moment before the pavement had been—and where now there was nothing" (550).

In "After Holbein," the servants play key roles in abetting Anson Warley and Mrs. Jaspar in their delusions. Warley's manservant,

Filmore, cautions Warley to slow his pace; yet he continues to do as Warley dictates. Mrs. Jaspar's young night nurse, Miss Cress, is only too aware of how deluded the old woman is and sometimes tries to burst her balloon by contradicting her; however, the old maid, Lavinia, who may not even out-live her mistress, persists in doing her duty to serve Mrs. Jaspar and honor her wishes. Lavinia's greatest desire is to live long enough to take care of final arrangements for Mrs. Jaspar when she dies. The older servants are loyal and caring, understanding their masters or perhaps sustaining their own delusions as Stevens does in Kazuo Ishiguro's *Remains of the Day*. The older servants "mother" the "small poor creature[s]" that live within Warley and Mrs. Jaspar allowing them to re-repress what they have become. For Warley, this re-repression suffices until death.

As in "All Souls," the servants become very powerful. They choose to nurture or to withhold nurturing and, in effect, hold the fates of their em-ployers in their hands. Without the shield of the servants, the main charac-ters' identities dissolve and denied selves surface weeping in "powerless misery" like Mrs. Jaspar, who is lost without her diamonds: "Her ruined face puckered up in a grimace like a new-born baby's, and she began to sob despairingly" (540). Wharton was only too acutely aware of the power of her servants to sustain the orderly surface of her life. In "All Souls," she explores her own denied self projected into the character of Sara Clayburn. The loyalty of her servants who have been with her so long is reflected in Sara Clayburn's smooth life at Whitegates. The All Souls' eve retreat of the servants reflects, as Barbara White points out, "the aristo-cratic writer's guilt and fear" (97). Here the revenge of the servants who have repressed parts of themselves to minister to the desires of their mas-ters and mistresses break loose. As in "A Bottle of Perrier" when the repressed Gosling murders his master, in "All Souls," the servants free themselves and temporarily abandon their mistress. In "After Holbein," the younger generation nurses, Miss Dunn and Miss Cress, are thinly com-mitted to the doddering Mrs. Jaspar and her fantasies; they are clearly committed to self-interest in keeping up the charade because "we're very well off here" (537). The master-servant life portrayed in Wharton's work is a tenuous one based on the hierarchy of dominance and submission. Annette Zilversmit points out that "All Souls" turns on role reversal. Sara, the dominant and independent, becomes the powerless and submissive when she arrives at the narrator's apartment. Bested by her servants, she and the narrator are cast as "mother and child, one submissive, one controlling" ("Last Haunted House" 325). Here the cultural and personal converge in

Wharton's work: the dilemmas of patriarchal and capitalistic power structures juxtaposed with unresolved parental issues, definition of selfhood,
and connection with others.

Wharton invests her conflicts in the ambivalent portrait of Sara
Clayburn. Sara's regressive dependency and her strident independence
both are unappealing. Sara gains a sense of control over her life only
through sacrifice. Independent, she is also alone and lonely. She represses
her sexual and dependency needs which increase the feeling of their ur-
gency when they surface. The uncanny horror she experiences stems from
the awakening of her repressed desires. In her work, Wharton experiments with the role of woman in the patriarchal society by creating traditional, dependent women and "new," independent women, both of whom
never seem to have fully found the answers on how to develop their potential to live free lives and yet live fulfilling lives connected to others. For
example, in the earlier novel *The Fruit of the Tree* (1907), Bessie Westmore,
the traditional woman "develops into more than the clinging, petulant wife,
whereas Justine [Brent] moves from freedom to conformity" (McDowell,
"Feminism" 531). Ironically though, neither woman finds the right for-
mula for a more satisfying life.

Similarly, Wharton never seems to have found the right balance in her
own life. Eager to embrace independence, she resisted giving up the attractiveness of femininity; eager to build her own career, she regretted
giving up the embrace of lovers, who might be jealous or competitive, and
the bonds of marriage. At times the bonds of marriage seemed to her like
chains, at times like ties of intimacy and warmth and companionship which
she considered essential to happiness. Like Dorothea Brooke in
Middlemarch, she agreed that "Marriage is so unlike anything else. There
is something even awful in the nearness it brings." But Wharton also told
Charles du Bos: "Ah, the poverty, the miserable poverty, of any love that
lies outside of marriage, of any love that is not a living together, a sharing
of all" (qtd. in Lewis, *Biography* 317). Sara Clayburn's conflicts over her
role as a woman, like the conflicts of so many of Wharton's other female
characters, reflect Wharton's own defeated struggle to create a balanced
life that would blend the best of tradition and the best of transition.

The use of absence and silence in "All Souls" is a familiar technique
from Wharton's supernatural fiction which again shows her ability to make
the invisible of the culture visible. The "unseen" surfaces symbolically.
Smith points out that "Mrs. Claymore's 'illicit' desires are projected
onto the servants but kept offstage and by their absence are intensified

in suggestiveness" (150). The servants' absence, Sara Claymore's reticence to talk about what happened, even with her cousin, and the silence of Whitegates with only one-way communication through the wireless indicate the constraint of society's codes and conventions on the individual. The individual's needs and desires are not met, not discussed, not heard. Undoubtedly Wharton felt, at times, as though she were working in a vacuum trying to depict the struggle of the individual, especially women, to solve problems of gender and balance in a patriarchal society intent on maintaining the status quo. And undoubtedly, at times, she must have felt that in choosing her path as a writer, a communicator of what lies below society's surface, she had chosen only another form of isolation.

The role of the narrator becomes a key factor in "All Souls" as it did in *Ethan Frome* and "Kerfol." The narrator's interpretation of Sara's story expresses her own biases, concerns, and limitations. She does not tell the tale in her "cousin's words, for they were too confused and fragmentary." The narrator relates Sara's story in her own way. "If the thing happened at all . . . I think it must have happened in this way . . . ." (254). Annette Zilversmit points out that the gender dilemma that traps Sara Clayburn also traps the narrator.

> If in *Ethan Frome* the main story can be seen as the inner fears, the nightmare "vision" of its nameless male narrator, even this last short tale must be read as the unspoken conflicts of the unnamed modern woman who boldly lives by herself in an apartment in New York City in the 1930s. The inner narrative becomes her internal possibility that she [like Sara Clayburn] has chosen isolation rather than independence. ("Last Ghosts" 301)

The narrator's preoccupation with interpreting Sara's story according to the luridly supernatural also tells us about the narrator's "internal possibility." Sara Clayburn will not return to Whitegates, but she keeps insisting that "there must be some natural explanation of the mystery" (274). The narrator, however, seems convinced that the supernatural, not the natural, caused the events at Whitegates. She says that her version of Sara's story will set the record straight since "stories about [Sara's experience] have become so exaggerated, and often so ridiculously inaccurate." After eschewing exaggeration and saying that she is more "likely than anybody else to be able to get at the facts, as far as they can be called facts, and as anybody can get at them," she proceeds to reveal herself as a believer in the occult traditions of the past and unravel the mystery by attributing events to wild superstition (252). She says matter-of-factly that she supposes that

> Even in this unimaginative age, a few people still remember that All Souls' eve
> is the night when the dead can walk—and when, by some token, other spirits,
> piteous or malevolent, are freed from their restrictions which secure the earth to
> the living on the other days of the year.

She thinks the appearance of the woman recurring on All Souls' eve "is
more than a coincidence" (273), identifies her as a fetch, connects her to
Agnes, and suggests her mission as the summoning of a Coven. Shock-
ingly, "the affinity with the unknown forces" exists in this modern woman's
reality. For all her modernity and independence, the myths of the past still
control her interpretation of the present.

Again Wharton shows us that tradition shapes the future. Superstitious lore and traditional conventions, which we only vaguely understand
or which we unconsciously retain as a part of ourselves, continue to dominate our present and our future and will do so until we attempt to face
ourselves, to find a "natural explanation of the mystery." The narrator,
potentially more the New Woman than Sara Clayburn, ironically offers the
least promise. She says that Sara did "not believe" but "at least feared" the
supernatural forces at work. She notes that "such moral paradoxes are not
uncommon." Such paradoxes, actually psychological, are common. Perhaps Sara comes closer to understanding her internal conflicts than her
younger cousin. Fear or stress forces Sara to an examined life; however,
finally, in her regression, she denies or represses knowledge of herself.
The narrator skirts the truth, not understanding at all, believing myths at
face value. Unfortunately, she does not experience fear—for fear might
bring her to genuine knowledge.[24]

As mentioned earlier, tradition is not always thought of as a villain in
Wharton's fictional world. James Tuttleton writes:

> In her best, most representative works, Mrs. Wharton continually returned to
> the idea of tradition and the need of viable modes of cultural transmission as
> important factors affecting the character of man's [sic] social history. She con-
> tinually argued the necessity of the individual's commitment to the cultural tra-
> dition; the danger of alienation from it; the catastrophe which ensues when social
> upheavals like revolution, anarchy, and war destroy the slowly and deli-
> cately spun web of that tradition; and the necessity of imaginatively pre-
> serving—if necessary even reconstructing—the precious values of the past.
> ("Archaeological Motive" 564)

But Wharton's attitude towards tradition was like her attitude towards feminism—ambivalent. Caught on the proverbial horns of the dilemma,
Wharton both cherished tradition and welcomed refreshing change. For

instance, the lassitude of her old New Yorkers is dispelled by the vitality of the dynamic new merchant class. Elmer Moffatt (*Custom of the Country*) is in many ways more admirable than Ralph Marvell; Newland Archer's son (*Age of Innocence*), who will marry one of Beaufort's bastards, shows more promise than his father. In the ghost stories, Wharton's subtext about tradition and feminism is more clear cut than in much of her other work. Wharton shows that women will have a difficult time finding fulfilling roles in the new society, but she seems to be suggesting changes in gender roles for men and women. She suggests that relationships must change to accommodate new patterns of gender identity. The patriarchal modes of thought of the past that enslave us must give way to new modes of thought and conduct that will create a new world, one where men and women can share love and companionship, and freedom and growth, without the debilitation of domination, submission, and manipulation, and where isolation and repression are not the only alternatives. Wharton suggests that we must retain traditions that afford us some stability and continuity, but we must divorce ourselves from the oppressive myths of the past.

Notes

1   "Pomegranate Seed" was originally considered by editor Loring Schuyler for publication in the *Ladies Home Journal*, but he found the story puzzling. Wharton revised the story, but Schuyler still refused it.   In a letter to Rutger Jewett, her editor at Appleton, January 31, 1931, Wharton reports that she has written a requested "modified ending" to "Pomegranate Seed," which she is submitting to him.   Not particularly happy about the modification, she notes that she read the manuscript at Christmas time to five friends who thought the previous ending "was perfect."   The new ending, however, she hopes will be "sufficiently explicit. I could hardly make it more so without turning a ghost story into a treatise on the supernatural" (*Letters* 532).

2   R.W.B. Lewis writes that "All Souls" was meant to be part of a volume called *The Powers of Darkness*, the volume which was to include the story about Beatrice Palmato.   Lewis dates the Palmato fragment as around 1935.   He writes, "In 'All Souls,' Edith Wharton's association of the powers of darkness with the irresistible power of unbridled sex was virtually complete" ("Powers of Darkness" 645). I agree with Cynthia Griffin Wolff's dating of the fragment as written about 1918 or 1919.

3   All page references for "Pomegranate Seed," "All Souls," and the preface to the ghost stories refer to Scribner's edition of Wharton's ghost stories, 1973.

4   See Singley and Sweeney, "Forbidden Reading and Ghostly Writing: Anxious Power in Wharton's 'Pomegranate Seed'," for discussion of Charlotte's attempt to appropriate male power through the reading of the letters.   They read "Pomegranate Seed" as "a parable about women's ambivalence toward the power of reading and writing" (178).

5   Margaret McDowell ("Edith Wharton's Ghost Stories") points out the similarity in plot to James's "The Friends of the Friends" (1896) wherein "a jealous woman finds herself impotent in the struggle with a dead woman for the affections of a living man" (139).

6   Kenneth Ashby provides another version of Freud's theory of the "psychically impotent" male who is drawn to the wild, forbidden female.   Also see Richard A. Kaye in "'Unearthly Visitants': Wharton's Ghost Tales, Gothic Form, and the Literature of Homosexual Panic" for a discussion of Ashby's homosexual disposition.   Kaye suggests that Kenneth Ashby, like Ned Boyne in "Afterward," may be summoned by a "male paramour" to a "deadly underground" (12).   He cites as part of his argument the references in the tale to the masculine character of the handwriting in the letters.   Charlotte observes that "in spite of its masculine curves, the writing was so visibly feminine. Some hands are sexless, some masculine, at first glance; the writing on the

gray envelope, for all its strength and assurance, was without doubt a woman's" (*Ghost Stories* 201). At another point in the story, Kenneth in reference to the writer of the letters asks, "Why do you assume it's a woman?" to which Charlotte replies, "It's a woman's writing. Do you deny it?" Kenneth's provocative response is "No, I don't deny it. I asked only because the writing is generally supposed to look more like a man's" (209). The possibility of this alternative reading of Wharton's story suggests again, as Kaye points out, Wharton's awareness from situations in her own life of the danger of male homosexuality for women .

7   The concept of the double, as in "The Lady's Maid's Bell," suggests again the incongruity between the public self and a private self. In Wharton's early ghost stories, women's independent, separate selves are stifled by convention. In the later tales, a reversal occurs: women assert their independent selves and struggle with internalized conventions.

8   For discussion of Elsie in relation to writing and the appropriation of power, see Singley and Sweeney. In *Edith Wharton's Letters from the Underworld: Fictions of Women and Writing*, Candace Waid presents Elsie as representative of Wharton's world of literature (reading and writing) which she longed for in childhood, wanting to leave the conventional world of her mother behind. Waid notes that "Wharton was haunted by conflicting calls within herself by two worlds which seemed sharply divided" (198). In "Life and I," Wharton writes that she was drawn to the "almost tangible presences" of words which had

> faces as distinct as those of the persons among whom I lived. And like Erlkönig's daughters, they sang to me so bewitchingly that they almost lured me from the wholesome noon day air of my childhood into the strange supernatural region where the normal pleasures of my age seemed as insipid as the fruits of the earth to Persephone after she had eaten of the pomegranate seed. (1075) [Allusions in this quote are (1) to a German folk tale incorporated in a poem by Goethe, "Erlkönig," in which a young boy riding through the forest with his father is lured by an elf king to his lair where he promises the boy his daughters will take care of him and (2) to the myth of Demeter and Persephone. When Persephone ate the pomegranate seed, she was required to remain half the year in the underworld with Hades and only spend half the year on earth with her mother, Demeter.]

The association of Elsie with Wharton's "forbidden" world of reading and writing suggests the complexity of Wharton's own unresolved conflicts in regard to her profession and raises the question of whether any male/female relationship is capable of providing closeness and freedom for independent direction. Finally, I think Wharton answers no to this question. Charlotte, the potentially New Woman, as I will show, like Elsie, is caught up in conventional constructs that destroy her relationship with Kenneth. Her independent efforts to "read" the text of the letters and gain some control over her life are as futile as Elsie's efforts to write to gain control. Elsie and Charlotte, whose efforts at writing and reading, suggest positive alternatives for female roles are still mired in the past and function ineffectively in relationships, killing them. In Elsie's underworld, efforts of expression are faint, illegible; she suffocates in a world where open communication is still illegitimate, and she draws Kenneth back to this misery. This could well represent the strange world Wharton herself inhabited as a struggling writer and wife of Teddy Wharton.

9   Charlotte's assessment of herself as she looks in her mirror reflects one of Wharton's perennial themes in her fiction: women look to men for validation. Because esteem and value become tied up with appearance, all other women who might catch a man's eye become rivals. In a late tale, also with supernatural overtones, called "The Looking Glass" (1935), Wharton shows how women are conditioned to devote themselves to men and to see their value mirrored in men's eyes. Distraught because her beauty is fading, the aging Mrs. Clingsland feels her life misses affirmation from one man, a young man whom she perceives worshipped her beauty and went down on the Titanic before having the chance to declare the love she is sure he felt. Cora Attlee, Mrs. Clingsland's masseuse, with the help of the writing skills of a dying young scholar, fraudulently produces supposed messages from the dead beloved. Mrs. Clingsland becomes addicted to the affirming messages which give her self-esteem and hope. Unless beautiful in the eyes of a man, adored by a man, devoted to a man, she is nothing. Mrs. Clingsland's folly is accentuated by Cora Attlee's deceit. Cora rationalizes that "women had to have news of their men." Her misguided sympathy for Mrs. Clingsland feeds the woman's debilitating habit of basing her sense of esteem on the adoration of a man.

In "An Economy of Beauty: The Beauty System in 'The Looking Glass' and 'Permanent Wave,'" Sherrie A. Inness discusses the complex system of cultural practices which might be called the "beauty system." She notes that "because beauty, at least as our society has constructed it, requires the omnipresent male gaze with its implicit desire, it encourages women themselves to pursue their own objectification in order to win the admiring glance that reassures them of their value in the beauty economy" (9). This concept of a beauty economy meshes with the requirements of a capitalistic society which keep women on a treadmill always trying to find "better products or changing styles to insure their personal beauty capital." Inness concludes that "the beauty system [is] such an omnipresent entity that no woman can escape its dictates" (7). If a woman is not caught up in the system itself, a woman is caught up in reaction to it.

"The Looking Glass" did not appear in the 1937 edition of *Ghosts*, but when Scribner's reprinted Wharton's ghost stories in 1973, the editors deleted "A Bottle of Perrier" and replaced it with this tale, presumably because it has a more overt supernatural connection through mediumship and spiritualism than "Perrier," which appears as more of a murder mystery. "The Looking Glass" was originally published in a Hearst publication as "The Mirrors" in 1935 before it was included in *The World Over* in 1936.

10   Elsie, however, has an advantage over Charlotte and Prudence Rutledge; she occupies the forbidden realm and exerts erotic influence.

11   "The Moving Finger" first appeared in *Harper's*, March, 1901 and was included in *Crucial Instances*, 1901. All page references for *The Moving Finger* are from Lewis, *The Collected Stories of Edith Wharton*, vol. 1, 301-313.

12   I think that these attitudes are still with us. In the 1960s and 1970s, women's liberationists, and finally all feminists, were reported by detractors of feminism to be dangerous castraters, and they were, to boot, castigated, like witches, as being as ugly as toads. Thus popular cultural sentiment develops new labels that linger like their traditional counterparts.

13   Wharton's relationship with Morton Fullerton, who was bisexual, raises again a homoerotic interpretation in reading the tale, suggesting a contest between a woman and "a male paramour" for the love of a man (Kaye 12).

14   "Pomegranate Seed" is a title used previously by Wharton. In 1900 in *The Touchstone*, Wharton's first novel, the character, Margaret Aubyn, writes a novel called "Pomegranate Seed." *The Touchstone* and the 1931 ghost story "Pomegranate Seed" have similarities. *The Touchstone* is also a two-women-one-man plot. The love letters of the dead Mrs. Aubyn have influence over her former lover, Stephen Glennard, and affect his marriage. See Candace Waid for a discussion of *The Touchstone* as a ghost story anticipating "Pomegranate Seed," 192-194. In a story also written in 1900 called "Copy," a successful writer named Helen Dale, who like Wharton, gains power through co-opting the male prerogative of reading and writing, produces a work titled *Pomegranate Seed*. In 1912, Wharton wrote a dramatic poem titled "Pomegranate Seed" based on the Demeter/Persephone myth. In the poem, the "daughter chooses to leave the world of the mother and dwell in the underworld of experience," as Candace Waid points out, and basically mimics Wharton's attempt to leave the socially constraining world of her mother to go to the underworld of reading and writing (3, 201-202). As Susan Goodman notes, the "mother and daughter are forever divided, forever attuned to different voices" (147). Singley and Sweeney point out another use of the symbol of the pomegranate seed connected to *Age of Innocence* (1920). "An allusion to the pomegranate seed also appears in an early abandoned outline of *Age of Innocence*, in which it signifies a woman's loss of sexual and intellectual freedom" (191).

15   Candace Waid sees Charlotte as the Persephone figure who eats the pomegranate seed, and the underworld as a place where women may appropriate male language and power (through reading and writing). She reads the Persephone myth as the story of a "daughter who chooses to leave the world of the mother and dwell in the underworld of experience (3) . . . Persephone, for Wharton is the figure for the woman writer who dwells in the underworld savoring the supernatural fruit of letters and books" (199). I agree with Waid's interpretation in terms of Wharton's life and in terms of her earlier use of the Demeter/Persephone myth. Also a number of Wharton's characters, Lily Bart and Ellen Olenska for example, seem to me to be Persephone figures in this sense, who dabble with the forbidden, and who, like Wharton, suffer exile. Ellen, like Wharton, builds a new life in the more hospitable nether regions.

Josephine Donovan (*After the Fall: The Demeter-Persephone Myth in Wharton, Cather, and Glasgow*) claims that "The Persephone-Demeter myth allegorizes the historical mother-daughter transition that occurred towards the end of the nineteenth century in the Western world." Women began to reject women's culture (Demeter) and to try to become a part of the larger patriarchal culture. "The daughters . . . were eager to expand their horizons, to engage in new systems of discourse, like Perspephone, unaware that such involvement entailed patriarchal captivity." Donovan sees the Demeter-Persephone myth as central to Wharton's work and replayed in plot after plot as Wharton herself rejected her mother's world and faced the dangers of trying to establish an independent life in the patriarchy (usurpation of men's language and power and the consequences; power struggles; isolation; losing contact with women's culture and the healing power of the cooperation with women). In line with Donovan's reading, I see Wharton using the Persephone-Demeter myth in "Pomegranate Seed" to struggle with questions of how to maintain relationships given repressive societal constructs. Charlotte does not choose exile, like so many of Wharton's earlier characters do; she tries to find a way to maintain a relationship and looks to new resources (female cooperation) for possibilities. Neither Charlotte nor Wharton ever resolve the dilemma of how to move to a new basis in male/female relationships.

16   In the Demeter/Persephone myth, Hades abducts and rapes Persephone.

17   Annette Zilversmit connects the tale with Wharton's *Ethan Frome* and Hawthorne's "Ethan Brand" ("Last Haunted House" 317-318). Leon Edel says that the story is reminiscent of Hawthorne, James, and Le Fanu ("Nature of Literary Psychology" 461).

18   Annette Zilversmit ("'All Souls': Wharton's Last Haunted House") connects Whitegates with the Mount, noting that Wharton's home in Lenox, Massachusetts, had two sets of white gates and was called White Lodge by subsequent owners. Zilversmit also notes that Wharton took walks through Shaker's Wood which is where Sara Clayburn goes for walks.

19   Critics have disputed the identity of the narrator because the gender and age of the narrator are not clearly defined in the story. It is only clear that the narrator lives alone "in a small flat in New York" (*Ghost Stories* 269). The fact that the narrator undresses the frightened Sara suggests the female gender. R.W.B. Lewis erroneously refers to the narrator as Sara Clayburn's "niece" ("Powers of Darkness" 645). In the first paragraph of the tale, the narrator refers to Sara as "my cousin" (252). Margaret McDowell says the narrator is Sara's cousin, a woman, not necessarily younger. She describes the narrator as an "unattractive maternal figure" ("Ghost Stories" 311). Annette Zilversmit identifies the narrator as a "younger cousin" ("Wharton's Last Ghosts" 301).

20   Barbara White says that Wharton "creates a powerful metaphor for sexual abuse" in "All Souls" (*Edith Wharton: A Study of the Short Fiction* 101). "The empty house . . . represents the abused body" (105). The male voice coming from the radio represents the threat: "one-way communication, low and secretive, passionate

and threatening, and in a language foreign to the victim, is a perfect paradigm for child sexual abuse . . . . The aftermath is also much like child sexual abuse, as Mrs. Clayburn feels that 'a tissue of lies was being woven about her'" (102). Susan Goodman interprets the metaphor another way. She sees "All Souls" in relation to Wharton as capturing "the loneliness of being the 'extraordinary woman' . . . . Sara feels both formless and imprisoned in the sealed tomb of her own body" ("Inner Circle" 57). The man's voice represents "the appropriation of the female voice" (58). Another possibility is that Sara Clayburn has repressed homoerotic impulses. The fetch comes to the house "only to see one of the girls" (255). The witches' coven and Sara's quest to find the women who have disappeared suggest the possibility of homoerotic desire. The man's voice representing heterosexuality is a threat to homosexual desires.

21 Although Wharton uses realistic detail rather than fantastic dream imagery, the following tales come to mind: Irving's "The Bold Dragoon" (which uses the motif of furniture moving during the night), Poe's "Ligeia," and Hawthorne's "Young Goodman Brown."

22 Annette Zilversmit sees "All Souls" as "a psychological study of a woman's deep-felt loneliness and long-denied desires" ("Last Haunted House" 316). She sees Sara Clayburn as a "repressed and controlled woman" who is facing her "buried dependence and needs" (317, 319). Sara Clayburn never touches her

> real needs, never openly expresses them, only attempting to fulfill them indirectly, through controlling, though "order [ing]", her life, her house, and her maid . . . . she never knows the satisfaction of closeness, the expression and response of such desire to women she is inextricably involved with . . . . She cannot envision saying that she wants Agnes to stay or ask where they are going or, even most bravely, if she might join them. Unable to understand that the sharing of feeling is the premise of intimacy, she concedes greater, perhaps supreme power to these women, perhaps even supernatural gifts, to women who seem to have such connectedness (320, 324).

These interpretations emphasize both Wharton's dependence on her servants and her oft repeated sense that other women have some ability to experience life which she lacks. Zilversmit notes that "Wharton exposes that women too may be forever barricaded from their inmost life and fear that other women have powers and communication that stay forever mysterious and forbidden to them" ("Last Ghosts" 304).

23 "After Holbein" first appeared in *The Saturday Evening Post*, May, 1928. All page references for "After Holbein" are from Lewis, *The Collected Stories of Edith Wharton*, vol. 2, 532-550.

24 In the contrast of views between Sara and the narrator, Wharton neatly addresses both of Freud's interpretations of the uncanny: discarded primitive beliefs once more confirmed and repressed infantile complexes revived by some impression. The nar-

rator in discussing and affirming primitive beliefs reveals her own repressed state. She becomes then Sara's double: sexually repressed, denying her "buried dependence and needs" (Zilversmit, "Last Haunted House 319). Margaret McDowell ("Edith Wharton's Ghost Tales Reconsidered") points out that both Sara Clayburn in "All Souls" and Charlotte Ashby in "Pomegranate Seed" rush "to a motherly figure for reassurance." Yet this proves to be ineffective, for the maternal figures, traditional and culture-bound themselves, are struggling with the same conflicts and are in no position to mentor their "daughters" (304).

Conclusion

As my work reaches its close, I feel so sure that it is either nothing or far more than they know . . . . And I wonder a little desolately, which?

Edith Wharton,
Letter to Margaret Terry Chanler,
June 9, 1925

In 1925 in a letter to her friend Margaret Terry Chanler, Wharton comments that her work may be "far more than they know," hinting that there may be significant aspects of her writing that readers and critics are missing. In *The Writing of Fiction* (1925), she notes that "True originality consists not in a new manner but in a new vision."[1] In the fall of 1922 writing to Sinclair Lewis about his novel *Babbitt*, she clarifies that a new vision may not always be evident to the public, but a writer must nonetheless stick to her course. "I wonder how much of it [*Babbitt*] the American public, to whom irony seems to have become as unintelligible as Chinese, will even remotely feel? To do anything worthwhile, one must resolutely close one's ears and eyes to their conception of the novel . . . ." (*Letters* 455). In *A Backward Glance* (1934), Wharton emphasizes her own course as a writer which she adopted early in her career. Noting that Edwin Godkin, the editor of the New York *Evening Post*, had "said that the choice of articles published in American magazines was entirely determined by the fear of scandalizing a non-existent clergyman in the Mississippi Valley," she writes "I made up my mind from the first that I would never sacrifice my literary conscience to their ghostly censor" (139). She says that "the greatest service a writer can render to letters is to follow his conscience [and] write only for that dispassionate and ironic critic who dwells within the breast" (140, 212). What dwelled within Wharton's breast, as evidenced by the ghost stories, was a personal vision drawn from her experiences as an upper-class woman and writer in a patriarchy. Yet Wharton's work defies formulaic biographical connections and unitary interpretations as does the work of any fine writer working "in the round." She grapples with the complexities of human nature and relationships. Her work encompasses polarities, paradox, irony, and change; it is the product of a complex creative process.

Wharton developed early in her life a sensibility for unseen currents around her. She reports in an autobiographical fragment that as a child, very ill with typhoid, she had been scared by a "robber-story" she read which caused her for years "to enter a world haunted by formless horrors." She was unable to sleep in a room with a book containing a ghost story, and often she burned these books. The "chronic fear" was "like some dark undefinable menace, forever dogging [her] steps, lurking, and threatening." It disturbed her sleep. When she returned from walks, as she stood on the threshold waiting for the opening of the door, she "was seized by a choking agony of terror." She writes: "It did not matter who was with me, for no one could protect me; but, oh, the rapture of relief if my companion had a latch-key, and we could get in at once, before It caught me!" ("Life and I" 1079-80). Wharton's symptoms indicate her artistic sensibility as well as her neuroses which have been variously interpreted as a fear of her cold, unaffectionate mother or undue love for her father. Whatever the actual circumstances of her childhood were or whatever the psychoanalytic explanations are, Wharton's childhood fears demonstrate her sensitivity to the nuances of her environment. Her eagerness to return to a "safe" environment may well reflect the cultural and emotional threats of the life that lay outside for her as she grew up in repressive Old New York.[2]

Wharton did not openly declare a feminist mission. In discussing what Blake Nevius calls Wharton's "lurking feminism," Diana Worby observes, "Her feminism, sometimes lurking, sometimes equivocal, sometimes absent, is indeed ambiguous" (88).[3] The ambiguity of Wharton's feminism lies in her reluctance to simplify life and in her struggle with her own personal conflicts. As Susan Goodman notes, "Wharton, as Virginia Woolf would have said, was neither 'this' nor 'that,' and it is in these more ambiguous, hard-to-pigeonhole details that a fuller picture of a complex woman begins to emerge" (5). Sandra Gilbert and Susan Gubar, although noting that Wharton is "not a feminist in the ordinary sense of the word" (137), emphasize that "her major fictions, taken together constitute perhaps the most searching—and searing—feminist analysis of the construction of 'femininity' produced by any novelist in this century" (128). They point out that her anger over the "exploitation and infantilization of the female," which is a "product of the patriarchal family," permeates the ghost stories.

Wharton's feminist vision well fits the province of the ghost story. Cleverly adopting the oppressive Gothic atmosphere for her own purposes, giving it new integrity, and relying on the rich symbolic potential of fantasy, Wharton develops a critique of femininity as well as a critique of masculinity and relationships. As Margaret McDowell notes, "Wharton's feminism is implicit and cumulative ("Feminism" 523). Indeed, the ghost stories suggest a progressive vision challenging cultural gender roles and codes that negatively affect individual lives and relationships. Her frequent use of "the fictional perspective of the male," which gave her advantages in the male-dominated field of literature, ingeniously underscores her feminism; her male narrators and registers are either mouthpieces for their unquestioned biases or ironically victims themselves of patriarchal codes. Wharton's fictional world of ghostseers and feelers is a complex culture. The ghost functions as an intruder, a disrupter of everyday life who brings suppressed or repressed information out into the open. Along with knowledge of the world and others, the ghost forces percipients to confront denied selves. In this world of ghostly intrusion, men dominate women and younger men, and women suffer in isolation, powerless and voiceless. Women may overcome their silence and achieve power through finding voice, through manipulation of men, through competition with other women, through establishing independent lives as men do, through sexual aggressiveness, through escape, through revenge. Yet all these avenues lead to the pain of not being heard or understood, to the loss of self and connectedness to others, and to further oppression, isolation, and suffering. Women and men lack positive parental nurturing and role models. Men and women, who both seem "unsatisfactory," face problems with identity, sexuality, power struggles in relationships, stagnation in marriage. Traditional roles are stultifying; new roles are risky. Patterns of domination and submission (including incest), passivity and regression, oppression and manipulation, exacerbated by capitalism and class, haunt both genders. No one escapes the debilitating effects of these patterns. What Wharton begins as an exploration of women's desire for expression and rebellion against patriarchal authority leads to the exploration of the effects of traditional patterns and resulting internal conflicts for both men and women.[4]

Clearly, Wharton desires a new social order. This is reflected in her entire canon. Margaret McDowell notes "The thrust of her fiction is in the direction of a more flexible, dynamic social order in which women can be active agents" ("Feminism" 538). Carol Wershoven posits that female intruders (such as Ellen Olenska in *The Age of Innocence*) frequently show characteristics of a new path. Susan Goodman suggests that Wharton sees female cooperation as a way for women to change the system and cites the unfinished novel *The Buccaneers* as potentially the fullest flowering of this idea. David Holbrook sees Wharton working from an "unconscious hope for a rebirth of the psyche and the achievement of the possibility of fulfilled relationship not possible with one's present 'condition' in the society of the time" (37). Unfortunately, Wharton did not achieve "rebirth of the psyche" for her characters or fully for herself, but she did express and embody hope for women in the appropriation of language and finding voice, expatriation and independence, and the idea that women might heal and grow by cooperating with each other rather than competing with each other. As a male-centered writer with female concerns, her positive course for women sometimes seems clearer than the possible positive course for men. It is by absence rather than by example that many of her "positives" unfold. In human relationships, she implies moving to open communication and the effort to fulfill each other's needs by acknowledging them and speaking of them. For men, she implies a new path: the abandonment of immoral domination, the development of sensitivity to others, the investment of self in relationships with others. Caught between traditional role models for men and women that do not work (the trapped, victimized woman or the competitive, vengeful woman; the trapped, victimized man or the dominating man) and new models of independence that seemed to foster insensitivity, lack of connectedness, and sexual repression or alternative sexual arrangements, Wharton could only dimly envision a future that would allow the development of individual identity and the forming of relationships in creative and sensitive ways.[5] This is not so surprising, as in the late twentieth-century, we continue to struggle with these issues. Wilson Follett laments, "For all her achievement one must regret that her growth was interrupted" (2).[6]

In her ghost stories, Wharton objectified her terrors, projecting them onto a vast screen where they could be scrutinized. The possibilities of the ghost story to reflect complex revelations about the self, society, and tradition offered Wharton a means to analyze and, to some extent, to exorcise her intuitions and fears. As Alan Gardiner Smith has pointed out, "In her ghost stories, the horror of what is, of the suppressed "natural," is greater than the horror of what is not, of the conventionally 'supernatural'." The terror and horror of Wharton's perceptions of the deleterious effects of life in a rigidly defined culture and her struggle with internal conflicts are bound up in the "dozen or so stories of the macabre and the supernatural"[7] which shall surely endure as a testimony of her feminist sensibility and as a guide from the past which may yet help to open the doors of the future.

Notes

1   Wharton also writes

> That new, that personal, vision is attained only by looking long enough at
> the object represented to make it the writer's own; and the mind which
> would bring this secret germ to fruition must be able to nourish it with an
> accumulated wealth of knowledge and experience. (*Writing of Fiction* 18)

2   Lewis ("Powers of Darkness") analyzes Wharton's symptoms as a response to her
mother, Lucretia Jones. However, I interpret this slightly differently from Lewis.
Wharton was eager to get back in the house where it was supposedly safe. Coming
from a repressed environment, she found the emotional experiences of the outside
world terrifying; she longed to return to her safe, repressive environment where
emotions were always in control. Ironically, of course, this "safe" environment was
emotionally retarding and destroying her (especially if indeed she were a victim of
incest). In this sense, Lucretia Jones and George Frederic Jones, as the ministers of
this environment, did constitute the genuine terror. In the ghost stories, the house
motif is predominant. Terrors lie inside in repressive environments that stunt growth,
but unlike Wharton, who as a young woman feared outside terrors and was eager to
enter her house, the characters in the ghost stories are reluctant to enter the houses or
to stay in the debilitating environments. I think this reflects Wharton's mature awareness of the double dangers of her heritage, within and without.

3   Diana Worby ("The Ambiguity of Edith Wharton's 'Lurking Feminism'") prefaces
this comment with the following observations:

> Although she has much to say about contemporary themes of women's
> socialization, their objectification as ornaments, the double sexual stan-
> dard, the effect upon women of male domination or male passivity, she
> remains unrecognized. One reason could be that in adopting the fictional
> perspective of a male in most of her writing, she cuts herself off from that
> feminine sensibility about which she had such ambivalent feeling. An-
> other could be that she had ambivalent feelings about women, and that this
> ambivalence crept into her fictional portrayals. (88)

4   Other critics have commented on the focus and progression of Wharton's stories.
R.W.B. Lewis sees the ghost stories focusing on marriage problems, sexual repression, and the fantasy of personal revenge (Introduction to *Collected Stories*). Cynthia
Griffin Wolff writes that "Virtually all of Wharton's ghost stories focus on one of two
themes. The first is the problem of the spectral double—a secret self or alter-ego
who is the reflection of some evil or forbidden impulse . . . . The second has to do

with a jealous love triangle . . ." (*Feast* 300). Margaret McDowell sees the later stories as more complex in ideas and techniques. She sees the stories of the 1930s shifting to problems of relationships. In the later stories, she sees Wharton exploring aging; death; "spiritual sensitivity; the longing for independence; concern for others or the lack of it; the misuse of power by the strong over the powerless; the juxtaposition of gossip, superstition, or custom with accurate historical information; the breakdown of communication, particularly among the members of families; and the dangerous temptation to live in a serene past rather than to face a disturbing present" ("Ghost Tales Reconsidered" 312). Kathy Fedorko sees a progression of stories: the ones from the 1890s-1910 focusing on the "mute claustrophobia of suppressed women"; the ones from 1910-1920 focusing on characters who understand the horrors they encounter; and the ones from 1920-1937 focusing on the "fear and suppression of female sexuality" and the power of the "regenerative Female" as a "source of creativity and growth rather than terror" (*Edith Wharton's Haunted House*). Barbara White sees Wharton using female registers, lower-class types, and, in general, more categories of the dispossessed heavily in the late stories. The characters also tend to be older (88-89). She also refers to "female vengeance in the late ghost tales" (98). Gilbert and Gubar (*Sexchanges*) comment on Wharton's "anti-utopian cast of her feminism" (137); her lack of faith in the New Woman (128); her conflict, rage, and revenge reflected in her stories over the "hopeless incompatibility between 'the established order of things' and 'the individual [female] adventure'" (136); and the fantasy of supernatural and quasi-supernatural vengeance (160)." They write that the ghost story

> More than any other kind of writing, incarnate[s] the power of the *forbidden word*, the word that refuses to be limited by the 'laws of nature and culture' . . . . Some of [Wharton's] best ghost stories illuminate one source of her terror: the unleashing of female rage as well as the release of female desire. Others document another source of fear: the expression of female pain at the repression of rage and the killing of desire. (159)

5   Alternative sexual arrangements were negative for Wharton. They were dangers to her romantic notions of a full relationship (intellectual, emotional, sexual, spiritual) with a man who would be a soulmate. Her work, by absence, reflects the bankruptcy of the soulmate concept.

6   Irving Howe writes that she "understands how large is the price, how endless the nagging pain, that must be paid for a personal assertion against the familiar ways of the world, and she believes, simply, that most of us lack the strength to pay" (17).

7   Evaluating Wharton's most "enduring" work in contrast to the "ephemeral," E. K. Brown lists as one of seven items likely to endure her "dozen stories of the macabre and supernatural" (Howe 72). The other items that Brown lists are *Ethan Frome*; *The Custom of the Country*; *The Mother's Recompense*; *The Reef*; *The Age of Innocence*; *Old New York* ("some *nouvelles* in the series"); *The Writing of Fiction*; and other articles on the "exploration of her art." Lewis concludes that Wharton is among the "modern masters" of the ghost story (Introduction, *Collected Stories* xxiii). "Edith

Wharton was certainly one of the ablest practitioners in her time of this probably underrated genre, for which she had a career-long addiction" ("Powers of Darkness" 644). McDowell notes that the ghost stories "reveal her extraordinary psychological and moral insight." She writes: "In fact, these stories achieve ultimate distinction . . . to the degree that she explores in them . . . human situations of considerable complexity" ("Ghost Stories" 134). The critics who have commented on Wharton's ghost stories agree that they are far more than "nothing"; in fact, they see them as an important contribution to the supernatural tradition and a significant extension of Wharton's themes.

Works Cited

Ammons, Elizabeth. *Edith Wharton's Argument with America*. Athens, Ga.: University of Georgia Press, 1980.

_____. "Fairy-Tale Love and The Reef." *American Literature* 47.4 (Jan. 1976): 615-628.

Anon. "Ghosts and Ghost Stories." Rev. of *Ghosts*. *Times Literary Supplement* 6 Nov. 1937: 823. Also included in Tuttleton, Lauer, and Murray 541.

Auchincloss, Louis. *Edith Wharton: A Woman in Her Time*. New York: Viking Press, 1971.

Bendixen, Alfred and Annette Zilversmit, eds. *Edith Wharton: New Critical Essays*. New York: Garland, 1992.

Benet, William Rose. "Fiction." Rev. of *Ghosts*. *Saturday Review of Literature* 6 Nov. 1937: 19. Also included in Tuttleton, Lauer, and Murray 541-42.

Benstock, Shari. *No Gifts from Chance*: *A Biography of Edith Wharton*. New York: Scribner's, 1994.

_____. *Women of the Left Bank*: *Paris, 1900-1940*. Austin: University of Texas, 1986.

Bernard, Kenneth. "Imagery and Symbolism in Ethan Frome." *College English* 10 (Dec. 1961): 178-184.

Blum, Virginia. "Edith Wharton's Erotic Other World." *Literature and Psychology* 3.3 (1987): 12-29.

Briggs, Julia. *Night Visitors: The Rise and Fall of the English Ghost Story*. London: Faber, 1977.

Carpenter, Lynette. "Deadly Letters, Sexual Politics, and the Dilemma of the Woman Writer: Edith Wharton's 'The House of the Dead Hand.'" *American Literary Realism* 24.2 (1992 Winter): 55-69.

_____ and Wendy Kolmar, eds. *Haunting the House of Fiction: Feminist Perspectives on Ghost Stories by American Women*. Knoxville: University of Tennessee Press, 1991.

Cohn, Jan. "The House of Fiction: Domestic Architecture in Howells and Edith Wharton." *Texas Studies in Language and Literature* 15 (Fall 1973): 537-49.

Cuddy, Lois. "Triangles of Defeat and Liberation: The Quest for Power in Edith Wharton's Fiction." *Perspectives in Contemporary Literature* (1982): 18-26.

Dooley, R.B. "A Footnote to Edith Wharton." *American Literature* (Mar. 1954): 78-85.

Donovan, Josephine. *After the Fall: The Demeter-Persephone Myth in Wharton, Cather, and Glasgow*. University Park: Penn State UP, 1989.

Downey, June E. *Creative Imagination: Studies in the Psychology of Literature*. New York: Harcourt Brace, 1929.

Duplessis, Rachel Blau. "For the Etruscans." Showalter, *New Feminist Criticism* 271-191.

Dwight, Eleanor. *Edith Wharton: An Extraordinary Life*. New York: Harry N. Abrams, 1994.

Edel, Leon. "The Nature of Literary Psychology." *Journal of the American Psychoanalytic Association* 29 (1981): 447-467. Also in *Stuff of Sleep and Dreams: Experiments in Literary Psychology*. New York: Harper and Row, 1982. 36-41.

_____. "A Stone in the Mirror." *The New American Scholar* 45 (1976): 826-830.

Elbert, Monika. "T.S. Eliot and Wharton's Modernist Gothic." *Edith Wharton Review* 11:1 (Spring 1994): 19-23.

Eliot, T. S. "The Love Song of J. Alfred Prufrock." *The Complete Poems and Plays*. New York: Harcourt Brace, 1971.

Erlich, Gloria C. *The Sexual Education of Edith Wharton*. Berkeley: University of California Press, 1992.

Fedorko, Kathy A. "Edith Wharton's Haunted Fiction: 'The Lady's Maid's Bell' and *The House of Mirth*." Carpenter and Kolmar 80-107.

_____. *Edith Wharton's Haunted House: The Gothic in Her Fiction*. Diss. Rutgers, 1987.

_____. "'Forbidden Things': Gothic Confrontation with the Feminine in 'The Young Gentlemen' and 'Bewitched.'" *Edith Wharton Review* 11.1 (Spring 1994): 3-9.

Follett, Wilson. "What Edith Wharton Did—And Might Have Done." *New York Times Book Review* 5 Sept. 1937: 2, 14.

Fracasso, Evelyn E. "Images of Imprisonment in Two Tales of Edith Wharton." *College Language Association Journal* 36:3 (March 1993): 318-26.

Freud Sigmund. "The Most Prevalent Form of Degradation in Erotic Life." *On Creativity and the Unconscious*. New York: Harper, 1958. 173-186.

_____. "The Uncanny." *On Creativity and the Unconscious*. New York: Harper, 1958. 122-161.

Friedman, Henry J. "The Masochistic Character in the Work of Edith Wharton." *Seminars in Psychology* 5.3 (August 1973): 313-29.

Gilbert, Sandra M. "What Do Feminist Critics Want? A Postcard from the Volcano." Showalter, *New Feminist Criticism* 29-45.

_____ and Susan Gubar. *No Man's Land: The Place of the Woman Writer in the Twentieth Century*. Vol. 2: *Sexchanges*. New Haven: Yale UP, 1989.

Goodman, Susan. "Edith Wharton's Inner Circle." Joslin and Price 43-60.

_____. *Edith Wharton's Women: Friends and Rivals*. Hanover: University Press of New England, 1990.

Gribben, Alan. "Edith Wharton's Letters to Morton Fullerton." *The Library Chronicle of the University of Texas* 31 (1985): 7-71.

Heller, Janet Ruth. "Ghosts and Marital Estrangement: An Analysis of 'Afterward.'" *Edith Wharton Review* 10:1 (Spring 1993): 18-19.

Heller, Terry. *The Delights of Terror: An Aesthetics of the Tale of Terror.* Urbana: University of Illinois, 1984.

Holbrook, David. *Edith Wharton and the Unsatisfactory Man.* New York: St. Martin's, 1991.

Howe, Irving, ed. *Edith Wharton: A Collection of Critical Essays.* Englewood Cliffs, N.J.: Prentice-Hall, 1962.

Howells, William Dean, ed. *Shapes That Haunt the Dusk.* New York: Harper, 1907.

Inness, Sherrie. "An Economy of Beauty: The Beauty System in 'The Looking Glass' and 'Permanent Wave.'" *Edith Wharton Review* 10.1 (Spring 1993): 7-11.

Jackson, Rosemary. *Fantasy: The Literature of Subversion.* London: Methuen, 1981.

James, Henry. *The Art of Criticism: Henry James on the Theory and the Practice of Fiction.* Eds. William Veeder and Susan M. Griffin. Chicago: University of Chicago Press, 1986.

Joslin, Katherine and Alan Price, eds. *Wretched Exotic: Essays on Edith Wharton in Europe.* New York: Peter Lang, 1993.

Kaye, Richard A. "'Unearthly Visitants': Wharton's Ghost Tales, Gothic Form, and The Literature of Homosexual Panic." *Edith Wharton Review* 11.1 (Spring 1994): 10-18.

Kellogg, Grace. *Two Lives of Edith Wharton: The Woman and Her Work.* New York: Appleton-Century, 1965.

Killoran, Helen. "Edith Wharton's Reading in European Language and Its Influence on Her Work." Joslin and Price 365-387.

_____. "Pascal, Brontë, and 'Kerfol': The Horrors of a Foolish Quartet." *Edith Wharton Review* 10:1 (Spring 1993): 12-17.

Kolodny, Annette. "Dancing Through the Minefield: Some Observations on the Theory, Practice, and Politics of a Feminist Literary Criticism." Showalter, *New Feminist Criticism* 144-167.

Lawson, Richard. *Edith Wharton and German Literature.* New York: Frederick Ungar, 1977.

Leonard, Garry M. "The Paradox of Desire: Jacques Lacan and Edith Wharton. *Edith Wharton Review* 7.2 (Winter 1990): 13-16.

Levi St. Armand, Barton. *The Roots of Horror in the Fiction of H.P. Lovecraft.* Elizabethtown, N.Y.: Dragon Press, 1977.

Lewis, R.W.B. *Edith Wharton: A Biography.* New York: Harper and Row, 1975.

_____. "Introduction." *The Collected Short Stories of Edith Wharton.* Vol. 1. New York: Scribner's, 1968. vii-xv.

_____. "Powers of Darkness." *Times Literary Supplement* 13 June 1975: 644-46.

Lidoff, Joan. "Another Sleeping Beauty: Narcissism in *The House of Mirth.*" *American Quarterly* 32 (Winter 1980): 519-39.

Lindberg, Gary H. *Edith Wharton and the Novel of Manners.* Charlottesville: University of Virginia Press, 1975.

Lovecraft, H.P. *Supernatural Horror in Literature.* New York: Dover, 1973.

Lubbock, Percy. *Portrait of Edith Wharton.* New York: Appleton- Century- Crofts, 1947.

Mariano, Nicky. *Forty Years with Berenson.* New York: Knopf, 1966.

McDowell, Margaret B. "Edith Wharton's Ghost Stories." *Criticism* XII (Spring 1970): 133-52.

_____. "Edith Wharton's Ghost Tales Reconsidered." Bendixen and Zilversmit 291-314.

_____. "Viewing the Custom of the Country: Edith Wharton's Feminism." *Contemporary Literature* 15 (Autumn 1974): 521-38.

McGinty, Sarah M. "Houses and Interiors as Characters in Edith Wharton's Novels." *Nineteenth Century* 5 (Spring 1979): 48-51, 73-75.

Messent, Peter B., ed. *Literature of the Occult: A Collection of Critical Essays.* Englewood Cliffs, N.J.: Prentice Hall, 1981.

Murray, Margaret P. "The Gothic Arsenal of Edith Wharton." *Journal of Evolutionary Psychology* 10.3-4 (Aug. 1989): 315-321.

Nevius, Blake. *Edith Wharton: A Study of Her Fiction.* Berkeley: University of California Press, 1953.

Olin-Ammentorp, Julie. "Edith Wharton's Challenge to Feminist Criticism." *Studies in American Fiction* 16.2 (Autumn 1988): 237-44.

_____. "Wharton's 'Negative Hero' Revisited." *Edith Wharton Newsletter* 6.1 (Spring 1989): 6, 8.

_____. "Wharton's View of Woman in *French Ways and Their Meaning*." *Edith Wharton Review* 9:2 (Fall 1992): 15-18.

Ostriker, Alicia. "The Thieves of Language: Women Poets and Revisionist Mythmaking." Showalter, *New Feminist Criticism* 313-38.

Ozick, Cynthia. "Justice (Again) to Edith Wharton." *Commentary* 62 (Oct. 1976): 48-57.

Penzoldt, Peter. *The Supernatural in Fiction.* New York: Humanities Press, 1965.

Punter, David. *The Literature of Terror: A History of Gothic Fictions from 1765 to the Present Day.* London: Longman, 1980.

Rabkin, Eric S. *The Fantastic in Literature.* Princeton, N.J.: Princeton UP, 1976.

Radcliffe, Anne. "On the Supernatural in Poetry." *New Monthly Magazine* 16 (1826): 145-52.

Rank, Otto. *The Double: A Psychoanalytic Study.* Chapel Hill: University of North Carolina Press, 1971.

Raphael, Lev. *Edith Wharton's Prisoners of Shame: A New Perspective on Her Neglected Fiction.* New York: St. Martin's , 1991.

Robillard, Douglas. "Edith Wharton." *Supernatural Fiction Writers: Fantasy and Horror, 2: A.E. Coppard to Roger Zelazny.* Ed. E.F. Bleiler. New York: Scribner's, 1985.

Rose, Alan Henry. "'Such Depths of Sad Initiation': Edith Wharton and New England." *New England Quarterly* 50 (1977): 423-39.

Sapora, Carol. "Female Doubling: The Other Lily Bart in Edith Wharton's *The House of Mirth.*" *Papers of Language and Literature: A Journal for Scholars and Critics of Language and Literature* 29.4 (Fall 1993): 371-94.

Scarborough, Dorothy. *The Supernatural in Modern English Fiction.* New York: G.P. Putnam, 1917.

Schriber, Mary Suzanne. "Convention in the Fiction of Edith Wharton." *Studies in American Fiction* XI (Autumn 1983): 189-202.

Sensibar, Judith. "Edith Wharton Reads the Bachelor Type: Her Critique of Modernism's Representative Man." *American Literature* 60 (Dec. 1988): 575-90.

Showalter, Elaine. "The Death of the Lady (Novelist): Wharton's *House of Mirth.*" *Representations* 9 (Winter 1985): 133-49.

_____. "Feminist Criticism in the Wilderness." *New Feminist Criticism* 243-270.

_____, ed. *The New Feminist Criticism: Essays on Women, Literature, and Theory.* New York: Pantheon Books, 1985.

Singley, Carol J. "Gothic Borrowings and Innovations in Edith Wharton's 'A Bottle of Perrier.'" Bendixen and Zilversmit 271-90.

Singley, Carol J. and Susan Elizabeth Sweeney. "Forbidden Reading and Ghostly Writing: Anxious Power in Wharton's 'Pomegranate Seed.'" *Women's Studies* 20:2 (1991): 177-203.

Smith, Allan Gardiner. "Edith Wharton and the Ghost Story." *Women and Literature* I (1980): 149-59.

Spiller, Robert E. et al., eds. *Literary History of the United States.* New York: Macmillan, 1959.

Stengel, Ellen Powers. "Edith Wharton Rings 'The Lady's Maid's Bell.'" *Edith Wharton Newsletter* 7:1 (Spring 1990): 3-9.

Stoker, Bram. *Dracula*. New York: Dell, 1974.

Sullivan, Jack. *Elegant Nightmares: The English Ghost Story from Le Fanu to Blackwood*. Athens: Ohio UP, 1978.

Thompson, G.R., ed. *The Gothic Imagination: Essays in Dark Romanticism*. Pullman: Washington State UP, 1974.

Thomas, Jennice G. "Spook or Spinster? Edith Wharton's 'Miss Mary Pask.'" Carpenter and Kolmar 108-16.

Todorov, Tzvetan. *The Fantastic: A Structural Approach to a Literary Genre*. Trans. Richard Howard. Ithaca: Cornell UP, 1975.

Trilling, Lionel. *The Liberal Imagination*. New York: Doubleday, 1953.

Tuttleton, James W. "Edith Wharton: The Archaeological Motive." *The Yale Review* 6 (1972): 562-74.

_____, Kristin Lauer, and Margaret P. Murray. *Edith Wharton: The Contemporary Reviews*. Cambridge: Cambridge UP, 1992.

Varma, Devendra. *The Gothic Flame*. Metuchen, N.J.: Scarecrow Press, 1987.

Waid, Candace. *Edith Wharton's Letters from the Underworld: Fictions of Women and Writing*. Chapel Hill: University of North Carolina Press, 1991.

Wershoven, Carol. *The Female Intruder in the Novels of Edith Wharton*. Rutherford, N.J.: Fairleigh Dickinson UP, 1982.

Wharton, Edith. *A Backward Glance. New York: Appleton-Century, 1934*. New York: Charles Scribner's Sons, 1985.

_____. *The Collected Short Stories of Edith Wharton*. Ed. R.W.B. Lewis. 2 vols. New York: Scribner's, 1968.

_____. *The Custom of the Country*. New York: Scribner's, 1913. New York: Charles Scribner's Sons, undated reprint.

_____. *Ethan Frome*. New York: Scribner's, 1911. New York: Scribner's, 1968. Ed. Blake Nevius. Includes text of Introduction to Modern Student's Library ed. 1922: 70-71.

_____. *French Ways and Their Meaning*. New York: D. Appleton, 1919.

_____. *Ghosts*. New York: Appleton-Century, 1937. *The Ghost Stories of Edith Wharton*. New York: Charles Scribner's Sons, 1973.

_____. *The House of Mirth*. New York: Scribner's, 1905. New York: St. Martin's, 1994. Ed. Shari Benstock.

_____. *The Letters of Edith Wharton*. Eds. R.W.B. Lewis and Nancy Lewis. New York: Charles Scribner's Sons, 1988.

_____. "Life and I." *Edith Wharton: Novellas and Other Writings*. Ed. Cynthia Griffin Wolff. New York: Library of America, 1990. 1071-1096.

_____. *The Reef*. New York: D. Appleton, 1912. London: Penguin, 1994.

_____. *A Son at the Front*. New York: Scribner's, 1923.

_____. *Summer*. New York: D. Appleton, 1917. New York: Harper and Row, 1979.

_____. *The Writing of Fiction*. New York: Scribner's, 1925. New York: Octagon Books, 1966.

White, Barbara. *Edith Wharton: A Study of the Short Fiction*. New York: Twayne, 1991.

Wolff, Cynthia Griffin. "Cold Ethan and 'Hot Ethan.'" *College Literature* 14.3 (Fall 1987): 230-245.

_____. "Edith Wharton and the 'Visionary' Imagination." *Frontiers* 2.3 (1977): 24-30.

_____. *A Feast of Words: The Triumph of Edith Wharton*. New York: Oxford UP, 1977.

Worby, Diana Zacharia. "The Ambiguity of Edith Wharton's 'Lurking Feminism.'" *Mid-Hudson Language Studies* 5 (1982): 81-90.

W.R.B. See Benet, William Rose.

Zilversmit, Annette. "'All Souls': Wharton's Last Haunted House and Future Directions for Criticism." Bendixen and Zilversmit 315-29.

_____. "Edith Wharton's Last Ghosts." *College Literature* 14.3 (1987): 296-304.

Index